Eularia Clarke
Painter of Religion

Eularia Clarke
Painter of Religion

Rebecca Sherlaw-Johnson

Eularia Clarke   *Painter of Religion*

First published in 2017 by
Books with Spirit
Malton Croft, Woodlands Rise, Stonesfield OX29 8PL
Email: rebeccasj@btinternet.com

ISBN 978-1546576976

Contents

Acknowledgments

My grateful thanks to all those who have contributed to this biography, especially to my mother Rachael Sherlaw-Johnson and my uncle James Kenelm Clarke for putting up with my endlessly dredging up their past; to my sister Griselda Sherlaw-Johnson for correcting the grammar; to Christopher Baines for some delightfully funny anecdotes; to Lindsey Thornton, Geraint Lewis, and Dale and Richard Morris for their help in publishing it; to those who are too modest to wish to be named – they know who they are; and in memory of Felicity Belfield who found time before she died to share her warm and heartfelt memories of Eularia.

Illustrations

Unless otherwise stated all illustrations are reproduced by permission of the Eularia Clarke Archive and the Clarke and Sherlaw-Johnson families. All the artwork is by Eularia Clarke. Photography by Geraint Lewis.

For a more extensive look at Eularia Clarke's work visit her online gallery at www.eulariaclarke.com

Eularia Clarke   *Painter of Religion*

Preface

M any British Artists have painted religious subjects as part of their collection but few have devoted their whole work to it. Even fewer have done so with no intention of making any money from it because they saw it as a vocation, an extension of their own faith and spirituality. Eularia Clarke stands alone in the history of British Art for this very reason. That on its own should rank her as an important British Artist, but when you set it alongside the fact that she was a Catholic painting during the 1960s, a decade that saw seismic change in the Catholic Church, her work takes on an even more profound role as a reflection of one of the most significant periods in recent Church history, not only for Catholics but for the whole of the Ecumenical movement. She is, to my knowledge, the only Catholic Artist who truly captures the struggle of moving from centuries-old traditions to a new way of practising faith.

Also unique is the extent of archival information that Eularia left us, especially her diaries. It is a record of the very human struggles she faced in terms of her own spiritual journey and the motivations behind her work, allowing us to walk her path with her as she painted.

I was the first person to read her diaries since her death and it immediately became clear to me that the public should once again have access to her paintings and that her story should be told. It is not an easy story, her life was a hard one: deserted by her husband, often penniless, she nevertheless managed to successfully raise two children and, having decided to become a Religious Artist at the age of 16, a calling as singular as it was lonely and unfashionable, she achieved it in the last ten years of her life.

Why is she not better known? For the very same reason that makes her unique: she rarely sold any of her paintings, wanting them to be freely available for everyone to see, but on her death her children took charge of the ninety canvases that are her collection and stored them away. Only two remained on public view (two of only five that she ever sold, despite many offers for them) and they are two of the most popular works in the Methodist Collection of Modern Art.

Eularia Clarke is my maternal grandmother and she died when I was ten years old, so my personal memories of her are those of a child. She was eccentric and fun, totally unlike any of the grandparents of my contemporaries, including my father's parents who were all very solid and respectable. It never occurred to me to question the fact that she painted religious pictures and had no husband, I was never curious about my grandfather: she was Grandmother, and that was enough.

She always had time for children, playing and singing with us, making us extraordinary dolls with her stylistic painted faces and knitted and hand-made clothes – just like the figures from her paintings. I was the only child I know who had a family of dolls that included a family priest!

Unlike my northern grandparents' house in Newcastle, which was full of dark, heavy furniture, ornamental china, spotless upholstery and where we could never jump around or make much of a mess, Eularia's house was damage-proof. There were paints and musical instruments galore; walls hung with old violins and guitars, an Autoharp, harmonicas, ukuleles and of course her religious paintings. I learnt many of my Gospel stories from these paintings and it seemed perfectly reasonable to me that Jesus and the Apostles should be inhabiting the same world that I did.

When I look back on her now it is chiefly the joy I remember, the joy she brought to my life, her extraordinary creativity and force of character, her tactility and vitality. She could be fierce and sometimes I was in awe of her, even slightly afraid. I remember telling my mother one day, 'We like grandmother. She looks as if she's going to say no, but she always says yes.' She was one of the most vital and alive people I have known. It is a shame that she herself never fully understood just how much she meant to me, and to so many others. Having read her diaries it is clear that she wasn't capable of understanding it because she didn't believe it could be so.

Eularia was at heart a believer raised by a family of intellectuals. At her core was an unshakeable faith in something that she found hard to define, most of her family (though very clever and talented) did not particularly believe in anything, unless it was music. Her life and work were a journey to give shape and form to a deep sense of spirituality that she was aware of from childhood, to know what it was. In the end her greatest obstacle was the conflict between the intellectual thinking she had been brought up with and the belief she sought, a struggle between heart and mind, between the quantifiable and the unseen, the rational and the unknowable.

She was a prolific letter writer, many of which survive thanks to a family obsession for hanging on to paperwork, but it is her diaries that are the most revealing about her inner life. These do not begin in earnest until 1954 when she was 40, but from then on she wrote consistently until just before her death in 1970, leaving eighteen volumes of densely packed, handwritten streams of consciousness. There are two types of diary writer: those who record factual events and happenings and those who record their inner thoughts and feelings. Eularia belonged to the latter. She rarely mentions dates, except for Catholic feast days, and, whilst events were mentioned, most of the detail relates to her thoughts and feelings about what was going on, rather than the facts of the events themselves. Piecing together the picture was greatly helped by her correspondence, especially to my mother, Rachael. These letters were far more factual, often very funny, and they were usually dated.

What emerges is a woman of two layers: the confident, intelligent, lively, creative, sometimes tactless, snobbish, moody and difficult Eularia that most people knew; and a far more sensitive, frightened, lonely seeker who longed for love and God and often felt completely inadequate in the face of life and the blows it brought her. Eularia knew that her choice to be a religious painter was a lonely, unfashionable and difficult one. For over twenty years she avoided it, wanting to be normal and have what everyone else had – a husband and family, security, someone to share life with – it was never to be. By the end of her life she had accepted this, indeed preferred the freedom of being on her own, becoming almost hermit-like as her health began to fail. By this time she had painted over ninety canvases of Gospel stories, Church worship and the more mystical aspects of faith. It is an extraordinary legacy.

A Note About The Diaries

As Eularia's biographer I have included excerpts from her own diaries wherever possible, to allow her to speak, because she describes her own journey far better than I can summarise it. My only regret is that, because her diary runs to eighteen volumes, it was not possible to simply publish them as they are. Passages quoted in the text with no reference are all dairy excerpts.

Rachael and James (her children) have always been of the opinion that she wrote her diaries intending them to be read, but this was not her primary motivation. Indeed she made an active choice not to destroy them before her death, something she seriously considered. This suggests strongly that she did not write her diaries for public consumption, but the fact that they may well be read after her death was something she came to accept. Eularia's primary motivation for writing her diaries was as a way of helping her to see herself: she tells us as much. As a woman who spent most of her life alone, with no husband or close friends that she could openly talk to or confide in, her diary was her substitute confidante. She did not always like what she saw when she reread them, but they did help her to reflect on herself and change what she could.

The art of the diarist has changed in recent years. Now we have bloggers, but the difference with blogging is the obvious intention that it is public. A diary in written form is intensely personal, especially when it is not simply a recording of daily events, but a way of seeing our deepest selves. By nature this is very exposing and Eularia's are raw in this sense. She hides nothing of herself and she could be brutal, about herself, her friends, her enemies and life – even God.

Political correctness did not exist in Eularia's day and some of her comments must be seen in this light. Eularia belonged to a world that has largely passed now and the way it used language was different.

Prologue

The works of Fra Angelico and Giotto gazed down from the walls of San Marco, vividly coloured frescoes of angels and saints, of the Annunciation and the Last Supper, of the Madonna and of Christ; timeless and poised; an age old story brought to perfection by the skill of long dead artists.

Room after room, fresco after glorious fresco emerged before the young Eularia as she trailed after her superior Aunt Sylvia and her beautiful cousin Alicia, whose hand-me-downs she was reduced to wearing, but none of that mattered anymore. For here was something more vivid and infinitely more compelling. There was nothing like this in England, no great tradition of Religious Art, only the watered down agnostic Anglicanism practiced by her family which gave no sense that these subjects could inspire such glorious works. A previously undreamt-of world was opening up before her, in which faith in something could inspire great work.

'This is what I want to be,' she said to herself, 'I want to be a religious artist, like Fra Angelico.' She was 16 years old and she would have to wait thirty years before she began to realise her ambition.

Eularia Clarke   *Painter of Religion*

Part 1

The Search for Answers

1914 – 1938

1

'Cheppers'

Elizabeth Eularia Baines was born on 4 May 1914 at 21 Chepstow Villas ('Cheppers'), Notting Hill, London, a relatively affluent neighbourhood of white-stoned villas built for the professional classes. She was the second child of four of Cuthbert Edward and Margaret (Peggy) Clemency Baines (*née* Lane Poole) and their only daughter.

The Baines family were mostly liberal intellectuals and great talkers. Anyone who knew Eularia would know how true this was. She could talk for England and what she said was always engaging, interesting, sometimes challenging, and occasionally very tactless, but you had to be a good listener because, when she was in full flow, it was very difficult to get a word in. Put two Baines' in a room together and there was no hope.

There were clerics and artists on both sides of the family. Cuthbert's grandfather was Vicar of Yalding in Kent and his grandmother, Catharine Eularia, after whom Eularia was named, was a direct descendant of the engraver Richard Cooper of Edinburgh[1]. Catharine Eularia was an accomplished water colourist although, as a Victorian Vicar's, wife it was not considered proper for her to exhibit or sell her work.

Some of Catharine Eularia's work survives within the family, most notably a series of pastels of her children, which are extremely fine examples of Victorian portraiture, capturing perfectly the dreamy innocence of youth. It was from Catharine Eularia that the family artists' motto came, 'Never a

---

1   Cooper was an early experimenter in lithography and his artist son (also Richard) was drawing master at Eton and taught art to the daughters of George III.

day without a line.' And despite a creeping paralysis that dogged her after one of her daughters drowned, she continued to paint and draw every day until ten days before she died.

Peggy's family also had distinguished artistic connections (her mother was descended from the sister of Thomas Gainsborough) and Peggy made many beautiful watercolours of botanical studies, something that the young Eularia would certainly have watched her do. Another influence was one of Eularia's favourite aunts, Vera Lane Poole (*née* Dendy), who was married to Peggy's brother, Austin. Vera was an accomplished artist and, unusually for a woman of that time, had trained at the Lambeth School of Art, privately with Walter Sickert, and in Paris. She taught alongside both Stanley and Gilbert Spencer, and Paul Nash at the Ruskin School in Oxford. Eularia visited Austin and Vera frequently and was great friends with their surviving daughter, Catherine.

Eularia's youngest brother, Christopher, said that:

'At least one member in each generation demonstrated a latent, almost instinctive skill at some stage... in our generation Eularia was the more dedicated artist.'

By the time Cuthbert's generation came along the clerical aspect of family tradition had been dropped in favour of agnosticism and the Civil Service. Cuthbert was the only son of the distinguished Civil Servant, Sir Jervoise Athelstane, and Lady Constance Baines. Cuthbert's upbringing was traditional upper middle class with a childhood in India before attending St Paul's School and then Corpus Christi College, Oxford where he studied Greats[2], after which he went straight to the India Office in Whitehall. Cuthbert, however, was far too unconventional ever to be happy behind a desk. In his heart he was an engineer, inventor and writer (his Short History of English Literature was published by Longman in 1909). The daily grind of Whitehall administration was to contribute to bouts of depression during Eularia's childhood, something she was later to say she had inherited from him. The fear of frustrated talent, of never achieving anything and having to be responsible for the care of others was something that haunted Eularia all her life.

It was Cuthbert's older sister, Sylvia, who did most to fulfil Sir Athelstane's expectations for his children. Where Cuthbert was a mild-

---

2 Name given to the Oxford Degree in Classics covering Ancient Rome, Ancient Greece, Latin, ancient Greek and philosophy.

tempered, imaginative and sensitive idealist, Sylvia was ambitious, forceful and fully prepared to set aside personal talents for the sake of doing what was right and ensuring her future. She made a good marriage to Philip Percival, a barrister who was a key figure in the Indian administration, and by 1906 had produced two children before Cuthbert, only three years her junior, had even thought about marriage. At this stage Cuthbert's yearning was to write, being good friends with many of the well-known writers of his generation including Rupert Brooke, G. K. Chesterton and Hilaire Belloc (he was an early member of Chesterton and Belloc's Distributist League and wrote regularly for Chesterton's *G.K. Weekly*).

When Sir Athelstane retired in 1902, he and Constance moved from London to a large house in Kidlington, Oxfordshire called Home Close, so Cuthbert (anyway an Oxford man) was familiar with Oxford social circles. In 1910 or 1911, just when his parents must have been despairing of him ever finding a wife and settling down (he was 33), Cuthbert met Peggy, then 25 and the daughter of an Oxford History don, Reginald Lane Poole, who was Vice-President of Magdalen College. Reginald's wife, Rachael, was also something of an intellectual, being the author of the first catalogue of all the portraits in the Oxford colleges. Margaret was the youngest of four children. Eularia was often later to refer to a Lane Poole streak of cruelty in this branch of the family, which possibly went back to Reginald who was also dogged by depression, especially in later life.

Peggy had a keen interest in botany but in the early twentieth century women were not allowed to be undergraduates so she studied biology privately with J.S Haldane[3]. She was working as a biologist at the Oxford Museum when she met Cuthbert. Peggy and Cuthbert, being similar in temperament, had an immediate rapport so it was no surprise that they fell in love. They were married at St Giles Church in Oxford on 2 January 1912. Nine months later Anthony Cuthbert was born.

Peggy, ever the biologist, kept a diary that recorded the early development of her children. Other events, such as the war, pass almost

---

3   John Scott Haldane, a physiologist living in Oxford, was famous for self-experimenting and had a home laboratory. Peggy almost certainly worked alongside the Geneticist and Biologist Jack Haldane, John's son, as he was Peggy's contemporary and was close friends with John's daughter Naomi (Mitchison).

unacknowledged next to the number of words Anthony could now say or Eularia's dietary preferences. Peggy and Cuthbert were unusual parents for their time. Neither were great disciplinarians and both were keen to encourage their children's creativity. The net result was that Eularia and her brothers ran wild.

This drove their aunt Sylvia to distraction (her own children, Alicia and David, were very well brought up). On good days Sylvia referred to her brother's family en-masse as 'the Cheppers'. On not so good days they were 'the Pegginses' (Peggy, being the mother, was assigned the blame for their lack of manners and good behaviour) and on very bad days simply 'the Brats'!

Sylvia may have had a point. Eularia was sandwiched in age between Anthony and younger brother Francis and these two together made a formidable force for disobedience and destruction. Anthony was known to climb the apple trees in the Home Close orchard and pee on people passing underneath. He also took great delight in removing the cover from the well on the day that a blind guest was being shown round the garden. Francis, who was referred to by Sylvia as Francis Disgustus, once spent a happy hour looking up names in the telephone directory and on finding someone with the surname 'Smelly' rang them up and asked them, 'Are you smelly and what are you going to do about it?' Nowadays these incidents might seem tame but in the early 1920s children were still supposed to be seen and not heard, well behaved and polite. The Baines children didn't come close to this ideal.

Eularia was barely two months old when war was declared in 1914. It was an ominous beginning and it coloured her approach to life, which she always saw as a kind of battle. Cheppers was shut up and the family left London, moving from house to house for the duration. Little is known about Cuthbert's war record as his was one of the many destroyed in the fire in the records office during World War Two[4]. At 35 he was initially

---

4   In September 1940 the War Office repository in Arnside Street, London, where many of the service records for World War One were held, was bombed, destroying more than half of them. Cuthbert's were among those destroyed.

Anthony, Eularia and Francis outside 'Cheppers' (circa 1920)

considered too old to be sent to the front, although it is likely that he
spent a few months there in 1917. Eularia found his discharge papers after
his death which listed him as a sapper[5], discharged in 1917 and assigned
to the Ministry of Food, after which he returned to the India Office. Like
many who went through the Great War he never spoke about it.

5   Sappers perform a wide variety of military engineering duties from general construction to bomb
disposal. Their remit is to facilitate the movement of the allies and hinder that of the enemy.

Peggy initially took the children to stay with her parents in Museum House, Oxford. The family was lucky in that they had a number of large houses, rented or owned by various relations, where they could stay. Apart from Museum House there was Home Close, and in Gloucestershire, Dixton Manor, which was rented by Peggy's grandmother Elizabeth Malleson (the pioneer of the District Nursing system) and her husband Frank. Dixton was a wonderful house complete with a secret room that had a window but no door, a working farm, and assorted aunts and uncles. Not far away in the Forest of Dean was Hudnalls at St Briavells where Cuthbert's Aunt Lucy Eyre lived with her daughter, Margaret, and Aunt Rose lived just down the road at Sitting Green. Of all of these houses it was Dixton that was Eularia's favourite.

The peripatetic nature of Eularia's early years stayed with her. She never found it easy to settle in one place or become part of a specific community. Even when her own children were small she travelled during their early years, taking them with her much as Peggy had done.

Peggy's first entry in her diary about Eularia was made twenty-three days after her birth:

'Eularia was born at three o'clock on the morning of Monday, May 4th. From the moment she was born she was most active and wide-awake, opened her eyes and looked about her, and sucked her thumb very vigorously and noisily. She weighed the next day six and a quarter pounds only, but was beautifully made, with a well shaped small head covered with silky brown hair, large well-shaped nose and chin and very pretty mouth. Her eyes are dark grey, and she has remarkably long fingers which she uses very daintily.'

Eularia always insisted that she had a terrible childhood with no support from her parents, especially her father. While there is no direct evidence of this in Peggy's diary or in any of Cuthbert's surviving letters, Eularia's cousin Ursula stated that she was appalled at Cuthbert's attitude and lack of support for Eularia. It was probably the collective vagueness of her parents that annoyed Eularia most. She had a life-long dislike of people who didn't react to what she said or did, assuming that they weren't interested in her. Christopher, Eularia's youngest brother, quite cheerfully stated that it was his Aunt Sylvia who taught him table manners, as he never got any guidance from his parents.

One of Eularia's abiding problems (which was to follow her all her life) was that she was always 'one of the boys' stuck in the middle between two very boisterous and rather bullying brothers who Peggy could not control. Eularia grew up haunted by the belief that boys were more important than girls. At heart she was a sensitive and creative person, much like Cuthbert, but survival meant being as tough as the boys in a world in which girls really needed to be the opposite to be accepted by society. Her own rather difficult character (those who knew them both said that she was like her Aunt Sylvia, whom she loathed) did not help. She was to complain that her brothers got the best of everything while she had the hand-me-downs.

Peggy was to say much later that she always felt that Eularia did not like either of her parents very much. Towards the end of her life Eularia wrote:

'I often speak and act with no dignity at all, quite childishly, my parents didn't go in for dignity or being respected, and Francis and I *are* eccentrics; often thought mad. We have spontaneity, often without enough self-control.'

Eularia was the first to admit that she was not a particularly endearing child. She was a solid, sturdy girl who was rarely ill, with her Aunt Sylvia's notoriously difficult temperament and superiority complex. She learnt to stand up for herself against two bullying brothers from an early age. Michael Gedge, a family friend, wrote to her in 1962 saying, 'You must remember that one expects a woman who brews her own beer, and whose favourite expletive is "Bugger!" to be tough.'

Aunt Sylvia remarked in 1923 that Eularia 'never speaks and only scowls'. To Peggy, Eularia was 'robust and handsome', often charming but with a very strong will which she seemed to delight in using to defy Peggy. But Peggy always considered her to be much more imaginative than the clever and talented Anthony. She wrote in her diary that Eularia was like she remembered herself to be:

'Her passion for little things – anything as long as it's small – I well remember. Also she gets wrapped in thought at unsuitable moments – in the middle of drying herself, or lacing up her boots, or with a spoonful of food halfway to her mouth. I remember being chivvied for just such things in my youth.'

Eularia's own recollection of these instances was less romantic; ' Everything seemed far, far away – a sensation I used to have in childhood; it used to scare me.'

There was always amateur music at Cheppers. Sir Athelstane was an accomplished violinist known as 'Paganini Baines' in the Civil Service, and Lady Constance was a keen musician who would have made a formidable music teacher. She went through a period of inventing new ways to teach music to children and her own grandchildren were often unwilling guinea pigs. Sylvia was an accomplished pianist and used to irritate the children by sweeping around in flowing garments, criticising them and playing endless Chopin. It gave Eularia a life-long dislike of both the piano and Chopin. Eularia taught herself to play the penny whistle and by the time she was five could play fifty tunes on it, and as soon as she was old enough she began to learn the cello.

The Lane Pooles were musical in a very specific way. They were obsessed with Bach and played an important part in the Oxford music scene. Reginald was a keen amateur cellist and musicologist who wrote the first English biography of Bach. Rachael, Dorothy and Peggy were all members of The Bach Choir and Bach reigned supreme in their household.

Peggy remained an enthusiastic singer all her life and passed the passion on to Eularia who showed a love of singing from an early age, and whenever the St Matthew or St John Passion were played on the radio Eularia would insist on playing the cello part along with it, much to the annoyance of her own children. But Eularia later commented that, 'St Matthews Passion, ... was my first childhood "book of devotions" – my first intimation that Christ was to be loved and longed for and served – yet only the music mattered to my family.'

Once the war was over the family returned to Cheppers and Cuthbert to his desk at the India Office. Eularia was later to say that he supported his large family by propping his feet up on an open drawer in his desk and snoozing away the afternoons. Cuthbert endured his job because he had a family to support but what he really wanted to do was write, so he did – often surreptitiously at that desk at the India Office. His first novel, a political thriller called *The Black Circle*, won a Hodder and Stoughton prize in 1921. His dream was to become a best-selling author so that he could leave the India Office and support the family on his royalties. In the end he published five novels (all now out of print) but his first was always the most successful.

The early years at Cheppers were challenging for Eularia, stuck in the middle, a girl and not a very attractive one at that, but it was not all bad. As children they had wonderful holidays running wild at Home Close, Dixton, Hudnalls, and later Rathmore and then Detmore where Peggy's aunts Hope and Maude Malleson lived. Anthony, Eularia ('Malaria' or

'Lair' as her brothers called her) and Francis were a self-contained unit of mischief and trouble. Then in 1920 Anthony started senior school.

It was to prove a decisive break between Eularia and Anthony. Much later she was to write that she did not know him from this time on. The closeness of their early childhood, the big brother that Eularia had so valued and wanted to impress, was lost to her. She never regained an easy relationship with him, often feeling judged by him and pushed away as he began to grow up and make his own friends outside the family circle. For Eularia it was Anthony, more than anyone else, who embodied the Lane Poole streak of cruelty.

2

School

In 1920 Cuthbert and Peggy gave up trying to teach Eularia at home and in despair hired a governess for her, with 'lamentable results'. As a result, in 1921, Eularia joined Mrs Kettle's class (a small infants' school in Notting Hill) and she finally began to make progress.

By the time Eularia was seven she had taken to writing poetry. She would say, 'May I have some paper, I have a poem in my head.' and write it down straight away without altering a word, maintaining that they came into her head complete. Peggy considered Eularia's mind to be old for her age and poetry was something she would continue to write for much of her life, often being published in later years in the Catholic Press.

Eularia began to attend Oxford High School, staying with Peggy's parents who were, since Reginald's retirement, living in Banbury Road. Eularia always considered that Rachael Poole (Granima) was one of only two adults who loved her unreservedly, the other being Peggy's sister, Dorothy. Despite this, Oxford High School was not a success for Eularia and she was only there for a couple of terms before returning to Cheppers where she eventually took the entrance exam to St Paul's Girls School, Hammersmith.

One of Eularia's lifelong crosses was that she always felt the odd one out. Certainly being the only girl in a family of boys made that unavoidable, and she seemed to be the only member of the family who could be relied upon not to get ill, which was a theme that was to follow her all her life. St Paul's was one of her few respites from this: a chance to escape the family and be with other girls her own age, and of similar background and intelligence. Until now most of her friends had been boys. The only real exception to this was, from Eularia's point of view, a poor one – her cousin, Alicia, Aunt Sylvia's daughter.

Alicia was eleven years older than Eularia and everything Eularia was deemed not to be. She was constantly held up to Eularia as an ideal to be attained and which she always fell short of, especially by her Aunt Sylvia and Grandmother Constance. To be constantly compared to Alicia from a young age did nothing for her self-esteem. They were unalike in almost every possible way. Where Eularia was dark, strong-boned, rather lumpy, gauche and somewhat difficult, Alicia was a beauty, with flowing red-golden hair, a flawless complexion and a svelte figure. She was also highly intelligent and very sweet natured, cultured, and well mannered. Understandably Eularia felt that she would never be able to achieve success as a woman, that she was gauche and clumsy in her relationships and, in fact, would never be free of the shadow that was Alicia. For Alicia's part she always seemed to have been most fond of Eularia and was to be a great help and support to her in later years when Eularia most needed it; she was even godmother to Eularia's daughter, but it is impossible to escape the sense that Eularia always felt wrong-footed by her.

On Christmas Eve, 1923, Christopher Richard was born. Christopher was, without doubt, Eularia's favourite brother. He didn't bully her and she didn't feel as if she was in competition with him. She felt very maternal towards him, giving him much of the affection she originally had for Anthony. Eularia was very good at playing the role of big sister and, being the only girl, she was expected to look after him. It is likely that this is the origin of her later tendency (once she had been rejected by her older husband) to fall for much younger men.

Christopher quickly became the much-loved baby of the family, with his blond curls, bonny looks and a gentle character very similar to his father's. Eularia would do anything for him and her moodiness was always dispelled by his presence.

During the summer of 1926 circumstances began to improve for Cuthbert at the India Office when he returned to a department and a job he preferred after four years of 'chronic boredom' involved in 'beastly non-descript work'. Poor Cuthbert, he was the last person in the world that should have had a desk job. He had an intelligent and lively mind, he could recite vast sections of Shakespeare and Moliere (in French) from memory and he had imagination. The daily routine of administration was excruciating, but he had discovered landscape gardening, thanks to a holiday remodelling a relation's garden, a passion he passed on to Eularia.

Cuthbert considered that Eularia was 'a dud' at most of her work, which is a little unfair as her school reports are not that bad. He did observe, however, another passion that was lifelong for Eularia, which led him to think (wrongly) that she might excel at athletics. Eularia loved water and swam like an otter. Cuthbert referred to her as 'really rather a superb little figure'. Eularia was known for swimming anywhere, even in the filthiest, coldest pools, but most of all she loved estuaries and the sea and would swim in them whenever she got the chance. Both my mother and I have memories of wading through mudflats and reed banks after her in order to reach cold and uninviting water, which she would immediately plunge into, leaving everyone else on the edge shivering.

In 1926 Cuthbert attended an inaugural meeting of the Distributists League[6] arranged by his friends G. K. Chesterton and Hilaire Belloc. Despite being friends with the Catholic Chesterton, Cuthbert was a committed agnostic all his life and never took on its Catholic ideals. He did, however, like the emphasis on self-sufficiency and was later to put much of it into practice in retirement.

It is likely that Eularia met Chesterton and Belloc as a child but the origin of her own fascination for religion is something of a mystery. It may have been a side effect of a family tendency towards interest in the supernatural. The strongest exponent of this was her Great Aunt Rose, who, while not especially religious, had a reputation in St Briavells:

'They thought she was something of a witch up there – quite possible. She knew the past – hundreds of years – more familiarly than the present, and the supernatural better than the visible.'

Eularia's own words, and it is possible that it was through her interactions with Aunt Rose (she was a gifted story-teller) that her awareness of the unseen was opened up. It certainly was not something she experienced at home.

Eularia was later to describe the religion at Cheppers as being agnostic or the shallow type of Anglicanism that had very little below the surface. She maintained that she had no instruction in faith but was avidly

---

6   They embraced the economic ideology of Distributism, which was based on principles of Catholic Social Teaching.

interested in it from a young age and sensed Christ as a child. But as Michael Gedge was later to point out to her, having been confirmed an Anglican she must have had some instruction. It is more likely that the kind of instruction she received didn't answer her increasingly deep urge to know more about faith and the supernatural, so she discounted it.

Certainly something did call to Eularia from a fairly young age. She wrote that she greatly irritated her family, especially her brothers, by constantly seeking out 'high' Anglican services in her quest to understand, and spending hours watching the nuns at the Zion Convent opposite Cheppers from the nursery window. She wrote in an article published in 'The Universe' just after her death:

> 'When I was small, my elderly relations took me round art galleries, and I wondered why Italians kept painting Jesus, while English painters stuck to views, and ordinary faces, and dogs? They showed me English religious painting; I dismissed Joshua Reynolds' "Heads of Angels" and "Infant Samuel" as just little girls, nor did Blake seem interested in Jesus, nor did Stanley Spencer. Only Holman Hunt's "Light of the World" seemed to be of Jesus, not just a man but "Light" like in the Creed.'

Though Peggy and Cuthbert may have found their daughter's passion for religion odd, inexplicable and difficult to deal with, they did recognise Eularia's artistic talents. Eularia said that sketching in the family was taken for granted because everyone did it and so it is rarely mentioned. Music, on the other hand, was mentioned much more frequently as Anthony brought his enthusiasm for it home and transmitted it to his siblings.

In 1926 Eularia passed the entrance to St Paul's Girls School. St Paul's suited Eularia completely. She loved it, showing an aptitude for both art and music (she was taught music by Gustav Holst). Her school reports survive and the 1927 report marked her out, somewhat predictably, as a talker and suggested that she try to be more controlled in speech and action. This was something that she never felt she achieved and saw as one of the roots of her problems in social interactions all her life. Her teachers accused her of acting before she thought, something she worked hard to control in later years. This often caused her to doubt her own actions, assuming that she would always make the wrong choice. She was always too aware of her faults compounded by a lack of patience with herself, but she never shied away from attempting to change for the better.

In general, she was a fair student academically, but it was in Art in particular that she began to excel. In 1927 and 1928 she won honours in the Royal Drawing Society's examination and in 1929 the school prize for drawing and painting. She painted a large mural of a fairground on the wall of the basement dining room at St Paul's in her usual mixture at the time of pigment and size, and it remained there well into the 1960s before it was finally painted over.

By the beginning of 1928 both Anthony and Eularia were settled in their respective schools but then in February what was to become an *annus horribilis* for Peggy and Cuthbert began. Anthony was rushed to hospital with appendicitis where he had an emergency operation. Eularia was sent to stay with a friend, leaving Peggy, now nannyless, to cope with a sick Anthony as well as Francis and Christopher (who had just turned four). Whilst left temporarily unattended in the nursery Christopher moved too close to an electric bar heater with no guard and set his jumper alight. Horrifying for any mother, but particularly so for Peggy whose own paternal grandmother died this way.

It took six weeks for Christopher's wounds to heal but he then developed a condition that caused his mouth to contract seriously, which was very disfiguring. On top of this he caught measles. Numerous further skin graft operations followed to help his mouth but Christopher was scarred for life. After this event photographs of Christopher as a child are rare and where they exist he is usually hiding his chin and mouth.

Typically, and quite within character, Eularia blamed herself for this accident. She felt she should have been there as she believed Peggy was too vague to cope on her own. Then Cuthbert fell ill with pneumonia and Peggy was worried for his life.

The last few years had been a struggle for Cuthbert. His first novel had done moderately well but none of the others had lived up to that success and money was increasingly tight. The elusive best seller was never to materialise. Once the fifth novel had been published he stopped writing. The pneumonia was probably the culmination of years doing a job that bored him to tears, never having enough money and never achieving the success he hoped for.

In 1929 Constance died (Sir Athelstane had died four years earlier). That, along with the fact that Anthony would shortly be leaving home to attend Oxford, prompted Peggy and Cuthbert to rent a small cottage called The Green, initially for weekends, in the village of Great Rissington, Gloucestershire. The family started to downsize in London as they began to spend more time at Great Rissington. They sold Cheppers in 1932 and rented a three bedroom top floor flat at 24 Esmond Gardens, Chiswick.

Anthony's passion for collecting musical instruments began at this time (he would later found the Bate Collection of musical instruments at Oxford). He bought a cheap job lot of brass instruments that he found lying neglected in a junk shop in Hammersmith and formed a family band, oddly name the 'Unhappy Family Brass Band', which rehearsed at Esmond Road.

The Unhappy Family Brass Band at Great Rissington (circa 1932)
From top left: Anthony, Ralph Henvey, Francis, Eularia, Christopher

This consisted of Anthony leading on the F trumpet, Francis on the tenor trombone, Eularia on the horn, Christopher on the B-flat cornopean, Ralph Henvey (their cousin) on the bassoon, Anthony Spurgin (a lifelong friend of Anthony's) on the E-flat bass and a long-suffering Cuthbert struggling with a B-flat baritone (a German hybrid instrument with rotary valves). They played traditional airs all arranged by Anthony such as *The*

Beer They Brewed at Burton. As none of them were particularly practiced at any of these instruments (except Ralph on bassoon) the noise must have been extraordinary. It certainly found its way into the neighbouring flats and became a constant source of complaint. Typically neither Anthony nor Francis cared at all and it was only when Peggy and Cuthbert were threatened with eviction that they had to take notice. Given that all three of the brothers grew up to become recognised authorities and performers on old musical instruments, this eclectic mix of junk shop instruments, and the family band, can be seen as formative despite the inconvenience to others. Eularia made some wonderful pen and ink sketches of these musical sessions, which still survive.

Band

In 1931, while Eularia, Anthony and Francis continued to blossom, tragedy struck when their cousins (Austin and Vera's oldest two children) both died of scarlet fever within a month of each other. The tragedy hit the whole family hard and was never talked about, although the memory of it stayed with Eularia. Vera all but gave up her art after this. It was a tragic precursor to possibly the most formative event in Eularia's life.

3

'Like Fra Angelico'

By 1931 Aunt Sylvia was living in Florence and, despite Eularia never measuring up to her exacting standards, Sylvia invited her to join her there with Cousin Alicia for the Easter of that year. Eularia was approaching 17 and Alicia 27, still unmarried and old enough to be considered a good chaperone for Eularia on the journey out there. Alicia's inability to find a husband, despite her obvious good looks and accomplishments, was a source of great distress to both Sylvia and her husband Philip. Sylvia now began to turn her attention towards her young niece who was living mostly in hand-me-down clothes from both Alicia and Sylvia.

Eularia's approach to clothes was always laid back and rather eccentric. It would be wrong to suppose that she did not care about her appearance, she did (she went into ecstasies in a long letter to Alicia when the latter supplied her with the means to buy her first Gossard corset in the 1950s), but it wasn't an all-consuming passion for her. As there was little spare cash in the family (less once Eularia married) she made many of her own clothes, which she enjoyed doing, and she became a master at making do and restyling old garments, the results often bordering on the eccentric.

Both Sylvia and Alicia had had a coming-out season and had been presented at the palace but there was never any question of Eularia taking this route. The family couldn't afford it and Cuthbert and Peggy had no inclination for it. So, like Eularia's clothing, they were going to have to make do. Sylvia felt that she could at least contribute towards ensuring that her niece had some kind of education in culture and antiquities, on which she herself was very keen.

Eularia was very excited to have the chance to go to Florence despite the combination of Sylvia and Alicia. It was to be her first trip abroad. The first of Eularia's many letters to survive is the one written in January 1931 to Sylvia thanking her for the opportunity:

'I simply can't tell you how excited I am at the idea of going to Florence! I can scarcely believe anything so wonderful could possibly happen. Thank you a thousand times for thinking of it. I don't know how I am going to live until the end of term! ... I am longing most of all to see the pictures.'

The Florence visit was fundamental to shaping Eularia as an artist. She was to cite it many times in interviews and gallery biographies as being the point at which she decided to become a religious artist. In particular it was the frescoes in San Marco by Fra Angelico and Giotto that inspired her:

'I was determined, as a child, to be a religious painter; very natural, as my family up to the (18)90s was full of vicars and professional painters and engravers. It was typically pagan by the time I was born, 1914, but I persistently longed for religion, and on a visit to Florence, I was so fired by the San Marco frescoes that I began to illustrate the Gospels with paint box and cartridge block in the regrettably artistic Art Nouveau manner of those days.'

Florence was a turning point. It inspired her, already showing talent as an artist, to begin to express some of the inner feelings that she had about God and religion, and she wrote that the main subject of her paintings from this point until her marriage were the Gospels. Only two unfinished sketches from this early period survive. The first is of the Crucifixion (thanks to Eularia's cousin Nan who she sold it to for a guinea). Its perspective is dramatic – seen from ground level, behind and to the right of the cross on which the silhouette of Jesus hangs. The second is almost certainly an early study of Jesus walking on the water with St Peter reaching up towards him. Both show Eularia's flare for the dramatic and both do reflect the Art Nouveau style but there is something about the boldness of line and the flat colour that brings to mind the frescoes of the early Renaissance painters.

After Florence, Eularia began increasingly to frequent churches and religious institutions in search of answers to her questions and her feelings. She wanted to know what worship was about, especially the Sacraments themselves. She wanted to understand why she was so inspired by those frescoes, why she felt so drawn to paint this subject.

Crucifixion

She never had any support from her family in this. Cuthbert was convinced by his agnosticism and would not have understood, or had much time for, his daughter's passion. Peggy was, and would remain, a gentle and vague Anglican and probably felt completely unable to answer any of Eularia's questions. Anthony and Francis were convinced agnostics just like their father and were scathing about their sister's interest. Anthony always remained so, but Francis had his own eccentricities and was happier to live and let live, even investigating Catholicism himself for a brief period in 1950s. Christopher was not yet at an age where his opinion mattered much to his siblings.

Eularia, unlike her more mild parents, was deeply passionate and tended towards the dramatic. She really *felt* things and wasn't prepared to let them drop. Once she had a passion about something she was like a dog with a bone. She would hang onto it until it was quite dead to her and sometimes she'd hang onto it even then. But their cynical attitudes and criticisms hurt nonetheless.

Even today her family are uncomfortable with the idea that Eularia had a calling and that they have a religious artist in their midst. Her children would much prefer to have had a safe landscape painter as a forebear. Eularia herself found it hard, inexplicable, lonely and often contrary to what she would have chosen for herself, but when it came down to it she was unable to deny it. There was something deep at work that defied the intellectual and it found its expression through her art.

Eighteen months after returning from Florence Eularia took up her scholarship at St Ann's College, Oxford, to study Theology where her beloved aunt Dorothy was the Classics don. It is uncertain why Eularia did not consider a proper art training. For someone who wanted to be a religious painter it was the obvious choice and her aunt Vera had shown that it was possible for a girl. A clue perhaps lies in a letter Cuthbert wrote to his nephew Davy in March 1932:

> 'Eularia is having a good time during her last year at school. She may go to Oxford as a Home Student or she may not – it is all very undecided. Of course, Art is undoubtedly her line; but is there any chance of her making a living out of it? I doubt it.'

By this stage money was very tight. Cuthbert was of the opinion that the depression changed them more than the war did. In order to get any kind of education now his children needed to gain scholarships and be self-supporting afterwards. The shadow of his own failure to support his family as an author may well have contributed to this and influenced Eularia's choice. Art does not pay the bills: a family myth that still holds to this day.

By December 1930 Peggy and Cuthbert had finally bought the cottage in Great Rissington as a weekend bolthole. The Green was to be the place where Cuthbert was most happy. They loved the cottage from the first even though it had no electricity, running water or sewerage. They relied on water from a hand-pump across the road on the village green and an Elsan in a cubicle attached to an exterior workshop.

Space was tight so Eularia decided not to sleep in the cottage itself and instead bought a traditional gypsy caravan for £5, which she installed in the orchard at the bottom of the garden, allowing her to sleep out of doors, something she loved all her life.

4

Oxford

Eularia decided to study Theology in the hope that she would begin to find answers to her questions about faith and religion. Perhaps she would begin to understand what was calling her. She was to be disappointed. She wanted to understand the mystery and instead was confronted by mental concepts and wrangles about texts and historical criticism. She later wrote, 'I found no religion there, nothing supernatural, still less divine.'

St Anne's, in those days, was a Home Students College as it had no Halls of Residence. Eularia lived with her increasingly elderly Lane Poole grandparents at 19 Banbury Road, somewhat marred by the fact that Reginald, who suffered badly from depression by this time, had taken to his upstairs study with the whisky bottle and seldom appeared. What might otherwise have been a disastrous three years was lightened by her taking life drawing classes at the Ruskin School in her spare time where she was taught by Gilbert Spencer (who drew a very fine portrait of her), Albert Rutherston and Barnet Freedman among others, and she loved it. It made up for the rather lowly third she gained for her degree and her complete disillusionment with religion as a result of her Theology teachers.

While she was at Oxford she embarked on her first serious relationship with a young dashing South African Rhodes scholar called Bram Fischer. They grew increasingly fond of one another. Eularia was to say that he wrote the best love letters of any that she ever received, none of which survive. Bram asked her to marry him and go back to South Africa, but

Eularia (circa 1932)

although she was very fond of him she felt that she didn't love him enough to move so far away from her family and so she turned him down. She was later to say that she treated Bram badly, but it was a sound move as Fischer gave up all the rights and privileges of being part of a well-to-do Afrikaans family to become a prominent opponent of apartheid (Fischer led Mandela's defence in the Rivonia trials). Eularia, always so conscious of her status, would not have made a good revolutionary's wife.

Eularia loved Great Rissington. She had a powerful attraction to nearby Wychwood Forest and she described cycling regularly over to Westcote, near Stow-on-the Wold, where there was a small nunnery, and attending services there:

'... that thrilling bicycle trip to Stow, cold bacon sandwiches among the beeches, always alone. The trips to Westcote, to the church, over and over again, because of the lovely "services" and the nuns there, when I bought a rosary and said prayers by haystacks and in barns.'

Many of Eularia's landscape sketches are of the Cotswold countryside and she used it more than once as a background for her later religious works.

Cuthbert and Jasper the cat at Great Rissington (circa 1932-33)

In 1936 Cuthbert was made redundant, a fact over which he greatly rejoiced, and he and Peggy built an extension on The Green with the money and moved there permanently. Much as Eularia loved Great Rissington, her early twenties were the wrong time to want to be stuck in the country. Cuthbert and Peggy kept the flat in Esmond Gardens as a London base and when she left Oxford Eularia joined Anthony there. The brilliant Anthony, of whom his parents had had such hopes, had completely confounded them by chucking his Oxford Chemistry degree in his final year (because he found electro-chemistry boring) and gained a place at the Royal College of Music.

Whilst Peggy and Cuthbert loved music and had always encouraged it in their children, this was a real blow to them. Music was fine as an amateur pursuit but in those days it was considered to be a profession only suitable for the lower classes and foreigners. But they had no more control over Anthony now than they had when he was small. They were further confounded when a couple of years later Francis joined his brother at the R.C.M. and Esmond Gardens became home to all three of them. Needless to say, Eularia's job was to keep house.

Anthony and Francis were still a handful. Cuthbert had to pay a large fine to bail Anthony out of a police station after he had vandalised a closed garage on the way back to London from Great Rissington in order to get petrol. It is a testament to Peggy and Cuthbert's rather vague approach to parenting that they never seemed to have questioned the advisability of allowing Eularia to live in London with two very untrustworthy and unreliable brothers. Perhaps they knew their daughter well enough to realise that she was very different from Anthony and Francis. She was more sensitive, far less confidant in social situations than people thought, and she appeared to have 'got' religion.

5

Cyril

For Eularia, London life was wonderful even under the somewhat dubious protection of her brothers. During the mid-thirties London was a hive of activity and creativity. She painted her gospel scenes, looked after the flat and got to know other painters (such as John Nicholls who lived round the corner) and musicians. It is possible that she attended classes in oil painting at the Ealing Technical College as this is suggested in some notes of her own, but we do not know for sure.

In 1936 Anthony did something he would regret for the rest of his life and which would profoundly alter the course of his sister's. He introduced Eularia to one of his friends from the R.C.M., a clarinettist called Cyril Clarke.

Cyril was 28, tall, blonde, extremely charming, a great wit and raconteur and a very talented musician. His origins were humble by Eularia's standards but his history displayed a rather romantic wild side that would undoubtedly have attracted her. He came from a Norfolk farming family with the odd claim to notoriety that his grandfather had decided to branch out into horse breeding, gone to Spain to obtain stock and returned without a single horse but with a Spanish bride. Cyril's parents were very respectable, his father having left farming and Norfolk behind in favour of engineering and Mitcham in Surrey. Cyril attended Rutlish, a minor public school where he failed to shine (possibly because he was an undiagnosed dyslexic) but taught himself to play the saxophone in his early teens, displaying a clear talent for music. He shocked everyone by running away from home at 16, only

Cyril Clarke (mid 1930s)

turning up a few weeks later playing in a theatre orchestra in Edinburgh. He earned his living playing in theatre and dance bands including Geraldo's and Mantovani's, but by his mid-twenties he was beginning to compose and wanted to be a classical musician (he was a life-long fan of Delius on whose grave his ashes were later scattered). He finally won a scholarship to study clarinet at the R.C.M. and became a contemporary of Anthony's. To the young and somewhat impressionable Eularia he must have seemed very glamorous and she fell for him almost immediately. Cyril was hesitant at first, largely because she was his friend's sister, and he talked to Anthony about whether he should pursue it or not. Anthony, to his everlasting regret, urged Cyril to 'go for it', and Cyril did.

They were soon engaged and Cyril was quickly introduced to a less than ecstatic family en-masse at Cuthbert and Peggy's Silver Wedding celebrations in Great Rissington, a formidable introduction by anyone's standards. He faced a solid wall of disapproval, especially from the aunts, Sylvia and Dorothy. Peggy and Cuthbert were being presented with yet another musician as a prospective son-in-law, with absolutely no family connections and no prospect of being able to support their daughter. It wasn't what they wanted for Eularia; Cuthbert at the very least would have liked someone with an income.

Cuthbert's misgivings were well founded because once Eularia married Cyril money, or lack of it, were going to define the next twenty years of her life. But Cyril was easy to like: he was very personable, could charm anyone and could talk the hind leg off a donkey, another trait that must have been attractive to her. Here was someone who could hold his own in a room full of Baineses and match any of them word for word. But even Cyril's own mother had misgivings about the match. She warned Eularia that he would be a hopeless husband, but they were in love and, perhaps not surprisingly given that Peggy and Cuthbert never could put their foot down about anything, they married at the church in Great Rissington on 27 July 1937 and honeymooned in Annecy in the French Alps.

Cyril at Annecy (1937)

In Eularia's sketches of Annecy it is possible to see the more angular style of her earlier Art Nouveau years beginning to develop into something more fluid. Eularia was a great sketcher. She had a way of capturing moments in time with a vivid presence using simple, almost primitive lines and bright colours. She did use watercolour, but more and more she was turning to gouache, which lent her sketches their primitive immediacy and brilliance. Her daughter, Rachael, says that she would usually sketch in pencil, making colour notes and observations, and then paint them in when she returned home. She was very adept at doing this. Even in her writing her descriptions are always full of colour references.

Eularia threw herself into the marriage with all the passion that was typical of her and for the first two years she and Cyril were, as far as we can tell, reasonably happy. They moved into a flat at 11 North Road, Highgate, London and Cyril found work in local orchestras and bands in the evenings (he joined the new BBC Orchestra), and spent much of his day writing and arranging music. Money was tight. Cyril had an extraordinarily generous nature and would, on pay day, stand the whole orchestra drinks without giving any thought as to how Eularia would buy food, so there frequently wasn't any money left to take home to her.

How happy they actually were is uncertain. Cyril had an unpredictable and sometimes violent temper, which Eularia was certainly afraid of, but the evidence that remains suggests that they both did their best to make the marriage work in these early years and, in general, Eularia seems to have been content. It is likely that she overruled any worries she might have had. She was by nature a positive person and always tended to find the bright side in any catastrophe. It could take a great deal, especially in these early years before life had really touched her, for her to finally admit that the path she was on was not working. As she grew older it would become something of a self-fulfilling prophecy. Having had so much disappointment by then to deal with she would tend to write it into situations, especially relationships, before it had a chance to take hold on its own.

In August 1938 Rachael Maria was born in the flat at Highgate. Eularia did attempt to follow Peggy's example of keeping a development diary for baby Rachael, but it didn't last long. Her way of recording, especially in this period of her life, was to sketch and she drew Rachael right from the first, doing a little sketch, presumably from memory, of her lying on the table with the umbilical cord still attached. Eularia was never one to shy away from the messier sides of life in her art.

Cyril may not have been an ideal husband (Eularia later described being married to him as like being married to a 'sieve' because of the money situation) but he was very proud of Rachael. Eularia's sketches of this time are all cosy and intimate scenes of baby Rachael and of Cyril. But just as it had for Peggy and Cuthbert in their early-married years, history was to take a turn that would change everything for Eularia. On the 3rd of September 1939 war was once again declared on Germany.

Cyril with Rachael (1938)

Part 2

The Blank Slice

1939 – 1956

6

War

On the 3rd of September 1939 Cyril was in London and Eularia was at her parents' house in Great Rissington with her baby daughter, Rachael, where they gathered around the radio to hear the broadcast that declared we were at war with Germany. Eularia wrote in a brief diary that covers the first few days of the war:

'We all sat grimly in the drawing room, Joan (*the maid*) fingering her apron, Daddy tense and writhing in a chair, Christopher nervous but uncomprehending, Mummy very tragic. I only wanted to hear the speech.'

Cyril was working for the BBC in London and cracks were beginning to appear in the relationship. On 8 September 1939, after a week's silence, Eularia had her first news of him through her brother, Anthony, who wrote to her that, 'Cyril is providing my lunches'. Cyril was doing this on the cheque that Eularia had sent him to pay his fare to visit her in Great Rissington. Understandably this did not go down well.

Despite being close to an airfield Great Rissington felt very remote from the war and Eularia had nothing to do except look after Rachael, most of the housework being taken care of by Joan and Peggy. She was bored, effectively homeless and husbandless and desperately wanted to do something constructive:

'If it wasn't for Rachael I could join the Land Army, but even to leave her for an hour is to ask a great favour of Mummy or Joan.'

There was no work in Rissington, there was no petrol to travel elsewhere to find any either and it was considered too dangerous for her to go back to London with Rachael.

Sometime during early 1940 parts of the BBC were evacuated to Bristol, including the Music Library where Cyril was working. Much to her relief Eularia joined him there. Being flat-footed, Cyril was refused for active service so instead he joined the Fire Service, not a pleasant or easy job in heavily bombed Bristol and one for which he was not temperamentally suited.

Bristol before the bombing (1941)

Anthony gained a commission in the Royal Tank Regiment in 1941. He was wounded and captured in Africa in 1942 and spent the rest of the war as a P.O.W. Francis was also captured, leaving his wife Ann to cope with his young son, Jonathan, which she didn't seem to be doing very well according to Eularia. Christopher completed the first year of his Maths degree at Oxford and joined an engineering research firm based at Shoreham working for the Air Ministry.

By mid 1940 Eularia was expecting again with the baby due in early 1941. Her plan was to leave Rachael at Rissington with Peggy and go into the Radcliffe Infirmary in Oxford to have the new baby. In the end the war decided things for them. In November 1940 Bristol was heavily bombed in a night raid, the first of many it would suffer throughout the war. Eularia departed for Rissington where she gave birth to Thomas James Kenelm (always known as James) in February 1941. Cyril remained behind in Bristol.

Once Eularia had returned to Rissington for her confinement she and Cyril were never to live together again as a couple. Bristol was no longer safe for a mother with two very small children, so she stored all her belongings, furniture (mostly inherited from the family), paintings, sketches, letters, everything that would not fit at her parents' house, in a barn close to Rissington and moved back there full time.

Not long after James' birth the BBC building in Bristol was bombed and Cyril was evacuated at almost no notice, with what was left of the music library, to Bangor, making it much harder for him to visit. In the first letter he wrote to Eularia after this event he said, 'When can you safely leave James? Could you come and spend a few days here?' So initially the separation was a hard one. But Cyril was not a good correspondent; being dyslexic he probably found writing letters a chore and he rarely dated any of them so it is a little difficult to work out the sequence of events. He always seemed to be hoping that his next royalty cheque would solve all their financial problems and it never did (his sister, Rena, spent a lifetime bailing him out). Certainly by 1942 he was badly in debt, with no collateral of any kind having lost many of his belongings, presumably to the bombing in Bristol, and unable to get credit. He bemoaned the fact that if he was the son of Sir Athelstane Baines[1] the banks would not hesitate to lend him money, but as he was nobody they refused to look at him twice.

---

1   Eularia's paternal grandfather.

His feelings of not being quite accepted by Eularia's family come across in his letters very strongly. He was constantly apologising to Eularia for letting her down, for not being in touch, for not sending money. He gives the impression that he was genuinely struggling to make things work and that he was still very fond of the children, but he was afraid that they were forgetting him. His fear was well founded as Rachael and James did indeed grow up feeling that their Grandfather Cuthbert was their father figure. They both say that they never felt deprived of a father because, in their memory, he was never around, and they had 'Gassy' (their pet name for Cuthbert).

It is hard to know how compatible Eularia and Cyril really were. They undoubtedly both tried to make the marriage work but the enforced separation came at the wrong time. Eularia never handled the shortcomings of others very well. She tended to adore them in the honeymoon period and then feel completely let down by them when it was over, and there is a hint in Cyril's letters that what she interpreted as his lack of confidence with her family irked her. Being a great 'rescuer' of people sometimes caused her to appear condescending and patronising in the eyes of those she was intent on rescuing and Cyril, who anyway suffered from low self-esteem, would not have handled that well. Certainly, as time went on, he became very anti-Baines.

Money was always an issue. Cyril earned it but he just as quickly spent it, and Eularia was to say much later that they never had a good sex life. She felt cheated in this area because no one had taught her about it in advance and she did wonder whether things would have been better between them had she been less ignorant about it all. Although Cyril could be charm itself, his ferocious and unpredictable temper, over which he seemed to have no control, was always a problem. Eularia feared confrontations with him and, like many musicians, he was over fond of the booze which made it worse. In the end the parents proved right, they simply were not compatible and Cyril was far from being ideal husband material.

During the war it was easy to explain Cyril's absence. So many men were away and so many families divided, but by the time the war was over it was clear that the marriage was too. By then Cyril had a mistress, a French Canadian called Lorraine, who Eularia was not prepared to put up with. Worse than that, in 1944, desperate for money Cyril borrowed a van, broke into the barn where all Eularia's belongings were stored, loaded them up, took them to London and sold them all for a cheque that later bounced. Everything went: all the furniture she had been given, or left, by relations, the wedding presents, all her letters and diaries and worse still all her early canvases, all the early gospel illustrations, vanished in one rash action. She was left with virtually nothing. Eularia never forgave Cyril for this.

Anthony did try to advise Eularia over Cyril, being the only other member of the family who really knew him. He wrote to her in February 1942 having obviously had disquieting news from Cuthbert about the situation:

'Now the thing to avoid is the gay defiant attitude – in Poole lingo, "(*being*) very, very brave about it".... You *must not* be defiantly brave about it but vigorously offensive about it. We all know the excellent Cyril is engagingly mad, and it is up to the slightly saner wife to administrate and direct the connection. Perhaps you are, but in spite of your talk about the vitality of Baines womenfolk, you have the same old tendency to spoil a courageous outlook by a timidity of action. Baines courage is, as I know too well, apt to be cerebral – "brother, thy tail hangs down below" and all that sort of thing.

'Stage a demonstration. Borrow some candy, and go *with the kids* to Bangor, be a bit crazy about it. It is not so much that there shall be method in your madness, but that your method *is* madness. Confront Clarke in three persons, you Rachael and James and with transport – and kiddiekar and a pram – do it. For God sake don't sit pretty – stolidly defiant.'

Anthony knew his sister well. Stolidly defiant and brave were exactly what Eularia did best when confronted by bad situations. Those who did not know her well would never know just how much she might be hurt by something, or how lost she might be feeling in relation to situations like these, and she hated confrontation. When she was frightened of someone (and she was frightened of Cyril) she was quite capable of crumpling up inside and running away. Needless to say she did not follow Anthony's advice.

Meanwhile she had to earn money somehow and the only thing open to her was teaching Art or Music, the subjects that she was good at. During the war there was a shortage of teachers so she began taking jobs in schools wherever she could find them and, like Peggy in the previous war, was to spend the rest of it moving from location to location, taking her children with her by train. Rachael remembers (and still has to this day) the little rucksack that Eularia made for her in which she fitted all her belongings, and the endless waiting on station platforms.

Eularia began by moving to her Aunt Dorothy's house in Walton Street, Oxford, where she was supposed to be the home help and cook. She then went to work part-time in a munitions factory, but the arrangement with Dorothy didn't work out, despite them being very fond of one another. Having two very small children and a rather distressed niece in the house must have been hard work for the spinster Dorothy.

Eularia found a teaching job at Haileybury and the small family moved there but were under constant threat from flying bombs, so she found another job at a prep school in Harwell called Pillar House. By the time the war ended she had moved her small family to a prep school near Wincanton. During the school holidays they returned to Rissington and, thanks to Cuthbert and Peggy's self-sufficiency, a well-stocked larder.

In fairness to Cyril he was not a bad man. He was simply one of those who never seemed to discover how normal life worked. He never understood the concept of money or fatherhood, not because he didn't want to, but because it simply didn't seem to register in his world. Rachael described him as someone who could keep a whole room entranced just by talking, but who was totally incapable of talking to anyone about the practical issues raised by parenting. She said that in her memory he never paid for anything. She described being taken to a smart restaurant in London with James and being introduced to oysters by Cyril who could not then pay the bill. Cyril and money simply didn't seem to exist in the same dimension.

In the end the only two casualties in the Baines family during the war were the marriages. Both Eularia's and Francis's marriages were over. Eularia was left with two small children to raise on her own and Francis with one, as his wife, Ann, had left Jonathan with him and returned to her native Australia.

7

Survival

Eularia was to call the next fifteen years of her life her blank years, taken up with survival, supporting a young family and having no time to consider exploring religion or serious painting. She never stopped sketching but the subjects now become focused around her daily life, her children and local landscapes, a way of keeping her hand in and fulfilling her need to record everything visually.

Once the war was over she moved back to Great Rissington full time. A few short months later, in early 1946, Peggy contracted pneumonia and died at only 59. Always with a tendency towards asthma, the strain of the war years and the failure of her children's marriages had proved too much. Cuthbert was lost without her and it fell to Eularia to stay on and look after him. Rachael remembers vividly being taken down the garden by Eularia to tell the bees of Peggy's death and picking up the sense of defeat that Eularia felt about the expectation that was now on her to stay and keep house for Cuthbert.

For her children, however, this proved to be beneficial. They both loved Rissington and they loved their grandfather. It was the only real home they had known. For the next three years they enjoyed a stability that they hadn't yet had in their short lives. Eularia took a teaching job at a small prep school in Fulbrook, just outside Burford, called Cotter's Bow which just about paid for James and Rachael to attend as pupils. She would drive them there every day in Cuthbert's old, battered Austin 7, always a hair-raising experience despite her having had a few lessons from a man in the village.

It was during this time that Eularia got to know Ben and Bertha Boulter who lived in Burford. He was an artist and she a very good violin teacher to whom Rachael was duly sent. They became lifelong friends and their daughter Clare eventually married Eularia's brother, Christopher. The Boulter's reinforced Eularia's own view that the most important things in life that you could teach a child were Art, Music and Craftsmanship.

Another artist she came to know during this time was the potter Michael Cardew and his wife Meriel who lived at Winchcomb. They had children of a similar age and there are several sketches made by Eularia of the Cardews.

Eularia did her best to fund her family. She even tried her hand at pastel portraits of the children at Cotter's Bow, aiming to sell them to the parents (two of which survive), but she couldn't cope with Cuthbert. Being stuck at Rissington and keeping house for him stifled her. For some reason that she couldn't fathom, and certainly didn't blame Cuthbert for, she developed a state of nervous revulsion towards him. She wrote to Alicia:

'I must make excuses to be in a different room, or have my food later, because I can't eat when he is eating, or sit with him without an effort of self-control and pretence that becomes increasingly difficult with exhaustion and stress. I don't really think he knows - I have tried and tried to hide it, and I'm a good liar. He mustn't know because he is so good and kind and generous and good-natured, and really it is not his fault *at all* – that is what is so cruel about it.'

On the plus side her cousin Alicia, who had been Eularia's Nemesis for so long, was fast becoming something of a confidante and a guardian angel for her, and was to remain so for the years to come. They drew closer after her aunt Sylvia's death in 1941 and Eularia had achieved what the beautiful and intelligent Alicia had not – a marriage (albeit a disastrous one) and children. This put Eularia on a different footing with her spinster cousin, who was to remain unmarried all her life. Alicia, a true 'blue-stocking', was an academic and, working as a teacher herself, was much better off than Eularia. She never failed to help Eularia out financially and was very fond of Eularia's children: she was godmother to Rachael, and her brother Davey was godfather to James. Eularia was never able to return this sweet-natured tolerance but she greatly appreciated Alicia's support.

Eularia was very aware of the stigma of being an abandoned wife and a single parent, something she would never lose. So when, in 1947 (following her younger sister, Peggy, only a few months later) her aunt Dorothy died of stomach cancer, leaving Eularia a very modest income, she decided it was time for a fresh start.

This came in the shape of Cousin Ursula Gregory, eight years older than Eularia, who lived in a large, rambling, primitive and ancient house at Little Baddow in Essex called Bassetts. Ursula, who was not married, had a tendency to fill her house with discarded and rather odd friends and relations, so she offered Eularia some space.

Bassetts was originally a Tudor farmhouse and said to be haunted. Ursula gave Eularia and the children the large oak-panelled dining room as a living space and it was all very primitive. There was no electricity, gas or running water, just flickering candles and Aladdin lamps. Eularia cooked on a paraffin stove, or over the open fire, and they washed with jugs and bowls, or in a tin bath in front of the fire. Eularia made some very evocative sketches of life at Bassetts.

They were miles from the nearest village and school meant a great deal of walking, as, without Cuthbert's car, Eularia had no means of transport so finding a job was impractical. Money was so tight that Rachael remembers Eularia going without food or living on mashed potato so that she and James could eat. To try and alleviate this Eularia created a series of fabric designs, which ultimately came to nothing. They are typical of her style, bold, primitive depictions of nature.

For much of the day, while the children were at school she was stuck on her own in the dark and gloomy house, and she wasn't getting on as well as she hoped with Ursula or her brother Kit and his wife Marion. She could not escape the shadow of being the poor relation, 'poor Eularia, whose husband left her'. Another concern was James, now 8, who was running wild and spending altogether far too much time with the farm workers in the fields for Eularia's liking. She worried that living in an all-female house meant that he lacked discipline.

In the end it was Rachael's schooling that decided things. She was due to start senior school in the autumn of 1949 and without transport it just wasn't practical from Bassetts. So Eularia, with Cuthbert's support, began to look for a small cottage that she could buy somewhere close to a suitable school.

As luck would have it Grace Watt, one of Eularia's old teachers at St Paul's, was now headmistress at St Swithun's school in Winchester. With

Bath time at Bassetts (circa 1948)

financial help from Alicia and an arrangement whereby she would teach recorders at Medecroft (St Swithun's junior school) she was able to secure Rachael a place. Even though Rachael was eligible for a grant the Hampshire Education Officer refused it because Eularia did not want Rachael to attend the free County High School.

Eularia (as would occur again many times in her life) was caught between a rock and a hard place. On the one hand she was poorer than many working class people, but on the other she had all the inherited snobbishness of the upper middle class who never quite belonged in the true upper class but were damned if they were going to give an inch in the other direction. It was to define her approach to Winchester society and often left her out in the cold. Better an impoverished and intellectual gentlewoman than a Winchester 'aboriginal'.

Cuthbert agreed to support Eularia in buying a small cottage in the Winchester area and so the search began. With this help from her father, and the selling of some of the shares in the Trust that Dorothy left her to Alicia, Eularia had £1500 at her disposal. After several abortive trips to Winchester and almost despairing of finding anything she could afford, she stumbled across an old muse cottage and stable sitting amongst a collection of garages off the Romsey Road and not far from the city centre. This was 12 Middle Road and it was cheap because it was condemned, but Eularia took it anyway and builders were brought in to renovate it and make it safe.

Clemency Cottage, 12 Middle Road (early 1950s)

Eularia had spent a whole year living, with two children, on three pounds a week and remained undaunted, although she now faced having to live off an overdraft in order to pay the builders. Her years with Cuthbert and Peggy as parents now began to pay off. With no money she had to be very self-sufficient. Unable to afford luxuries like carpets she wove rush mats (just as Cuthbert and Peggy had done) and she made all her own soft furnishings and clothes, often with fabric supplied by sympathetic relations such as Alicia or Aunt Margaret. Cuthbert helped financially where he could and by the autumn of 1949 the family moved into 12 Middle Road, which Eularia christened Clemency Cottage in honour of her mother, although to the family it was always Middle Road.

All those who knew Middle Road remember it with great fondness. It was small and very primitive, an eccentric and shabby home, but it reflected Eularia perfectly. It was to morph over time but in those early days the old stable was converted into a parlour and the living room next to it proudly sported a cook-and-heat stove. Upstairs Rachael and Eularia had a bedroom each and James took over the attic above the old carriage room. The walls were hung with family paintings and broken musical instruments, the furniture was an odd, eclectic and rather ramshackle collection of cast-offs from other members of the family, and pot plants, often scented geraniums, sat around on window sills, but it was home, and it was their home.

Financial help from Alicia punctuated the next few years. Every letter that Eularia wrote to her relations during this period began with abject thanks for money. She had long since given up asking Cyril for any and none was ever forthcoming.

8

Someone to Love

Until 1953 Eularia's diary-keeping was patchy (a short account of Rachael's birth and a few days noted at the beginning of the war). By the time Eularia's diaries began in earnest in October 1954 (an earlier one begun in 1953 is either lost or destroyed), it is impossible to overlook the fact that she felt that life was passing her by. Lacking a partner to talk things over with she needed an outlet, a place where she could express all those feelings that she was unable to express in her daily life. She was extraordinarily good at it. It is in her diaries that we begin to get to know the Eularia behind the outwardly confident and coping mother and teacher and begin to see her inner turmoil. They are frank and revealing.

She turned 40 in the May of 1954 and the elusive grail of a loving husband, a man to partner her through life, had not materialised. The best she could say was that she had two children who seemed to be doing all right, a house, albeit rather primitive and basic, and a job teaching part-time recorders to whoever would pay her. Money was extremely tight and she was still reliant on help from her father, the ever-generous Alicia and Aunt Margaret. It is easy to forget that there was little in the way of income support at this time, with the exception of a small child allowance for those under 15. Without the help of her relatives, Eularia could easily have been destitute.

It was not the constant scrabbling for money and struggle to make ends meet, however, that was to define this decade of Eularia's life, but the hunt for that elusive love of her life. First, though, the problem of Cyril had to be resolved.

Eularia had contacted a solicitor about getting a divorce whilst in Essex. This was not an easy undertaking at the time. There had to be a sound basis for it and there was a hitch as no technical desertion could be proved until she actually asked Cyril to come back ('one has one's pride,' as she said in a letter to Aunt Margaret), so the solicitor agreed to write to Cyril to discover his intentions.

Cyril, in response to the letter from the solicitor, arrived on the doorstep for Christmas 1949 complete with two kittens and a distinctly 'off' turkey in an attempt to see if they could make a go of things. Rachael, now 11, and James, 8, were overjoyed and obviously hoped that there would be a reconciliation, but it wasn't to be. He only managed one night and then left.

In a letter to Eularia in 1952 Cyril wrote:

'It is certain sure that I am no use to you, or to the children – more especially to them. My views, my way of life, my complete inability to conform to the official or accepted standards of behaviour – with grinding axes and rolling logs – resulting in virtual ostracism from high musical places and the concomitant of little or no income – my average is about three pounds a week – has brought me to the point when I must seriously think of leaving the country.'

Incredibly talented, it was the unpredictability of Cyril's temper that always let him down, making him almost impossible to work with, exacerbated by an increasing drink problem. Rachael later said that:

'in the circles in which he moved everyone smoked and drank heavily… Cyril's drinking got to dangerous levels.'

On 17 July 1953 the divorce went through although Eularia was never to feel truly free of Cyril. Communication with him (usually over money or the children who he hardly ever saw) always ended badly, usually with Eularia in tears. She did attempt to sue him for maintenance later in the decade but ultimately gave up. He would never have paid it anyway.

Eularia was beset by unwanted relationships in the early 1950s. Cuthbert, who had spent a lonely couple of years at Great Rissington after she had left with the children, had rekindled a friendship with the daughter of an old friend of Sir Athelstane's from the Kidlington days. Now a widow and living in Oxford, Dorothy Harlow became his new partner (although they never married) and he was extremely fond of her. Struggling with bouts of depression and finding Great Rissington too much to cope with, he let it and moved in with Dorothy.

For Eularia it began a feud, which was to last until her father's death. She felt that Dorothy was always prejudicing Cuthbert against continuing to help her and the children financially. Dorothy had no love for Eularia either. She all but banned any lengthy visits by Eularia and the children to Oxford to see Cuthbert because, by Rachael's own admission, she and James didn't like her either and had behaved so abominably when staying there that poor Dorothy simply didn't want them back.

Eularia teaching recorders at Medecroft (circa early 50s)

Back in Winchester the family settled in to Middle Road and Eularia, who had taught herself to play the guitar, added this to the recorder teaching at various schools in and around Winchester and to private pupils. In between all this Eularia was finding time to sketch, although her output dropped in the early years at Middle Road. All her energy was going into keeping afloat financially.

She did enter a couple of landscapes into a local art exhibition at this time because Rachael organised the framing of them and their entry in her mother's absence (she was in hospital recovering from appendicitis and instructions were posted from her convalescence bed). No record remains of which landscapes these were and as only five landscapes in pigment or oils, mostly unframed, now exist it is likely that she sold them or over painted them.

Eularia had not given up on the grail of a relationship. During the fifties this subject eclipses anything else in her diaries including, as she was later to regret, her children. Eularia, very aware that her biological clock was ticking, desperately wanted to settle down and have a normal family. Being a single mother was hard and socially unacceptable at the time. She couldn't claim the respectability of being a widow, she was a divorcee, deserted by her husband and the rather conservative and provincial society of Winchester found her hard to accommodate. She had no one but herself to rely on with the children and the appendicitis incident, plus a further complication with adhesions in 1953, brought home to her how vulnerable the children were without her. She even wrote to Alicia asking her to be their legal guardian should anything happen to her. Everything depended upon her, a situation that she hated, and one cannot blame her for becoming a little obsessed with finding someone to share the burden with.

But Eularia was hopeless at choosing potential partners, and there were three potentials during the 1950s, all called John and all younger than she was. Having been spurned by the older Cyril she now turned to younger men just as she had when Anthony lost interest in his little sister and Christopher, the baby, came along to fill the gap.

She had begun to establish a steady friendship with John Hough (a friend of her brother Christopher) in the early fifties, but then in 1953 (the date is uncertain) she met John Amos, a submariner based in Portsmouth who contacted her about playing the recorder and flute. He was a keen amateur musician who was looking for chances to play in a group and so he began to come over to Winchester in the evenings, when he wasn't at sea, to play music, often bringing other musical navy officers with him to join in.

Eularia was attracted to John Amos immediately, falling head-over-heals for him, another good-looking blond and a good ten years younger than she was. As with all her potential partners there was a snag. John Amos was very much in love with another woman of his own age who lived in Cambridge and who, at the time Eularia met him, was not returning his affection. This left Eularia in a difficult position: she fervently hoped that John would forget Lucy and turn to her, but she also stepped into the role of being the maternal big sister and the 'rescuer': the one he could rely on when he needed a shoulder.

She developed a letter addiction (long before the advent of email, letters were the most common way of staying in touch) and she would hang the mood of her whole day around the morning post. If there was a letter from John Amos she would be elated and positive, if not, down and depressed, a constant fluctuation in mood nobly born by her children, especially Rachael (now a teenager) who was at home more than James and who sometimes became so infuriated with her mother over this that she would slap her.

None of Eularia's letters to any of these men survive, only some of their correspondence to her and her diary entries, so there is a certain amount of reading between the lines, but even she was of the opinion that she always overdid things in her letters. She was effusive, dramatic, and one can't help thinking that the average, rather stayed Englishman might have found them a little overpowering.

Then, from Eularia's point of view the worst happened. In the summer of 1954 Lucy finally accepted John's proposal of marriage and Eularia was devastated by it, although she never told him. She now received long letters about all their wedding and honeymoon plans, yet another couple of happy people for her to bear up to.

9

Chief Cook And Bottle Washer

Somewhat on the rebound and needing some kind of consolation, she renewed her friendship with John Hough and sought refuge in it. Reading between the lines again it seems fairly clear that John Hough was quite careful never to give Eularia any indication that he thought of her as anything but a friend and he was a terrible correspondent (he lived in Oxford), which for an ardent letter addict was persecution.

It is impossible to escape the impression, even through Eularia's own diary entries, that John Hough found her rather overwhelming and tried in various ways to put her off as gently and as politely as he could. She took this to be shyness on his part and, fatally, decided to 'rescue' him. If she couldn't be on the receiving end of his affection then she tried to compensate by loving him twice as much.

James was of the opinion that John Hough was gay but unable and unwilling to act upon it because it was still illegal, although there is no real evidence for this in anything that Eularia wrote. Once she was on a rescue mission it was difficult to stop her. It was the same passion and persistence that was later to produce so many religious canvases, but at this stage it had not found its voice.

Much later Eularia was to wonder frequently whether her attraction to God and to the Church was a replacement for a relationship. In all probability, given how much turmoil and lack of fulfilment she had in her relationships with men, it was the other way around. Society told her that as a woman she should be with a husband, but her early experiences with the supernatural and God suggested otherwise. The desperate search for a human love was probably an attempt to fill a gap that she didn't fully understand and to be socially acceptable at a time when to be a single, divorced parent was neither common nor entirely proper. It is easy to forget, and because she outwardly appeared so strong and positive many never realized, that Eularia was not the confident, robust woman that she appeared to be; she was deeply vulnerable.

Focusing on John Hough did help Eularia get over John Amos though, which is perhaps why it became so important to her. While she found John Hough's lack of response frustrating and inexplicable, it was John Amos's marrying Lucy that cut most deeply.

'I give and give and give, they take, and I am left unthanked and unloved... O, what a collapse of Mum! Tears pour into the sink again.... what's the use of doing things for people, or putting up patiently with their "worst sides", cheering depressed mothers, being nice to their children, trying so hard to be some use in the world!'

It was Eularia's strength of character that carried her through these dark times. The same character that caused her to feel domineering and inappropriate in the company of others, that meant that she would pursue men relentlessly and inappropriately, allowed her to raise two children on her own. Inevitably she always assumed that she was at fault. It was always her fall-back, the low self-esteem that had come from unhealthy comparisons and feeling inappropriately behaved as a child.

She had few confidantes in Winchester, never finding it very easy to make friends with her own sex, and it was female support that she really needed over the children and her loves. Erna Feuchtwanger was one and in the early 1950s there were two others, Joyce Gladwell and Mary King (who was married to the vicar at Stoke Charity). They were able to give her much more of the sympathy that she really needed. Erna, in particular, as a widow with a son, could empathise over Eularia's position and both families regularly spent evenings at each other's houses sharing food and music. The 1950s was a decade of music for Eularia. She never felt accepted by, or good enough for, Winchester's 'top flight' music group run by the Cowans. Instead she played cello once a week with a local orchestra run by (John) Jack Sealey, sang with a group at the Cathedral organised by Alwyn Surplus called Clausentums and there was regular music making at Middle Road. But Eularia, accustomed to the company of men, never valued her friendships with women in the same way. Very few survived for long as the women around her always showed her unwanted reflections of herself, which she found too uncomfortable to be patient with.

Eularia also felt that she was in competition for men with Rachael who was an attractive and vivacious 16-year-old. This was not helped by Eularia's increasing tendency to feel more comfortable with younger men, to the point that Rachael dreaded taking her boyfriends home because Eularia, ever the talker, would monopolise the conversation.

Eularia was always to credit Rachael with a balance and sanity that she felt she never had herself. She felt that her daughter was much better at life than she was. Rachael worked on the basis that someone in the household had to be, that dealing with it all very sensibly and unemotionally was her protection against all the drama. They didn't always have an easy relationship; Eularia was often to say that she felt Rachael treated her like dirt. In fact Rachael was probably no different from many teenage daughters towards their mothers.

1955 was largely taken up with her quest to 'save' John Hough, and his to avoid her, but she would not take the hint. The 'John Hough project' was a physical expression of a much deeper need: to have a focus for her life. Rachael and James were becoming much less dependent on her. Rachael was in her last two years at school and would soon be leaving home and James was settled at boarding school, thanks to an art scholarship, and really only needed her during the holidays.

The end of the 'relationship' with John Hough finally came after a visit to Oxford with Christopher when once again John Hough told her that he wanted to be left alone, he wanted to be free. Sad though Eularia was over this, she was more philosophical than she had been over John Amos. The end had been so long coming and so rigorously avoided by her that in the end she simply ran out of energy.

One positive aspect to come out of the John Hough years was an interest that Eularia developed for canals. During the 1950s the canal network was in sad decline and only a few enthusiasts like John Hough and her brother Francis had boats and bothered with attempting to navigate Britain's inland waterways. Eularia made a series of sketches of the canals at this time, showing their dereliction. They are evocative and in some ways reflective of her own feeling of being abandoned and left to decay.

Eularia was always at her worst when she was tired and Christmas was the time of year she found most tiring. Usually Christopher joined the family at Middle Road and Christmas 1955 was no exception. Eularia once again found herself in the role she hated most, chief cook and bottle-washer, while everyone else had fun making music, or in Christopher's case, taking his car apart and trailing motor oil all over the place. James and Rachael were both at the unhelpful, sulky teenager stage and by New Year's Day Eularia was at screaming point:

'Next morning I was so tired, I got up and wept at breakfast. R (*Rachael*) came down presently and told me how silly I was in a high, assured voice, without pity or understanding, and something triggered in my brain, I smacked her about the head. She howled and screamed, and attacked me, but I did not even want to resist, I was quite glad of her blows. J (*James*) came down and divided us, and said we were practicing for the sales, grabbing corsets from each other!'

Music at Middle Road (circa mid 50s)

Rachael said of her mother:

'She was one of those people who need more love than they are likely to receive. James and I, however, loved her devotedly and she was, in spite of her prickly personality, a wonderful mother. She was totally at ease with children, which of course made her a good teacher, and she not only gave us love, but a solid grounding in the things she thought would matter to us when we grew up... music, painting, drawing... What are we both still doing today, after so many years? Music, painting and drawing! She taught us how to look at things, and how to put paint onto paper and canvas. She made sure that we had good music lessons and made us practice in spite of battles. She encouraged us in all sorts of crafts... she had inherited Cuthbert's idiosyncratic craftsmanship. She was also an extremely stimulating and inspiring person to live with, tremendous fun but quite demanding. She was very vulnerable and I learnt how to avoid upsetting her. There were many times when we both, particularly James, found the relationship difficult.'

By the middle of 1956 Eularia was beginning to become fed-up with the constant round of teaching, playing and singing. She felt that it required too much courage, control and nervous stress from her, especially as the children were no longer really at home. She persevered because it was something to put her energy into and kept her socially engaged but she was finding it less and less satisfying. Increasingly it was her sketching and guitar playing that were the more satisfying and enjoyable. She especially began to rediscover the joy of sketching and painting alone, now that she didn't always have the children with her.

Her delight that Rachael gained entry to the Guildhall School of Music in London was equally balanced by her despair at James' poor end of term report: 'Does he never *try*?' Her worst fear was that he would end up like his father.

In the end Eularia came to an extraordinary conclusion over Cyril, which was as far sighted as it was generous, given the circumstances he had left her in, when she finally gave up any thought of attempting to sue him for financial support or divorce costs:

'I am glad I did the best and most useful thing – having the children. I am a vehicle for many gifts, and these will flourish best if diluted by the solider Clarke blood, and perhaps the children will have really splendid families of their own – Today I have decided not to get money out of Cyril. I really can, and should earn it. He really did me a kindness – most upper-class women of my generation fail to find husbands, and look at them!'

Eularia, rather like her father, had to take a practical line in everything, even though she would have been far happier focusing on her creative abilities. She still felt that she must keep a home for the children to come back to, which included being a respectable figure, earning money and maintaining a good reputation. She wrote in her diary that what she really wanted to do at this time was to camp and explore, to follow her wandering spirit, to begin again somewhere new. But like the good mother she was she instead paid £5 into James' bank account to cover the cheque that Cyril had sent him (which the bank had bounced) even though she couldn't really afford it. Increasingly she was feeling trapped in a life that was not of her choosing. Then something occurs in her diaries, which indicated the beginning of a profound change. Certain pages have an 'X' marked at the top of them calling attention to entries that she wanted to revisit easily.

In 1956 Eularia started playing cello for the Romsey Music Society orchestra organised by Cicely Card who was in charge of all the peripatetic music teachers in the Hampshire area. It was here that she met a young man who was to have a profound effect on the course of the rest of her life and the reason for the 'X' as all the marked pages are passages about him:

> 'I had noticed a young viola who looked just a little like JH (*John Hough*), and played beautifully, and when we all went to Miss Card's house for drinks, I approached him and found he was Stallard – and had played under Anthony in the International Ballet! He was so nice, I warmed greatly to him – shy, charming and sensitive – just a bit like JH must have been once.'

This was John Stallard who lived in London, but taught violin part of the week in various schools around Hampshire and, crucially for Eularia's future, was a Catholic convert.

Eularia's cousin Catherine Dupré (Austin and Vera's surviving daughter), and her family, had converted to Catholicism a year before, but as Catherine did not live anywhere near her Eularia seldom saw her and so hadn't taken much notice. Besides, she had been too involved in first John Amos and then John Hough to be distracted by religion. Now these two things came together in one person because she fell for John Stallard in the same way that she had with the previous two Johns, so the fact that he attended Mass now had relevance to her. In one of her later exhibition biographies she wrote, '… and in the middle of all this I heard a young violin-master say: "Damn, I've got to go to Mass." This remark brought me into the Catholic Church.'

It wasn't quite as simple or direct as this, but it was John Stallard who was the original inspiration for Eularia to investigate Catholicism and thus go back to her original vocation to paint religion.

Part 3
A Reluctant Catholic
1957 – 1963

10

'Not Quite My Son'

With Rachael in London at the Guildhall School of Music and James away at Leighton Park, Eularia increased her teaching, which brought in more money and left her less reliant on the goodwill of Cousin Alicia, Aunt Margaret and the rest of the family. But her teaching load was exhausting, with St Swithun's Junior School (Medecroft), Oakwood House School, Netherfield Prep School, Danemark and Totton in Southampton, as well as private pupils. None of the school holidays coincided which meant that she rarely had any time off, but she felt that she couldn't afford to turn down employment.

Her experience of teaching all ages and people from different walks of life helped her painting. Working with upper-class prep school boys and masters, girls in the local secondary modern, her guitar group of 'Teddy Boys' who she taught to play such epics as "Little Brown Jug" and "Rock Around the Clock" allowed her to bring a broad appeal to her work, especially through the characters that inhabit her paintings.

This flexibility showed in her music too. Whilst firmly rooted in her appreciation of classical music, one of her great appeals to young people was that she made the effort to keep up with what they were interested in. She was later to teach herself Beatles songs for this reason and greatly admired Cliff Richard and Dusty Springfield. This understanding of how music was moving forward at a popular level helped her to foresee the musical changes that were to begin in the Catholic Church in the 1960s. It was Eularia, in 1958, who recommended to Canon Sidney Mullarkey that his curates learn the guitar and he took her up on it. Musically, she was ahead of her time foreseeing the advent of guitar Masses long before they became a reality.

The beginning of 1957 was a confusing time for Eularia. She was at a crossroads in her life but not yet free enough to choose her path. She was suffering from empty nest syndrome and very aware of being alone, but the children, James in particular, were still dependent on her financially and needed a base during their holidays so she didn't feel able to lessen her workload, or attempt other paths and new starts elsewhere. She was finding the music scene, of which she was so much a part, increasingly irritating and stressful but it paid the bills, provided social contact and was the same world that John Stallard moved in.

She was increasingly aware of a void in her life, but was still convinced that a relationship with a man would fill it. John Stallard was the nearest she ever came to this and it was through her relationship with him that she finally realised that such relationships were not the answer.

During 1956 and 1957 the relationship followed a now familiar pattern. He was, of course, younger than she was (fourteen years her junior) being only 28 when they first met. She did all the running, the hoping and the loving and he remained friendly but aloof. John shared a London flat with theatre director and producer Dennis Maunder, only coming down to Winchester once a week when his classes brought him there, and by the beginning of 1957 he was a regular visitor at Middle Road on Mondays and Tuesdays.

Eularia was never to be quite sure what John Stallard was after and it is likely that he didn't really know himself. He was, by his own admission (and despite having had affairs with women), not interested in love or the physical aspects of relationships. So Eularia had gone from an enthusiastic heterosexual who loved someone else, via someone who had no interest in women, to a man who didn't have much interest in sex at all. Ironically John wasn't even a very good Catholic, despite being a convert. It was not in his nature to be enthusiastic about anything. He came from a very solid, provincial background and appeared to have little affection for his family, or even the luckless Dennis who was extremely supportive of him. Rachael thought him a somewhat self-obsessed hypochondriac. He was often bored by life, prone to cynicism, and probably one of the attractions Eularia held for him was her lively unconventionality.

For Eularia he was the natural successor to John Hough, someone she could focus all her bottled-up love and feelings onto, and once again he was interested enough in her for her imagination to build his friendship into something much greater. Unlike John Hough, they had much more in common. John Stallard was a regular visitor to Middle Road, they were both local music teachers, Stallard had enough spirituality about him to have bothered converting to Catholicism and they both suffered from migraines (something which cheered the hypochondriac Stallard up no end when he found this out; he loved nothing better than to sit and chat about his ills).

Eularia put all her energy into helping and supporting John Stallard and was instrumental in creating a small amateur orchestra for him to conduct, which met in Winchester on Monday evenings. He came to her on Mondays after he had finished his days teaching, they went to orchestra and then he would return to Middle Road with her for supper. He never stayed overnight though, lodging instead with a Mrs Honey who lived locally and returning to Eularia on Tuesday morning for coffee.

For all her unconventionality (and despite the fact that she would very much have liked there to be more romantic involvement with John Stallard) there was always awareness on both parts of how it would look to others in a small, provincial and rather conservative society. Eularia cared what people thought of her and she was very sensitive about her already precarious social position. Her diaries express the vacillation between very much wanting them to be more than friends, and how difficult and how inappropriate that would seem to her friends and neighbours. For that reason John Stallard's own reserve and insistence that he sleep at the respectable Mrs Honey's as a lodger acted as a reason never to pursue this question too deeply:

'Life for a divorced woman is a campaign of re-instatement, one fights inch by inch to be accepted. For me difficulties are greater as I am eccentric and free in my language and might be immoral.'

Although their friendship was always to remain platonic, John Stallard was the nearest thing Eularia ever found to a soul mate. It was a relationship that was hard for outsiders to understand but it was important to both of them and it would last on and off for nearly ten years.

Early in 1957 a diary entry reads: 'off to Bournemouth to see suicidal father.' Cuthbert, who was temporarily in a rest home in Bournemouth, had taken an overdose. The attempt had failed, but Eularia was concerned about his mental state and she heartily disliked the rest home. She felt guilty about not visiting him in Oxford but the problem of Dorothy Harlow remained. Eularia simply did not feel welcome there and Dorothy was one of the people that Eularia felt totally unable to stand up to. She was to regret this later, but even with hindsight it is unlikely that she would have braved it.

Eularia at Middle Road (mid 1956/57)

By the spring of 1957 John Stallard was the focus of most of her energy and this section of her diary is headed, 'Not Quite My Son.' Significantly she and John could and did discuss religion and faith. They would often sit after their Monday suppers together in Eularia's living room in front of the 'cook-and-heat' stove and talk for hours. It was the first time Eularia was able to really express her own beliefs to anyone. 'I told him how I had no faith, but practiced Christianity as a magic spell, he clearly hopes I shall be converted.'

Lack of faith was something that always bothered Eularia, even after her conversion. But often what she calls a lack of faith seems more like a lack of foundation. Her father's agnosticism and her mother's inability to pass on any belief she may have had meant that Eularia always felt she stood on rather shaky ground with regard to Christianity, as if she never quite belonged to it, an observer looking in rather than an integral part of it. As a 'cradle Catholic' I have always felt secure in the language and experience of my spirituality, even if the way I express it changes. Eularia never had this language or these roots and, despite her fascination for the history and traditions of the Catholic Church, she was never able to feel absolutely confident in it or supported by it.

What the lack of faith or roots did allow her to do was to come to Catholicism and religion with fresh eyes and I am convinced that this is why her work has such power and appeals to all denominations. On the one hand she understood the theology behind what she was expressing, on the other she had no history of experience and no sense of passing on something she had been taught to believe. It was entirely her own vision and interpretation, born from her own inner experiences of God and her drive to understand how they fitted.

With John Stallard Eularia made a concerted effort not to fall into the trap of over-attachment and addiction that she had with John Hough, but when she first heard that Stallard was Catholic it was still a blow. The first time he told her that he had been to Mass she wrote in her diary:

> 'That was it. He is a Catholic. I accepted the blow inside me. To him I am a married woman, so safe, such a safe friend. He badly wants me to be a Catholic too. But if I do this, then I am a married woman, not only to him but to everybody, and can't even settle down with elderly bachelors.'

In those days the Catholic Church did not recognise divorce. This was one of the biggest barriers to Eularia converting as it effectively meant she would have to give up any idea of ever having her dream of a partner. But John Stallard was persistent about Eularia becoming a Catholic, perhaps hoping for strength in numbers. At this point Eularia was not convinced that John would stay around, so she refused to commit, but her interest was peaked and the old memories of religion awakened.

11

A Question of Faith

Sometime during the first part of 1957 Eularia attended a Friday Mass at St Peter's Catholic Church, Winchester (her parish church) to see what it was like:

'Very quiet, like being at the bottom of the sea. Lovely plainsong chanting, and full of silent congregation. I had to go by myself, and felt very strange, like in a foreign country – but I did love the Offertory, full of half pennies and threepenny bits.'

Inevitably it was the choir that drew her and she joined them one Sunday for High Mass shortly afterwards:

'I loved singing, and the incense and everything, and when the organist asked me to come again whenever I could, I was astonished – so different from my usual reception.'

In the mid 1950s, apart from the priests themselves, it was the choir that did most of the work during Mass, the congregation essentially being 'audience' playing very little active role in the Mass itself. Eularia was already familiar with the plainchant and simple four-part Latin masses that the choir sang, having spent so many years singing in other choirs and more recently the Clausentums group at the Cathedral. She read music easily and she had a good strong voice, useful in any choir.

But it was her relationship with John Stallard that remained her most important focus, and an older, wiser Eularia began to emerge. She is far less frantic about it in her diary. The hopes and desires are still there but they are accompanied by more ability to let things develop naturally rather than constantly attempt to push them along.

For the first time she mentioned how she confused love and fear and how she only dared to love people who she knew would not be cruel. It is undoubtedly her brother Anthony that she had in mind here, followed by Cyril and perhaps even her own father. The cruelty was almost certainly verbal rather than physical but it undermined her, making it difficult for her to trust. It was the reason why she avoided people like Dorothy Harlow and could be so hypersensitive to what others said.

She, Stallard, Rachael and James spent three weeks in the August of 1957 motoring down through France and as far as Alicante in Spain. James and Rachael both have fond memories of this holiday today, although James recalls Eularia being very tense throughout, the irony being that, without realising it, he was the source of much of the tension. Eularia was in fact deeply torn between loyalty to her son's need for attention and wanting quality time on her own with John. John took the side of James and she boiled it up into such a state that she feared she was having a breakdown.

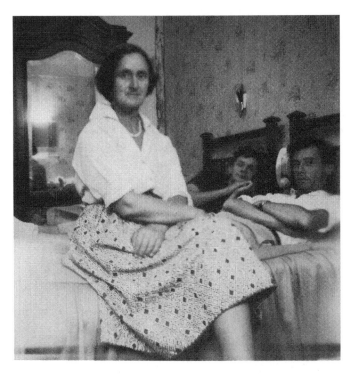

Eularia, James and John Stallard on the trip to Spain (August 1957)

Worse still, it affected her painting. She had been sketching as they went, but given the amount of time they were away and the number of places that they visited there are remarkably few, and those there are seem rather hurried and are often unfinished. She put this down to being too distracted by all the upheaval she was experiencing. Nevertheless the sketches are atmospheric examples of the East coast of Spain before the developers moved in.

Everything had calmed down by the time they arrived back in Winchester but it was something of a watershed. It was the last time that Eularia, James and Rachael would holiday together, and whilst it affirmed Eularia's friendship with John it was very clear to her after this that he would always back off from any kind of physical contact. It was the one place in which he and the much more tactile and demonstrative Eularia were different. Eularia quickly dissolved any real illusions about what she was to John Stallard and settled for what was on offer, which was probably why the friendship lasted much longer and, in the end, gave her more than either of the others ever had.

In fact its part-time nature came to suit her well. The easy friendship and companionship that they settled down to, rather like an old married couple when the spark has gone, seemed to calm down the inner angst she had about not having a proper partner, because John was someone who she could turn to and talk things over with. He gave her a sense of stability. She knew that (mostly) he would be there if she needed him. This allowed her to focus on her deeper feelings once again which were much more bound up with God and the non-corporeal.

Eularia was never to have an easy relationship with the Catholic Church either and yet it was the only organised Church that she ever felt drawn to. She was not the kind of person who fitted in well with rigid structures, and she would always remain something of a square peg. For a start she was female, and women in the late 1950s and early 1960s in the Catholic Church were either nuns; very traditional stay-at-home mothers with large families; priests' housekeepers; or meek and respectable spinsters and widows who stayed quietly in the background, or looked after the church cleaning and flower arranging. If divorced women were relatively rare and tainted by a suggestion of scandal in normal society, then divorced women in the Catholic Church were virtually unheard of and Eularia was very relieved when she was told that the Church would not make her go back to Cyril.

The female Catholic world was not her natural milieu. She was used to being part of a man's world, and felt very easy in their company. Her description to Rachael of a party she attended at around this time put it very clearly, she described there being a 'hammer-and-tongs debate among me and the men, while the wives drank silently.'

The gap between male and female was still very polarised. Few women dared to consider having an equal relationship as a friend with one of the priests. To Eularia it was entirely normal and she quickly became friends with the two curates at St Peter's by becoming their guitar teacher.

Eularia had strong doubts about converting at first:

'I don't know quite what it is. Dislike of joining a sect, being labelled – no label quite suits me – pretending to believe things I never *shall* feel convinced of, however much I believe in the rightness of the Church.'

In fact it was Rachael who converted first under the influence of Guildhall friends in London, but getting to know John Stallard had rekindled Eularia's interest in the religious and the supernatural, helped by the long trip through Catholic France and Spain. Added to this the Catholic Church in England, which since the Dissolution of Henry VIII had carried a stigma, had been going through something of a renaissance in the first half of the twentieth century among intellectuals.

In 1829 the Roman Catholic Relief Act was passed, and for the first time since the Dissolution Catholics in England and Wales were given almost equal Civil Rights (including the right to vote and hold most public offices). Catholicism in England had been reasserting itself after years of oppression, largely through its high profile intellectual converts who spoke up for it and made it popular during the nineteenth and early twentieth centuries. These included such notables as Dorothy L Sayers, Augustus Pugin, Gerald Manley Hopkins, John Henry Newman, Graham Greene, Evelyn Waugh, Thomas Merton, Muriel Spark, Malcolm Muggeridge and G. K. Chesterton who Cuthbert knew so well. The 1950s represented the last decade in which there was a real surge of conversions though, for the Catholic Church in general was on the verge of wide-sweeping changes that would, for a while, plunge it into confusion and ultimately completely transform it.

Despite the upsurge in popularity there was still a prevailing 'ghetto' feeling about being a member of a Catholic community in England, which appealed to Eularia's tendency to feel outcast. Winchester was no different, and because it was close to the ports of Southampton and Portsmouth it had a sizeable number of Irish and Italian immigrants.

After such a warm reception Eularia joined the choir full-time at St Peter's, Jewry Street in Winchester, under the direction of organist Will Thomas[1]. Her relationship with Thomas was later to become tricky but initially she liked him very much and they got on well. She had a good voice, could sing soprano or alto as needed, read music (not all the choir members could) and was extremely reliable in both attendance and performance. He was glad to have her.

At this time the Catholic Mass had very little congregational involvement. It was mostly spoken or sung by the priests (in Latin) and the choir responded in plainchant. The choir also performed what would later become the congregational parts such as the Gloria, Sanctus and Agnus Dei using one of the many sung Masses (three- or four-part) available and reasonably within their capability. To be a member of the choir was to be in the most active part of the congregation and Eularia, by her own admission, was never very good at simply being audience. Being part of the choir was something she really enjoyed as she wrote to Rachael in July 1957:

'We stand in a little high stone gallery, I and Anne Drummond, and Mary White and various girls, and a lot of robust plain-clothes men who are very hot on plainsong. There is no reverence except at special moments, most of the time the pretty girls whisper and gossip and the choir mens' children sit about drinking lemonade out of bottles, like on a bus, but of course at stated intervals we all kneel down and you could hear a pin drop.'

The priests often used to join the choir practices and through this and teaching them the guitar she quickly got to know them. It was completely natural for her to gravitate towards the men. Blissfully unaware of any kind of Catholic etiquette, she must have made a welcome change to priests who were more used to being treated with utmost politeness and demure respect, admired from afar or even being attractive to the women in their parish. The fact that Eularia was very familiar with the failings of men whilst, at the same time, being at ease with them, made her easy for the young priests, in particular, to confide in, which they did. To the younger curates she must have seemed like the mother/big sister

---

1   More commonly known as Bill Thomas, but Eularia always referred to him as Will. For that reason I have adopted Will throughout the biography.

substitute that their mostly male-centric lives lacked. For Eularia it must have been refreshing that they simply didn't care about any deficiencies brought about by her socially dubious status.

In the late 1950s and early 1960s Winchester was the administrative centre for the Catholic Diocese of Portsmouth by virtue of the fact that the then Archbishop, John Henry King[2], lived in the presbytery at 29, Jewry Street. King had been the parish priest in Winchester since the early twentieth century and was instrumental in the erection of the current church building, late Victorian Gothic in style and completed in 1926. He was made Auxiliary Bishop to the diocese in 1938 and appointed Bishop in 1941 at around the very time that the Bishop's residence in Portsmouth was bombed. It seemed easiest for him to remain where he was and run the diocese from Winchester, while the new house was built in Portsmouth. When it was finished, however, he didn't like it so he continued to live in the attic at Jewry Street where he would say daily Mass for the housekeeper and the presbytery cat. So, as well as the parish priest and his curates, Jewry Street was also the home of the Bishop and his secretary.

Canon David Mahy (who arrived in Winchester as a young curate in 1960) said of both Bishop King and Canon Mullarkey that they were very relaxed in their administrative style, allowing their curates a good deal of freedom which they much appreciated and which undoubtedly facilitated their friendship with Eularia.

---

2   The title 'Archbishop' was given to John Henry King by Rome in recognition of his service to the Catholic Church and was a personal title. Portsmouth remained a Diocese.

12

Priests

The first official point of contact for Eularia was the parish priest, Canon Sidney Mullarkey. He was in his fifties and Eularia described him as spiky but with an ironic sense of humour delivered with a twinkle in his eye. David Mahy described him as a very pastoral priest much concerned with those under his care. Assisting him were two much younger curates who were both to prove significant to Eularia: Pat Murphy-O'Connor (older brother of Cormac who would later become Cardinal Murphy-O'Connor) and Angus Mason[3], both in their early thirties.

Of the two it was Angus Mason, an intellectual and a convert like her, who Eularia related to most strongly. Pat Murphy-O'Connor was jovial, good-natured, from an Irish Catholic family who had strong links with the priesthood, loved a pint and was known to have a bawdy sense of humour and be a very good mimic. Angus, on the other hand, did not come from a Catholic background, but a broken one (his parents had divorced when he was a child), which Eularia could easily identify with. He did not convert until he decided to become a priest. He was a refined and educated Oxbridge man (who like Eularia played the cello), highly-strung, sensitive, possibly too prone to introspection, and in many ways rather like John Hough and John Stallard in character. One can see where this is going:

'I had a stomach chill and felt cold and miserable and utterly desolate and empty of faith, when in came Fr Mason – so appallingly simpatico and eager that I hardly remembered he was a priest.'

---

3 Angus Mason is a pseudonym.

Angus Mason and Eularia not only had interests in common but issues as well. In order to become a Catholic Eularia would have to give up any idea she might have of achieving her dream of another husband, because she was divorced. Angus, who had a natural love of women, was finding his vow of celibacy challenging.

Just because a priest takes a vow of celibacy does not make him immune to normal human feelings, desires and emotions, and priests who give up their vocation because they have fallen in love are not uncommon. It is not surprising, then, that the younger priests in particular might occasionally feel that their vow of celibacy was challenged and under threat. In a letter to Rachael Eularia wrote:

'I hope this isn't depressing – Angus came for *three hours* last week, sitting in the garden eating biscuits and talking... What he didn't tell me was what I learnt later – that his breakdown last summer was due to love for a nurse! She was asked to leave, and he was sent away to recover. Poor, poor Angus.'

Instead of being scandalised and judgmental about this revelation, Eularia was full of sympathy. She understood only too well the conflict between the need for human, earthly love and love of God because she struggled with it herself. It certainly didn't stop Angus Mason from becoming Eularia's favourite priest. Because of John Stallard it was easier for her to resist allowing her feelings for Angus to follow what would otherwise have been her normal pattern. She absolutely respected the fact that he was a priest, but she loved him nonetheless and expressed great sympathy and concern for him, which was shared by Pat Murphy-O'Connor who was his housemate and colleague.

Already, in 1958, she was beginning to observe in her diary the patterns of worship which would ultimately inspire her early paintings:

'Mass was without any feeling *at all*. But it was nice – the housewives with shopping bags, the mother with her little boy, taking him up the aisle and genuflecting with him in one movement.'

Her immediate instinct was to register the visuals, little details that are easy to overlook. Eularia was very good at observing the little details in a big picture, a fall-back to her mother Peggy's recollection of her being fascinated by the little things in life. It was these 'little things' that would later give her paintings, whose subject matter was so large, their intimacy and immediacy.

She often felt what she described as an 'odd emotion' especially when observing, or taking part in, Church ceremonies. She loved the ritual of service, the movement, the show and spectacle. It was what first inspired her to paint it all. It harked back to her youthful obsession for Church ritual and the interaction with the supernatural. For the first time in her life she began to gain an understanding of what lay behind her sense of the supernatural and what all the ceremonies were about, and it was the priests who supplied it:

'I can never have enough of the Benediction candles. The stoles, and the priests going out and appearing like Petrushka above the altar, and coming down with the silver monstrance and the adoration of the people and the Divine Praises. I doubt if I shall ever feel rightly believing about the Blessed Sacrament. I have to tell myself severely that the Host is really Jesus' body. Actually, I only feel, how nice, that if he has been revered all these centuries – I shall revere it too, because I am sure it is right to do so, and my unbelief bears no fruit.'

Eularia was always brutally honest in her diaries about the fact that intellectually she struggled with Catholic Doctrine. She never blindly accepted it although she did do her best to embrace it. She is not alone here. The history of faith among humans is a history of struggle to give voice to something experienced, but almost impossible to put into words. Something happens to it when we attempt to verbalise it, somehow it becomes diminished, and Eularia was aware of this, although she made attempts through her poetry to find the words. Her answer, ultimately, was to paint it, to attempt to illustrate in a visual way what she experienced, just as the early Renaissance and Byzantine artists who inspired her had done.

But she was still a couple of years away from doing this. 1958 was the year in which she took her first steps towards conversion, and they were often shaky steps. There was another issue that caused her to stall over her Reception and which took a lot of ingenuity on the part of the priests to overcome. She explained it in a letter to Alicia in early 1958 (the punctuation is hers):

'I was puzzled by something Daddy told me, and so got hold of a copy of the "Converts' Profession of Faith", rather sooner than I was supposed to (they keep it till last, when one is nicely hotted up). And when I found I'd have to "condemn, abjure and detest the heresy" which was producing people like Ursula, it really seemed laughable. I must say the priests took a *lot* of trouble over Ursula – and Mummy as well – and eventually decided that when people like that die, they go straight to heaven in spite of "Nulla salus extra ecclesiam" (*there is no salvation outside the Church*) BECAUSE they find that they were really Roman Catholics all the time without knowing it!!!!!!!!'

The priests had to find a way round Eularia's very natural concern that by becoming a Catholic she was admitting that those she loved, and in Ursula's case greatly admired, were somehow wrong and would be consigned to damnation because they were not Catholics. One can detect a rather ingenious creativity in the priests' conclusion, but these concerns led her to reconnect with a very old friend of Peggy's called Trixl Gray. Trixl, who had become a Catholic nun in 1916 and changed her name to Sr Mary Raphael[4], was at St Mary's Priory, Princethorpe near Rugby. In contacting her Eularia was reaching out to someone who had known her mother well, but who also understood what she was proposing to do by converting. It is intriguing that Eularia seemed to have been so concerned over what Peggy would have thought about her becoming a Catholic, given that she never seemed to think much of her mother's opinion when she was alive. Eularia's feelings about her mother seemed to mellow and take on a much gentler and tender quality once she was dead.

Trixl and Eularia began a correspondence that lasted until Trixl's death in 1963, which Eularia found very supportive. If Trixl had been the same faith as Peggy she would have been Eularia's godmother, so, although as a nun she was unable to stand as Eularia's official godmother at her Reception, she now assumed that role by proxy. Eularia's letters to Trixl do not survive but Trixl's answers do. In the first of these, dated May 1958, she reassured Eularia that Peggy would not have objected to her becoming a Catholic if it was what she really wanted to do.

Trixl was one of the very few nuns that Eularia really liked. She could be very rude about nuns, especially en masse ('the black bonnets' as she referred to them). This came from a deep fear of her own, which she also projected onto the middle-aged Catholic spinsters and widows at St Peter's. She saw in them a shadow of something she could become and firmly resisted (she hated it if they tried to include her as one of them). To her nuns, middle-aged Catholic widows and spinsters represented a kind of prison, a solid wall of disapproval, perhaps too closely related to the kind of disapproval she had faced from Constance and Sylvia.

---

4   Eularia always refered to Sr Mary Raphael as Trixl, so I have stuck to that.

Despite the fact that she had been reassured that she wouldn't have to go back to him, Cyril still remained something of a spectre at her feast. He had finally been sacked from Argo Records, which he had set up with Harley Usill, and had gone to Ibiza. As is often the case with alcoholics, he had become totally unreliable, often failing to turn up for work at all, and had left Usill no choice, although the ever-faithful Lorraine, who had remained in the background ever since the early 1940s, still stuck by him. Either Eularia did not know this at this time, or she chose to overlook it, because she half expected to have to look after him. This softening in feeling was enhanced by a postcard she received from Cyril and, perhaps, also by the fear that the Catholics might still insist that she return to him.

The whole question of marriage remained a vexing one for Eularia, especially in relation to the Catholic Church as she felt she could not win whatever she did. On the one hand she might gain legitimacy by returning to a husband with whom she had had such a disastrous relationship, and on the other the very fact of being married itself seemed to consign her to second-rate status.

Angus Mason was the first person Eularia met who really seemed to understand how she felt:

> 'After a bit of talk, we (*Eularia and Angus*) went into the garden and I poured out beer. He relaxed in the sun and we talked for an hour... He took me down to the town, and on the way down he poured out the troubles of celibacy... He has only just found what he's missed. I went on about husbandlessness, him about wifelessness, we fairly roared about it in the car, as we went down the High St'

Whatever part John Stallard played in her conversion, it was her feelings for, and affinity with, Angus Mason that influenced her most strongly:

> 'At four came Fr Mason – full of the cosiest appreciation of *everything* – the beer, the garden, having it out of doors, every blessed thing, and we had tea and he stayed from 4 till 7, full of eager talk. Well, I don't see how I'm going to get out of it now – this warm welcome from such a very kindred spirit. ... I have never known such appreciation...What will happen next I don't know – he seems in a hurry to get me in without the usual preparations.'

It was around this time that she met another man whose friendship, along with that of his wife and children, would prove very supportive to her in later years, especially in relation to her painting. She attended a talk by the Archbishop at Southampton University and was offered a lift home by

Eversley Belfield who was a lecturer at the University, lived in Winchester and was a Catholic. He and his wife, Felicity, were to become staunch supporters of Eularia and her work and she later became godmother to their youngest child.

Even pre-conversion Eularia was beginning to experience strange sensations. She described an experience whilst attending Mass at St Peter's:

'In the middle of Mass suddenly things go unreal. I saw their little heads all grouped round the altar and they seemed to be in a different sort of world. Not like a play or opera, but a different sort of air.'

The position of the Choir at this time in St Peter's was high up in the organ loft at the side of the Sanctuary, so Eularia could look down and see the communicants quite clearly:

'Every time I read about religion something seems to "give" inside me – a melting feeling. I don't know what it means; but somehow I can see how the devil speaks, and occasionally I chase him away angrily. I wonder if it is true?'

She described another experience at Mass during October Devotions:

'The Cannon elevated the Host so close, so purposefully, I looked up terrified, and felt he was shining a very strong torch, very close, almost on my eyes. Soon after I began sweating over my forehead and feared fainting, but just lasted out till Sanctissumum Sacramentum.'

All this was bringing her much closer to conversion and a growing sense of value about having her own space and time to reflect in. The crushing need to have a full-time relationship was finally dying. With that in mind she decided she needed to settle things once and for all with Cyril, to determine if there was any likelihood of him ever needing her, but fear of him meant that she chose to do this indirectly through Cyril's mother: 'I can't make a confession until I've settled about Cyril.'

Priscilla Clarke replied quite quickly to say that Cyril (now back from Ibiza) was very ill and in hospital. It was alcohol related and apparently serious. Eularia, typically, rose to the drama of the situation.

'I thought, Cyril took me, and made me all I am, a wife and mother... If Cyril needs me I'd better go, but I think he has somebody else looking after him. He won't want me.'

She was right. Cyril's care was falling to the ever-faithful Lorraine. It was John Stallard who kept Eularia's feet on the ground over this, although Eularia resented what she saw as his rather callous response, but he was right. Cyril and Eularia were divorced, she didn't owe him anything and, given their past history, probably wouldn't be wanted anyway. He accused Eularia very accurately of 'pointless and over-dramatized' emotions.

Eularia would always blow hot and cold over things that really mattered to her and her relationship with John Stallard was no exception. On any given day in her diary she could be complaining about him bitterly, convinced that he didn't care and not seeing why she should bother to put herself out. A day or so later everything had changed and she was all in favour of him again, ready to support him in anything and full of affection. The same mood swings were true of her relationship with the Church and the priests. She described her love for it all, her desire to have faith and to be received, and then something would happen (such as the priests forgetting to thank her for arranging Christmas music) and she would plunge into an anti-Catholic and anti-priest diatribe which could last anything from a morning to several days, always leaving her in 'a sort of shadow-land' with the feeling that nobody would help her.

13

A Year of Change

The next eighteen months were to be pivotal and life-changing for Eularia. At the beginning of 1959 she was still feeling very ambivalent about Reception into the Catholic Church (set for Easter). By Candlemas at the beginning of February, although she was still attending Mass regularly and singing in the choir, she was behaving rather like a bolshie, rebellious teenager. What happened next passes almost without comment in her diary and yet it was decisive to her future course in life:

'Down in bitter east wind to St Peter's (*Candlemas service*) − no singing at all, but a cold silent church, yet the candles looked lovely as we lit them from each other for the Gospel. Off to Danemark − in the spare half hour I found paper and chalk and drew the Candlemas.'

Although she did not turn this sketch into a painting until autumn 1960 it predates the Lourdes sketches (usually considered her first religious works since her early twenties) by almost eighteen months. She didn't take it further at this time though, as events overtook her.

First was concern over her children who were both looking for careers in areas where Cyril was well known. He was back in London, living openly with Lorraine, and was now in a position to influence their lives more directly. She was terrified that James, in particular, would make a similar mess of his life, or that Cyril would prejudice their careers, so in order to have as much financial resource as possible to support them Eularia took on another school (Shedfield) and more private pupils. Then Cuthbert suffered a mild stroke in March, forcing her to rush to Oxford.

Sketch of Candlemas (February 1959)

The question of her Reception still hung in the air and it seems, from her diaries, that she was still dithering about whether it was the right choice or not. Her old fear of always making wrong choices prevented her from committing to it and caused her to over-analyse her motives, all of which tended to lead her round in circles. Ironically it was her cousin Alicia who, indirectly, clinched it.

Eularia spent a week with Alicia being subjected to her 'Intellectual Truth,' which Eularia simply found 'no good' and she mentioned her proposed conversion. This brought them on to the subject of Michael Gedge, who they both knew from the Kidlington days and who had remained a good friend of Alicia's. He had become an Anglican Vicar, one of the 'working priests' who became a coal miner in Kent and combined this with being a vicar to the miners. He had then spent some time teaching, but, much to Alicia's disgust, had given it up to attend the Beda College[5] in Rome in order to become a Catholic priest. Eularia

---

5   The Beda College was founded in 1852 as part of the English College in Rome specifically to train older men, often clergymen wishing to convert, as Catholic priests.

remembered Michael from her childhood, so she wrote to him about her proposed Reception and noted in her diary:

'I shall write to Michael and I think become a Catholic, now that I know that this "affection" comes back even after a long absence. I still know to my shame that I don't really deeply reverence the Host – surely it *can't* be? Yet why is there this atmosphere of happy peace around it? It at any rate can't bring badness... I shall always pray badly and disbelieve and use the Church for showing off, but one thing is sure – that I've no real belief in the C of E – somehow it isn't the church for me. Because I like to be different? Because I want to hit them for despising me?... 'I begin to see that Catholicism will win eventually... I am now leaving it to Michael Gedge to see to.'

Michael Gedge didn't waste any time and replied to Eularia's letter indicating that he was intending to oversee her Reception. A tough and rather crusty character already in his late fifties, he was not easy to say no to. Although Eularia still wasn't entirely convinced about converting she was very glad to have someone take charge and put an end to her dithering.

The day of her Reception duly arrived, 24 March 1959, and John Stallard took Eularia to Winchester station to meet Michael off the train. 'Nobody seemed to be getting out of the train, but soon a sort of criminal type with a bicycle came, and said I hadn't changed much!'

The best and most concise description of Eularia's Reception is the one she wrote to her cousin Catherine Dupré (already a Catholic convert):

'A friend of Alicia's turned up here in Holy Week – one of the convert parsons of 1955 vintage – called Michael Gedge – whom I hadn't seen since we all acted at Kidlington 35 years ago. He bicycled here in *shorts* (aged 56!) and took me by the scruff of the neck and got me received (*b*)y main force – the Canon was very cross as they were doing overtime with confessions and he'd had no warning and he had to get an old lady (*anonymous*) who was praying in the church to be my godmother. Michael roared out the Penitential psalms and the little old lady clicked her rosary in great bewilderment and Michael had to practically kick me through the responses. There was no question of conversion; it was simply that Anthony had accustomed me from birth to doing what I'm told by the nearest thing in trousers that knows his own mind!'

It is very likely that without the push from Michael Gedge Eularia would have continued to dither about whether to convert, indeed she may never have taken the final plunge, but, as she said many years later, without her Catholicism there would have been no paintings. Michael was to remain a consistent support to Eularia over the next few years in her struggle with the Faith. In some ways they complemented each other. Michael was older, straight talking and stood no nonsense from her, whereas she was able to provide him with aspects of Catholicism which she felt he was too masculine and doctrinally-based to grasp. She wrote to Alicia in June 1959:

'I have just *one* most useful quality – that I can tell him about a whole side of Catholicism – the fancy side, with apparitions and shrines and things, and priestic practices – which an English public-school convert could never know, as they are told in childhood via mothers and nuns etc. I went straight for this side of things because it is so interesting to the female mind, and now after two years I am able to give him cosy lectures to fill these gaps in his knowledge, so that he can make Catholic noises to his parishioners.'

It was without doubt a rocky start and it would always remain a rather rocky 'marriage', but the fruits it bore were to rank among one of the most extraordinary bodies of religious work by any artist.

The family's reaction to Eularia's Reception was not, on the whole, positive, especially amongst those who had been her staunchest supporters and allies. Alicia was against it and Aunt Margaret wrote to Eularia most strongly about it. Anthony never approved, having taken on his father's firm agnostic beliefs, and it stood between them for the rest of Eularia's life. Francis was more magnanimous, maintaining that you could either be a Catholic or an atheist as nothing else in between washed. He himself chose atheism but was happy to allow Eularia her Catholicism. Christopher was too easy-going to express an opinion either way. Rachael showed no sign of minding at the time as she was also a recent convert, but James found it difficult to begin with.

Despite the family's reaction Eularia was beginning to settle into her Catholicism:

'Now that the reaction is over for the moment, I can feel what I suppose is Grace pouring into my heart. It is only a vague emotion, but it is mixed up with the thought of shrines and pilgrimage, and for the first time I think I am glad to be a Catholic.'

Eularia's main connection with St Peter's continued to be the choir. In 1958 a new Pope, John XXIII, was elected. It was this Pope that would initiate far-reaching changes within the Catholic Church, convening the Second Vatican Council in 1962, but changes began almost as soon as he took office. In mid 1959 Eularia wrote to Rachael:

'Poor St Peter's, it's been told by the Pope that the congregation must sing the Mass, so now we (*the choir*) all huddle in the back pews, with Mr Thomas (one finger poised on the harmonium) at our head. We all have leaflets, and we sing the Kyrie off them, and then the Congregation (i.e. the Canon *very loud* and a tiny wisp of voices) sing the Kyrie, then we sing the next Kyrie and so on. Miss Walsh loves it, and I rather like it, because it must be rather awful being congregation while the choir is up in the gallery being polyphonic! Unfortunately the congregation dug in their hoofs when it came to the Sanctus with rather a lot of notes, and out came the rosaries and little prayer books, and down went the Liturgical Movement!'

The Liturgy, which is the form the Mass takes (what is said, who says it and when), had remained unchanged for centuries. It is difficult to understate just how far reaching and impactful changes to it were. Pope John (later called the Blessed and now canonised) was considered by many to be inspired by God and just what was needed for the Church to take it forward into the modern world by recalling the simplicity and ideals of the early Church. David Mahy and Pat Murphy-O'Connor were very keen on the changes. They felt, as many did, that if the congregation were encouraged to join in and be a proper part of the Mass it would be a very positive move, a way of taking the Gospel to the people more effectively. Despite what many conservative thinkers maintain today about the health of the Church in the 1950s, there were many who felt that congregations were merely going through the motions out of habit and that the faith itself was dying.

The Pope was proposing to change the whole structure of how the Church worshipped, but many people, congregations included, did not see the need to take an active part and did not want to let go of the old ways. It was to divide the Church, polarising it into modern thinkers and reformers, and hard line conservatives. Archbishop King and Sidney Mullarkey made the decision very early on that they would implement whatever changes the Pope decreed as soon as possible. They supported reform, but, as Eularia's description shows, the initial attempts to institute it were not very successful. Put bluntly, many "Cradle Catholics" (those who had been Catholic from birth) had never had to bother with taking an active part in Mass before and didn't see why they should start now. If they wanted to sing they would have joined the choir. The choir was equally unhappy, as it had to sit at the back of the congregation (no chatting and drinking lemonade) and was losing the chance to sing its part Masses in favour of much simpler unison congregational participation.

Sidney Mullarkey's first valiant attempts to bring his congregation into the modern world fell flat and were abandoned for a couple of years, but the changes were coming. They were to underlie much of Eularia's relationship with St Peter's and would reflect in her painting. Being a convert and with no history in the old ways she had no particular attachment to them and, on the whole, favoured change. She was good at moving with the times, having become used to it with her pupils, and in many respects was even ahead of them. But pioneers are often exposed and vulnerable to criticism and Eularia was no different, especially in relation to the choir who didn't see why someone so new to their religion should then come in and demand and support changes that effectively eliminated them as a body.

14

A Wedding and a Funeral

Eularia, already in the middle of a busy summer term, was then plunged into arranging a wedding at very short notice and with very little money. Rachael had become engaged to the new man in her life, Robert Sherlaw Johnson. As he was on the short-list for a job in Canada, which would mean leaving in the autumn, they wanted to marry before they left. Robert was a graduate of the Royal Academy of Music, a very good pianist, a young composer and a Catholic convert. He was a very un-neurotic Northerner who disliked drama and had been raised to expect to be waited on by his women. Despite the fact that he and Eularia both had music and were Catholic converts in common, they never had an easy relationship.

St Peter's was to be the venue and Eularia was thrown into a quandary. As a very new convert she was about to be confronted by the wall of her own family's entrenched agnosticism in the one place she was beginning to feel safe. Robert's family were not Catholic either so the Catholics present were likely to be outnumbered ten to one.

'I ought to have explained to you about Cyril...' Eularia wrote in a letter to a rather alarmed Alicia. Once again Cyril had injected the dramatic into the arrangements by ringing James at school to tell him that he was dying. James felt so sorry for Cyril that he suggested that if Cyril pulled himself together he could walk his daughter down the aisle (it is fortunate that Rachael had always wanted Cyril to give her away), but Eularia now also had a potentially drunk ex-husband to add to the mix. Cyril maintained that he had only been given five years to live. In fact he lived another fifteen (and died after being run over by a motorbike, not as a result of alcohol) so he was almost certainly over-egging it to gain sympathy.

Despite Eularia's misgivings, the wedding went off without incident. Cyril proudly walked his daughter down the aisle looking very smart and was reasonably sober for the occasion. Poor Lorraine was condemned to wait in a teashop in Winchester High Street for the duration of the service and because of this Cyril did not stay for the reception.

The wedding is the only film we have of Eularia, a short, rather indistinct, amateur Cine film taken by a friend of Robert and Rachael's. For some reason Eularia chose to wear black and to top it all off with a luxurious lace mantilla, which makes her look like a Spanish matriarch at a funeral. The film is silent but she performs her hostess duties, greeting arrivals at the church, rather like the lady of the manor. There is a touching moment as the bride and groom exit the church of her standing above them on a step next to Cyril. It was the last time she and Cyril would ever meet.

With the wedding over life settled down for a few brief months. The only cloud on Eularia's horizon was Cuthbert's decision to finally sell Great Rissington, which meant that the house had to be cleared and the family could take what they wanted. This caused a row between Eularia and Dorothy Harlow that was never to heal and almost certainly came from Eularia's lack of tact over who should have what. But it was a rift that was to have consequences for her later in the year.

She began to settle much more easily into being a Catholic and get to know the more intellectual members of St Peter's congregation, which included Eversley Belfield and his wife, Felicity, and Adrian and Veronica Stokes. Angus Mason encouraged Eularia to join the Newman Society (founded in Oxford as a Catholic Club in 1878) and Southampton University had a branch that met regularly in members' homes. It was to prove a fruitful relationship when she did, as the Chaplain at Southampton University who ran it, Fr Robin Noel, was to become a friend and a keen early supporter of Eularia's work.

For the first time since beginning her diaries back in 1953, painting is mentioned as something she really enjoyed, but at this point she was more interested in writing. She had been working on a guitar book, although it came to nothing. Eularia was never a serious writer in the way that she was to become a painter. What probably inspired her in that direction in 1959 was connecting with Frank Sheed and Maisie Ward (who was another distant relation) who had a small Catholic publishing imprint. The first few years after her Reception and Confirmation saw her experimenting with writing (especially a return to poetry), music and painting as if her newly unleashed creative forces weren't quite sure in which direction to turn, but ultimately it was painting that would take over. In a letter to Alicia written in the autumn she expresses her feelings on Catholic Art:

'Alas, so much Catholic Art looks unmistakably as if it is done by happy art teachers in Sec. Mods – but nobody minds, and the days of apprentices are over. One misses depth and experience and hard-bitten craftsmanship – not to mention the *genuine artist* – but one gets jolly, colourful things, and R.C.s can't pay much anyway.'

By the time she began her eighth diary in the autumn of 1959 she had been in Winchester for ten years (the longest she had remained anywhere as an adult) and was still thinking of moving elsewhere. She wrote an assessment of her ten years there:

'I'm horrified at all the things I've started and stopped – the list is terrible. Recorders, Winchester *and* London, Clausentums (*Cathedral group*), Sealey's (*orchestra*), politics, Art Club, - I must stop this dropping things. I do it because everything disappoints, but must stick to things somehow.... It is never what I *want*. I want moonlight on stubble fields and myself *there* – I want singing round my table, not in London. I want the suck of water under my boat, the birds waking outside my tent – just like when I was a child. But I'm not going to get what I want, that is clear enough.'

Eularia's friendship with Angus Mason undoubtedly helped her through this period of transition. For the first time she had found someone who appeared to feel things as deeply as she did and who was going through similar struggles, especially with faith. It helped her to feel that she wasn't simply doing it all wrong and it was probably Angus who opened her up to the idea that God may work in ways that are contrary to what our human selves might desire. He certainly taught her about how dividing love can be. He helped Eularia to understand the difference between earthly human love and love of God by sharing his own story with her.

Then, at the end of October, all her issues were eclipsed by a far more serious and tragic event:

'All Souls' Day, and today Daddy really did die – not as he should, with a nice deathbed and lots of relations saying goodbye, but alone and by overdose. Francis rang up – Dorothy had told him, Daddy was found dead in bed. There is to be an inquest. Dorothy won't have me... The thought of such a sad despairing death, and no more jokes, no more Christmases, and such a good life all gone into darkness, is dreadful. He may have saved himself a lot of illness and misery, but that is our fault – mine more than most I suppose. I should have *braved* Dorothy, written more letters, cheered him up. All too late.'

On the morning of 31 October Dorothy Harlow found Cuthbert dead in his bed. He had taken an overdose of barbiturates, leaving a note giving his clear intention to end his life. Depression and increased lack of mobility since his stroke all contributed, he had simply decided that there was no point in continuing.

The first thing Eularia did on hearing the news was go to the presbytery and ask the priests to say a Mass. Once again Angus Mason and Pat Murphy-O'Connor did their best to be supportive but the impact on Eularia was doubled by her new faith. Being a Catholic, Eularia now subscribed to the belief that suicide was not only a sin but also a ticket to damnation, which in those days was still the prevailing belief. That she felt responsible for Cuthbert's suicide was entirely within character, just as it had been with Christopher's accident. Everyone else who knew Cuthbert thought that he was probably extremely practical about it. He simply decided he'd had enough of life and succeeded where he had failed once before. As an agnostic he had no problem with the morality of it and Eularia chose to forget that Cuthbert hadn't been on his own for several years thanks to Dorothy.

There are large gaps in the archives of Eularia's correspondence. Her letters to Rachael and to Alicia survive because both parties kept them, but Eularia herself rarely kept letters except in exceptional cases. Her correspondence from her clergy friends is one instance of this so, for the first time, it is possible to see (when compared with her diary entries of her reaction to these letters) just how she interpreted what was written. Angus Mason wrote a very sympathetic letter to Eularia just after Cuthbert's death, which is a good example of this. It is entirely professional, well written and full of concern and yet Eularia described it as, '…the priest holds predominance over the man, and his words were distant, prim and impersonal, though they give me some comfort over the death – not much.'

This is the conflicted Eularia who never quite knew what she actually wanted. The one person who would have almost certainly have given her the kind of very human comfort she thought that she wanted was John

Stallard, but she refused to tell him about Cuthbert's death (for that very reason). It is a glimpse of her being caught again between that fundamental rock and hard place that underlay so many of her relationships: the need for a very human love and affection, the saviour who would come and rescue her and wipe everything away but which ultimately always proved to be flawed and fleeting; versus the more all-encompassing unconditional love of the Divine which, being so much less tangible, she found hard to believe in, accept, or relate to. The idea that she could be loved 'no matter what' was at best a scary thought and at worst impossible because of what she saw as her flawed and unlovable character.

Cuthbert's death also brought to the surface another theme, which Eularia strongly identified with, that of her talents coming to nothing:

> 'I see the pity of the life coming to such a cold dismal end, the brilliant promise not harvested, the loneliness and depression of the last years. I want Angus to understand him, and the end of the family, and the need for a new sort of family – practicing Christians who can control impulses and face death and use their talents.'

Angus Mason, who was her favoured confessor at the time, seemed to instinctively understand the human touch that she needed. It helped her to feel safe to unburden herself to him about all her fears over being responsible for the suicide and that she didn't feel that she deserved absolution. The second letter that Angus wrote to her was full of concern. He told her:

> 'He, Our Father, is sheer goodness, love, understanding, all the attributes: one simply has to abandon helplessly such pain into His keeping.'

His message is simple and effective, but he mentions in it that his original draft of the letter to her was nine pages in length and he scrapped it because it wasn't going anywhere. Eularia was a nine-page letter person – lots of drama, lots of explanation but ultimately, as Angus explained, not really saying anything helpful, so initially she rather pushed aside what she saw as the poorer one-page version. But on reflection she realised that she had been wrong to do so. Angus's letter helped her to feel positive about her faith again. In the end she realised that it was, '... a letter to keep for comfort and help through anything in the future, a letter unlike any other, more powerful and strengthening than anything I've ever had in all my life.'

The kind of support she received from him and from the other curates at St Peter's over the next few years was to completely change her view of relationships with men, for these were men who both cared and who gave back without expecting anything in return. It was a whole new concept for her.

It was undoubtedly Angus Mason who began this change of approach in relating to men. She couldn't simply barge in at the presbytery. She had to think out her actions in a way she never had before. When she was worried about Angus's non-appearance at Mass it was Pat Murphy-O'Connor that she contacted and he was very matter-of-fact about there being nothing to worry about:

'I recognised in myself the shameful disappointment, the usual one. I hungrily seek out emotional situations, emotional thrills, excitement and each time I am quietly let down and find myself where I was, quite unneeded, not part of any dramatic situation.'

It was her tendency towards drama that gave her paintings their unique stamp and, in my opinion, makes them different from the religious art produced by male artists, including Stanley Spencer who she greatly admired. There is an uninhibited emotion about her work. Her characters readily express their feelings on their faces, with the exception of the Christ figure who holds the calm serenity so redolent of Byzantine icons, as if nothing any of the people around him can do will surprise or upset him. It creates an incredible stillness within so much dramatic movement and it was undoubtedly through her priest friends that she began to sense this.

Her struggle with the Church now became an uncertainty about whether it was her feelings for Angus driving her on or whether she genuinely had a positive relationship with Catholicism itself. The child who so longed to be the centre of attention and never was came through very strongly in her relationship with the Church. She recognised very clearly that there was a part of her that always wanted to shine, to be special, to be praised, to be the centre of attention. She found it almost impossible to be 'one of the crowd'.

One of the delightful highlights in what had otherwise been a very challenging few weeks was the news that she was to become a grandmother. Rachael was expecting the following summer, '…which is pure joy, and more than I dreamt of.'

Eularia was in a kind of limbo, a cusp between her old life and what would become her new one. It was marked by the death of Cuthbert. A suicide in the family is always hard and questioned by those left behind, doubly so if you believe that suicide means eternal damnation. The rather bumpy, dramatic sides of it were balanced by a growing friendship with people like the Belfield family. Eversley Belfield and Angus Mason both suggested again that Eularia join the Newman group, as they were keen to have graduates.

Angus backed this up when she explained a fear of being 'chosen' to him shortly afterwards:

'...and when I came to my dilemma about having to begin to be a saint or else always in a state of conflict, if it were all true I thought I was saying it to the right person at last, because he wasn't a bit surprised and seemed to think it would be all right and that I must stay myself and not worry about being original and therefore awkward. This was a shock at first, but a consolation after, it wasn't a warning to change. He explained why people kept asking me about the faith – he said when a person of my intellectual gifts took on an ossified, antiquated and strictly legal faith, people were always interested. I liked this. And he said help would always come, and when he'd been beyond reach of consolation, help had always come, from somewhere. I said I had no sense of God, and he said, don't try to – I'm glad to have got that one out.'

For the first time in Eularia's life someone, a man, was telling her to be herself. For Eularia the tide was turning.

From the beginning of 1960 Michael Gedge began a correspondence with Eularia that was to cover all his years of training at the Beda and beyond. There is no doubt that face-to-face Eularia and Michael found each other challenging. Michael stated in a letter in 1962:

'Indeed I think we get along better on paper than in life, for we always seem to scrap in a sort of ecclesiastical one-upmanship contest.'

Michael never was one to mince his words. In an earlier letter dated January 1960 he wrote:

'I much enjoyed your letter – like yourself it seemed to go on and on, but when reading and not listening I am able to get a word in edgeways whenever I like!'

Both Michael Gedge and Eularia were great talkers and both opinionated. If you listen to Michael, Eularia always won, never allowing him a chance to speak, but if you listen to Eularia it's the other way round, so we are left to wonder what an evening of conversation between them was actually like. Michael was to become a staunch if often outspoken and critical support to Eularia in her struggles with faith. He did not spare her anything. He told it as he saw it and his advice was often extremely sound. If Angus was supporting Eularia's more emotional and spiritual leanings, then Michael always helped to keep her firmly grounded. Gradually, with his help, she began to equate her bouts of unbelief with her moods. If she was down lack of faith was her default position, but when she was feeling optimistic and balanced faith came easily.

She continued to have strong feelings for Angus Mason but she was very careful about them. She didn't want to put him in an awkward position. It is as if this opened another doorway within Eularia. Unable to put her energy into the object of her affection in the way that she had with the three Johns (by relentlessly pursuing them and seeking to 'rescue' them) she had, instead, to allow her feelings to find a different expression and something began to emerge which surprised Eularia and certainly left her family uncomfortable even to this day. She first expressed it in a diary entry in early 1960:

'The funny thing about it all is that I speak to God more or less easily, some folks can't. And every now and then something crops up and seizes me and I stamp on it and strangle it at once because I am afraid it may be the love of God and where on earth would that lead...? I have to resist it strongly, but I know I won't always be able to.'

What is revealing here is how untrusting Eularia is of love and a sense that to admit the love of God might take her places that she is reluctant to go. This is a common symptom of a call to a vocation (not always religious). A sense by the personality that the soul may have an agenda currently beyond its understanding, and that is scary. The idea that we might give ourselves up to be consumed by something so much greater and which might take us to places that we fear can produce an antagonistic reaction that puts us in direct conflict with ourselves.

Throughout this period Eularia oscillated with increasing frequency between sensing a calling (which she squashed) and wanting to be seen as special by the parish, especially Angus Mason, then feeling that she had failed. She then fell back into her default pattern of judging herself for getting everything wrong and botching it up. It was a painful transition and one is left with the impression of a reluctant child being dragged kicking and screaming to a destination.

In fact Eularia's ability to love and care, which had been stuck for so long on personal romantic love, was shifting and expanding – and it confused her. Other parts of her, which had remained shut off for years, probably ever since her Theology days in Oxford, were beginning to reassert themselves again and long-shut doors were beginning to creak open. Rachael was settled and expecting her first child and James too would shortly be leaving for London. They no longer needed her in the same way, John Stallard did not need her, the priests did not need her. She was having to shift her focus to the idea that they might seek her out not because they needed her but because they wanted her, that they enjoyed her company, that she did actually have something to offer that wasn't based simply on need.

If Angus Mason began to encourage Eularia to step into forgotten areas of herself, in early 1960 James was the voice that mirrored the subconscious part of herself that was convinced she was a bad lot and unable to change. James had become very anti-Catholic since his mother's conversion, which, given that he was living at home while waiting for a possible BBC position, made life awkward.

> 'J (*James*) had pointed out that my character had not improved since I became a Catholic, and he pointed out that it would be fatal if I thought it had.'

Her relationship with James was deteriorating. Having him living permanently at home was proving difficult for both of them. Their relationship had depended on long absences making them glad to see each other, but familiarity was breeding contempt. It was time for him to leave and they both knew it.

Angus Mason frequently attempted to encourage Eularia out of her worst self and he was the first person who told her that she was 'alive and sensitive' (possibly the first person, since Peggy, who had recognised this side of Eularia). It was his job and his vocation, and Eularia understood that, but it was a complete revelation to her nonetheless. Angus, like a good therapist, was adept at remembering what Eularia's issues were which, for the first time, helped her to feel that she was of some importance, as she wrote:

> 'It is quite a new thing for me to be bothered about, and a comforting one.'

Someone was finally helping her by sharing her burden in much the same way as a good therapist would now. The fashion for therapists was a long way off in 1960 and attending one carried a stigma with it, but having a priest as a guide and confessor was far more acceptable. It is a service that has perhaps become somewhat forgotten in more modern times when so much publicity has been given to the more negative aspects of the Church:

'I shall find him disturbingly attractive always. But the blessing is, that I know my pattern. I love intensely and then suffer, and then hate and resent the lack of response – and after that, friendship and ease.'

14

Lourdes

Just after Ash Wednesday, 1960, Eularia was diagnosed with breast cancer. Since Christmas she had been experiencing what she described as 'claws' in her left breast but the doctor's first thought was mastitis and Eularia was convinced she was healthy, so it came as a shock. Her biopsy resulted in the removal of her left breast, something for which she had in no way been prepared.

Later she wrote to Alicia about the whole experience:

'I told Rachael to ring you up about this, as you are the family news centre! I didn't let anyone know earlier, if I could avoid it, because I thought I'd be quickly in and out in a few days, so, I only told my delightful neighbours, and John (*Stallard*) who did the necessary things like fruit and nightgowns; and nobody else knew except the priests (because of a morbid custom of confession-before-operation!). So of course the hospital was cross when it came to a full mastectomy for cancer, and nobody to inform except their reverences – but they got over it, and their revs. did it *beautifully* so no need to fuss, I thought... Of course the R.C nurses spoil me abominably and bring me secret cups of tea! It has all been surprisingly happy, although just at first it was unfortunate, as James wrote from Paris on the very day after the op, about how nice it was with Cyril and Lorraine, who are married and settled. He didn't know, of course, but I was quite unable to cope with the loss of both him (apparently) and a slice of myself, and I really don't know what I'd have done if good old Mother Church hadn't gathered round, and sweet little Irish nurses soothed and prayed all through the night and got hold of the priests next day. *They* got it all sorted out in no time, and saw to it all, and I even got my candles.'

Rachael (who had had no advance warning of any of this and was now seven months pregnant) suddenly found she had a potentially very sick mother. She rushed to Winchester to be at her mother's bedside and it was Pat Murphy-O'Connor who took on most of the pastoral work, Eularia would have preferred Angus Mason, but Angus had problems of his own.

Eularia had her own very clear ideas about what the cancer represented:

'I'd asked to expiate my father's suicide – not expecting anything to happen, then it grew from the breast and perhaps it has worked, in any case it is done by God and this is strange, to say the least.'

This explanation, as odd as it is, gave her satisfaction because she felt she had given it for a good cause.

Eularia's mastectomy was deemed a success and it was decided that she didn't need further treatment. She did feel self-conscious about being lopsided, but the ability to rebuild lost breasts artificially was a long way off and so she either had to wear a false one or adjust her clothes accordingly to disguise the fact. It is from around this time that she began to wear increasingly shapeless tops eventually resorting to her homemade smocks, which became such a feature of her later years.

With no one now at home pouring cold water on her religious activities, Eularia fell into a pattern of regular, almost daily, Church attendance, still bolstered by her feelings and admiration for Angus. Then one day:

'When I thanked him at the end (*of confession*), I was just going when he almost inaudibly said pray for me, and I had time to say yes, and then penance.'

It was the last time she saw him. After Easter she went for a short 'convalescent' visit to St Joseph's Convent at Woodchester and on her return she found Angus Mason absent. She assumed that he was on holiday, but now that Eularia was attending daily Mass more often Angus's absence was much more obvious to her.

She missed being able to talk over her conflicts about Faith with him and one arose in May after attending the Marian procession. May is a month traditionally devoted to Mary and includes the May Devotions to the Blessed Virgin Mary. In 1960 processions were often still held during this month, very similar to May Queen processions, though it is Mary who is Queen of the May. Eularia loved these processions, as she loved much of the theatre of the Church but she found herself struggling with Mariolatry:

'It is beautiful, but for me it is false… the whole impact is made by people, more and more of them, now including all the nuns and friars as well. They represent Christ, and this I follow because it is the best thing so far.'

The idea that the Church is its people and that they are the body of Christ is an underlying theme in all her religious paintings. That the gospel lives through us in our everyday lives, and not on some remote altar, was something she would come to believe passionately. The gift and value of her diaries are that we are able to see this journey gradually emerging, with all its doubts, hiccups, bumps and rocky bits intact. Her 'ministry', her inspiration and drive to paint came from a gradual evolving of life experience and of following her intuition, often without having the slightest idea why she was drawn in the direction she was going. She would frequently question the wisdom of it on an intellectual level, was often unhappy with it and even, from time to time, hated it. It makes her journey very real and easy to identify with in a way that perhaps the distant lives of the apostles and the saints are not.

By the time Whitsun arrived Eularia had given up hope of Angus Mason returning. At first the official line was that he was on holiday but as this turned from a couple of weeks into a month she began to realise that he might not be coming back. She was right. Early in June another parishioner told her that Angus was leaving and had applied for a religious order.

Eularia felt it deeply but she also recognised that it gave her an opportunity to see how well she related to the Mass and the Church without the sun of Angus always being in the ascendant. She did not shy away from this challenge, although the loss of Angus was to haunt her for a long while to come.

It was to Pat Murphy-O'Connor that she turned. Eularia's relationship with Pat was very different from her one with Angus. Angus Mason was the last man she would ever have a romantic crush on. Pat Murphy-O'Connor was much more like a brother and his jovial light-heartedness had caused her to overlook him in favour of the more serious and cerebral Angus, but as she began to go to Pat for Confession she found a much more empathetic, serious side to him and a very grounded spirituality, which she grew to appreciate.

If Eularia's diaries are to be interpreted correctly then it was their shared concern for Angus that initially stimulated Pat and Eularia's friendship. Pat missed Angus too. He knew more about the circumstances of Angus's leaving than Eularia did and it had raised issues for him. Both of them greatly appreciated having each other to confide in and Pat was the first man that Eularia became friends with without any kind of agenda at all. It was probably the most relaxed and natural of all her friendships.

June saw the birth of her first granddaughter (me) but it was a bittersweet time for Eularia. She was overjoyed at being a grandmother, but, due to strict hospital rules confining visitors to one person only, she was unable to visit Rachael or myself for two days. Inevitably she felt excluded, compounded by the news that her brother Anthony had finally married his current girlfriend, Patricia Stammers, without inviting her to the wedding or even telling her that it was happening.

She returned to Winchester with mixed feelings to a very full summer. She hadn't given herself a chance to convalesce properly, or adjust to the loss of her breast, and it was beginning to take its toll emotionally and physically, but still convinced that she was the indestructible member of the family, the robust one, she soldiered on.

Just after my christening in July (which she hosted) Angus Mason's replacement arrived at St Peter's. David Mahy was from Guernsey and newly ordained. At 23 he was much younger than Angus and Pat Murphy-O'Connor, but he was to become a significant part of Eularia's story as an artist.

Familiar with Pat's playful ribaldry through her brothers and Angus's intellectualism through her father and grandfather, David Mahy often confused her. She had not met anyone quite like him before, so young, but so committed and clear about his vocation. She often referred to him as a saint (something David himself feels is totally underserved) but she didn't always know how to be with him. She was old enough to be his mother (he was similar in age to Rachael) and yet felt that he had an authority that she admired and that seemed far superior to her own.

Towards the end of the summer an exhausted Eularia went on the trip that was to change the next ten years of her life: a pilgrimage to Lourdes with a local group led by a Fr Chadwick.

Eularia always cited Lourdes as being a turning point and the experience that re-inspired her religious painting. As was her habit she took sketching tools with her (she was rarely without them) and so it was quite natural for her to sit and sketch. It poured with rain much of the time but she sketched the flow of people around her. Four of her paintings are of the grotto from different angles and this is her description of her first sight of it:

Lourdes: Grotto from Outside (summer 1960)

'We went along the riverside, among the trees, and strolling silent crowds, and we saw it blazing with a whole tree of candles, people thick in front of it, and the statue of Notre Dame de Lourdes in her nitch, with a trail of ivy over her feet. We went right in and I said my first prayer for Angus kneeling in the mud among the devout folk, and Fr C (*Chadwick*) said, we'll say a rosary outside.'

She painted the grotto from both inside and outside and the act of pilgrims touching the walls:

'Then round the grotto alone in the silent slow-moving crowd, all the mixed nations, and I did everything the others did, rested my forehead on the cool rock, like the priests who seemed to get so much comfort from it, and kissed it and stroked the shining black surface experimentally. I sat for a long time loving it, it's nice sitting in a quiet cave among devout loving people in the Pyrenees.'

She also painted the collecting of water from the spring (*Lourdes:Water From the Spring)*, and following the Stations of the Cross up the mountainside in the early morning (*Lourdes: Way of the Cross*):

'The sun rose as we went up myself comfortably barefoot on the stones (less comfortable kneeling) past rather too statuesque statues, 1908 or so, praying the stations higher and higher, singing Stabat Mater with blue mountains getting larger and bluer beneath.'

Original sketch for Lourdes: Touching the Walls (summer 1960)

The final painting of the grotto was the *Communion for the Sick*:

'The sick lay or sat in rows, in stretcher carriages or chairs, and when it rained they were protected by hoods. Scouts, guides, seminarians stood about and prayed and helped, a woman yelled and had to be constantly covered up.'

She painted three almost identical versions of people waiting for confession inside the church which became *Confessions at Lourdes*.

Eularia, aware of her health scare and still not feeling really well, attended the Piscine, although she found the experience strange and rather off-putting:

'I was plunged with screams and much handling into murky darkness and (?) water, to kiss the virgin at the far end. I then dressed, my officious attendants astonished at my lack of clothing. On coming out of the water I felt very joyful, but I soon reflected that this is a normal reaction to cold water – I'm used to it, and putting on clothes without drying – but these devout inhibited women clearly never do it, so the results are exhilarating.'

Her reaction to the whole Lourdes experience was not entirely positive, but she was glad she had been. She was later to say that she had tried too hard at it and simply ended up exhausting herself. Once again there had been no Damascene experience, no clear inner sense of faith, and she had found herself unable to tolerate Catholics en masse, but Lourdes had opened some subtle doors. The previous year, so full of trials and drama, culminating with the pilgrimage, now began to do its work. The artist was finally beginning to emerge from her cocoon.

15

The Work Begins

After returning from Lourdes Eularia began to turn her sketches into paintings, probably using her usual mixture of size and pigments which gives her early paintings their flat, matt quality. The mediums Eularia used for her religious paintings are not always clear. Many are certainly in oil, but she also reported using gouache on canvas in her diaries. She rarely specified what medium was used for which painting, leaving us to guess, and she does not actually note using oils until around 1962 when James bought her some new ones. Used to money being tight, she often used up what she had available.

In a letter to Rachael she wrote:

'...nearly all day I paint away, and have done much the best things of my life, all of the Lourdes, all memory, all quite large and full of S. Spencer details.'

It is only after the visit to Lourdes and the beginning of the religious painting that she wrote regularly in her diaries about what she was painting and her experience of painting it:

'I painted all yesterday, the panels are nice, I shall perfect a technique on them and work *hard* – soon I shall be back to illustrating the Gospels as when I was young. I began St Matt. last night and immediately saw the Baptism in Fazeley Canal (*Coming up From Water 1965*). These days there is a sense of great urgency, I must get something *real* done everyday – it's not enough to see to the house and the chores and dress make and write letters and shop and teach. I must really *use* my life... I feel the terrific power rising in me, the power to make pictures out of everything I've ever seen, Heaven and Charing X. All England full of Gospel happenings.'

Very quickly after completing the seven Lourdes paintings she moved on to subjects much closer to home and this was when she turned the *Candlemas* sketch into a painting:

'It's the first non-Lourdes painting, and apparently the miracle continues – the Good Friday Kissing of the Cross, very S. Spencer but also very good.'

Kissing the Cross, Good Friday was set in St Peter's. Eularia's fascination with patterns of worship matched her sense of drama. When noting points for her own autobiographical notes for exhibitions, she wrote about this period in her life:

'Catholic Church and Grand Opera – candles, incense, processions and palms and vestments and the unselfconscious movements of worship by an enclosed family-type congregation.'

Despite the optimistic tone Eularia was far from confident about the Lourdes paintings. She knew that religion was a tricky subject, one that people often found embarrassing, and indeed the paintings met with mixed reactions among those she initially showed them to. But two of the Lourdes paintings, *Inside the Grotto* and *Way of the Cross* make up two of the only five paintings that she ever agreed to sell, and as with almost all the religious works she sold, she made copies for the collection.

Her relationship with St Peter's also underwent a subtle change after Lourdes, one that was to prove foundational to her art over the next six years. It began with her decision to attend early morning Mass on a daily basis as a discipline, rather than simply when she got round to it:

'But whenever I go to Mass here (*St Peter's*) I want to go again, as soon as possible, and although each going is a failure and disappointment, I still need to go and want to... Religion is the only steady thing in my life now, which is odd as I don't really like it, and it doesn't improve my lot.'

She still found it hard not to have Angus Mason around despite her growing friendship with Pat Murphy-O'Connor, and it still caused her to question her motives for being a Catholic:

'Do I believe that God cares about us, or do I just huddle in a heap with fellow humans to share their warmth and yet not have to entertain them or know them? I was taken back to Lourdes in memory, and what stands out is the utterly unsatisfactory set-up, the loneliness and drabness, tiredness, wetness, darkness, lack of direction – and yet the paintings have come mysteriously out of it, and I didn't actually lose faith, which is odd in itself.'

There was a part of her that, without Angus there to confide in or be guided by, was expecting to lose faith altogether, to wake up and find that she had made a big mistake. Her surprise was that this did not seem to be happening, in fact, quite the opposite. Her faith seemed, quite inexplicably to her, to be growing.

Eularia had to pluck up considerable courage to show the Lourdes paintings to Sidney Mullarkey, who appeared ambivalent about them but encouraged her to keep going. Throughout her painting career the opinion of the Catholic priests about her work mattered to her almost more than anyone else and she was very adept at reading negatives into responses, probably when they weren't even there. So, the lack of dramatic show on Sidney's part (never a man given to the dramatic anyway) reinforced her belief that they weren't very good. Veronica Stokes, who saw them a day or so later, loved them very effusively, which, of course, was exactly the reaction Eularia wanted, but from Sidney, not Veronica.

Everyone who remembers Eularia recalls a very positive and cheerful woman, but the cheerfulness was often a mask. Whatever she was feeling in the moment coloured the whole of her world and her responses and relationships with others. It was always personal. She found it very difficult to stand back and allow that the responses of others might have nothing to do with her at all, that they were simply feeling low, unwell, harassed or down themselves. It was the very fact that people found it so easy to be with her and to relax in her company that allowed them to be themselves. But no matter how tough or relaxed she appeared, everything that was said to her was under scrutiny to see if she had behaved badly or 'dropped bricks', to see if she was liked and accepted.

Eularia had already recorded having strange sensations during Mass but on 23 January 1961 she had an experience that was to underlie her inspiration and her work for the next nine years. She spent the evening at a meeting of the Newman Society and arrived back late to a cold house (Middle Road had no central heating) and so went straight to bed with two hot water bottles:

'I don't know what happened, but I got charged with a sudden sweep of love of God that I was about paralysed by it, it kept happening again and again until I was weak and shivering and begged it to stop, and sobbed between thanking and not deserving it and longing for it never to stop. It was so like human love only one could feel it beginning at the heart and containing one completely and kept happening again and again as often as I spoke and answered it. It was not frightening at all, it was as if he were laughing at me and showing me quite merrily and tenderly that He could do things with me almost like a lover, and produce the emotions that I always long to feel.'

She came to refer to this as passive prayer, er-prayer or just simply prayer. She described having this sensation and the joy that went with it quite frequently. It kept her going through very challenging times, crises of faith, rejections, disappointments, and illness. She only ever really lost sight of it again in her darkest moods, not because it went away but because she was too negative to allow it space.

16

Expanding Horizons

In March 1961 Eularia finally acquired transport as she wrote to her cousin Alicia:

'I am very miserable because I've got my first "car" – a darling cheap Citroen 2cv van which I love devotedly and long to rush around Hants in, but I've just failed the Test in spite of twelve excellent lessons…the clergy quite failed to cheer me by telling me I had a unique opportunity of sharing the failures and humiliations of the Way of the Cross – (though I quite see what they mean), but they meant well, bless them – but I do so want to take grandchildren to the sea some day.'

Eularia in Spo (1961)

Eularia had not driven since 1948, relying on trains, buses and walking. Now that the children had left home and were no longer in London (Rachael and Robert had moved to Leeds and James to Norwich to join Anglia Television) she decided that it was time to finally take the plunge and become independently mobile, but she needed to acquire a license to do so. She liked the idea of simply taking off at weekends and exploring. When Cuthbert's estate had gone through probate she received around £1,400, which in the early sixties was a reasonable lump sum and certainly more than Eularia was used to having, so she decided to put some of it towards her van which she called Spo after its license plate. She chose a van because she wanted to be able to camp in the back and she furnished it with a hay-stuffed mattress covered in her favourite black and white checked gingham, a primus stove and the basic necessities for camping.

Having been dependant on public transport, or friends and relations who had cars, for years, Eularia's new van and driving license (she did pass eventually) expanded her world and her sense of freedom. She spent the summer, when she wasn't teaching, travelling and exploring. She drove no more than around thirty or forty miles a day, avoided main roads and would park on a beach, a cliff top or on a verge at night and sleep in the back of Spo. She made tea on her primus stove and bought fish and chips from the nearest town or village. This was a pattern that she would frequently follow in the early 1960s and locations from these visits often appear later as backdrops for her paintings.

She was never a confidant driver, though, and long trips were always a trial. She frequently got lost (being very inept at map reading) and panicked, which made her more lost. Spo worked well for sleeping in if the weather was fine, but not if it was wet as it tended towards condensation and she would wake up soaked. Spo also proved to be a most unreliable van. It regularly broke down, leaving Eularia stranded in the middle of nowhere. She became quite adept at quick fixes, mostly through guesswork, and was frequently left waiting for the AA or the local garage to come and rescue her. She told Rachael in July:

> 'I've bought a cheap mandolin for the car, when it breaks down and requires the AA I play "Roses from the South", you need minims to practice tremolo, it is great fun.'

Pat Murphy-O'Connor, Sidney Mullarkey and David Mahy at
St Peter's, Winchester (early 1960s)

Her friendship with Pat Murphy-O'Connor blossomed. She thrived on
feeling needed and Pat became the younger brother substitute in her life,
but Pat was a man who was willing to give her support in return as a
confidant and priest, something she really appreciated:

'Pat was a dear... he said I'd never get anywhere in this business of myself
and God unless I managed it. I told him how I did all my pious acts from
entirely selfish motives, and he said I could make too much of this imparting
of impure motives – the important thing is that I do pray (I don't). I said it
would be so nice if just *once* I was nice to someone I didn't like. He said, do
you know what would happen to you then? I suddenly saw, and said I might
think I was getting somewhere, and he said, exactly.'

They both had a wicked sense of humour, which they greatly enjoyed in
each other. But it was not Pat who ultimately replaced Angus Mason as
Eularia's confessor. Instead she chose David Mahy.

David Mahy was only 23 when he first arrived at St Peter's and, by his own admission, naive and immature from spending six years enclosed in a seminary studying to be a priest. In looking back he said, 'It is only now, in retirement, that I have been able to reflect, and to realise the extent to which she (*Eularia*) was a mentor in my continuing formation as a priest.' So David was an interesting choice for Eularia as a confessor and speaks to something she divined in him even at that young age. But he ended up with the job quite by accident shortly after Christmas at the end of 1960:

> 'I went for a long overdue confession, not knowing which of them (*the priests*) it was, as it was pitch darkness, and doesn't even smell of tobacco or sherry (*Pat and Canon respectively*) – and as it was a rainy day I made an unusually good anonymous confession. I was a bit bothered when it turned out to be our new boy, because I'd rather avoided him as being very young, but he dealt rapidly with my transgressions and then got right down to it with a *lecture*. He said he'd been Angus's successor for long enough to know exactly how much I must be missing him, because he was quite exceptional and I'd never find anyone else at all like him, and I mustn't think it wrong to be thoroughly gloomy about it and he quite understood. But now it was time to find another priest who'd help me; (pause) now I'm *not* suggesting *myself* as that priest – in fact there's nothing to prevent you getting anybody, even outside Winchester (long pause). BUT – I should like to come up to see you soon about one or two things; when I come back from my holiday, because I shall need time to think it over and prepare for it, etc. etc. It was very touching, and rather like the child Jesus sitting up in the manger and giving me the works!'

Her friendship with David Mahy was very different from the one she had with Pat with whom she joked, played music, and commiserated. It took her longer to appreciate David because he was the first young man she had met who didn't seem to need anything from her, even as a confidante. David's insistence that she was an important mentor to him indicates how unaware she was of her value. Her first response on seeing such a young priest was typical, to try and support and help him in every way. She felt motherly towards him; in short she wanted to be needed by him. But David refused to be sucked into the more dramatic and emotional aspects of Eularia's character. David, unlike the more Celtic Pat and more complex Angus, did not do drama. This was extremely good for her, which she was later to acknowledge, but at first she didn't know what to make of it.

Much as she loved Pat she was convinced that she needed a hard taskmaster as a confessor and she felt that he would be too lenient on her. As with Michael Gedge, it was the very fact that David was so much less emotional about things that attracted her. She knew that it was a quality she needed, even if she found it hard to accept and she knew she would never have feelings about him in the way she had about Angus.

Just after Easter 1961 she joined Robert and Rachael at Spode Easter Music Week, held at Spode House, Hawkesyard Priory, near Rugeley in Staffordshire. Hawkesyard was a Dominican Seminary and in the early 1960s full of young trainee priests and novices. Spode House, once a boys school run by the Dominicans, was now a conference centre under the wardenship of Fr Conrad Peplar OP. Conrad was the son of Hilary Peplar who, with Eric Gill, had set up the Ditchling Community[6] and Conrad's early experiences of communal creativity and easy going community life pervaded the atmosphere at Spode. The Music Week was Conrad's own inspiration and was to see many of the new young Catholic composers pass through its doors over the next fifteen years.

Eularia enjoyed Spode, despite the fact that she often ended up being the babysitter. She loved the atmosphere of the rather tatty house with its wild gardens, the opportunity to spend time saying the daily offices with the Dominicans, and she enjoyed the music. She greatly warmed, as so many did, to Conrad himself, who was an exceptional man and priest and, through his work at Spode, touched the lives of many who remember his extraordinary tolerance and inclusiveness with great affection.

Here Eularia met people, many of them professional musicians, who were actively looking to the musical future of both the Mass and the Church, while balancing it with its history and with the secular world. There was none of the entrenched traditionalism that she encountered at St Peter's and it was another influence on the direction Eularia's own creativity would take.

Consequently Eularia began her next diary on a much more optimistic note and she gives a very accurate description of how her relationship with God and faith would continue:

---

6 The Guild of St Joseph and St Dominic was a community of Catholic Artists and craftsmen founded by Gill & Peplar in 1921. Gill was a member of the Distributists League (as was Cuthbert) and they put many of its theories into practice at the Guild.

'Apparently it wasn't a case for saying "Thy will be done." I was beyond that, and had to act like the widow and the judge – I wanted it and hadn't a hope of getting it by myself, and no hope in anything else. So I howled, and was allowed to have things my way.'

Her sense of always being at war, of always having to fight for what she wanted, comes across strongly here. For Eularia faith that came easily would have been no faith at all. She wouldn't have recognised it. She needed the drama generated by the conflict in order to feel that it was real.

It was during this summer that she began to write poetry again, inspired by a visit to the ruins of Netley Abbey:

'I said a whole rosary at the high altar, lay down looking up into the blue, blue summer sky and a poem came to me – first one for about 30 years.'

This was 'Netley in June', which was the first of her poems to be published in the Tablet later that summer.

Things never went smoothly for long. Eularia had the first of what were to become frequent quarrels with Will Thomas and the choir. This time it was just Thomas but she grumbled about it to Pat and said, 'Catholics don't care, and Pat said, now listen, you're a Catholic, and I said, I can't be, because I know what dotted crotchets are.'

Their immediate superiors and the direction the Church itself was taking supported Pat Murphy-O'Connor and David Mahy in their desire to take the Gospel to the people (by involving them), and they often discussed their ideas and plans with Eularia over cups of coffee at Middle Road. Eularia always said that without the Catholic Church there would have been no paintings and these conversations, along with the enthusiasm of these two priests, helped to give shape and form to her own sense that the Gospel is living in the modern world through the people, which she expressed so eloquently in her paintings.

She found inspiration for several of her paintings while out in Spo that summer, exploring. *Oblates at Compline, Taena Community* painted in 1961 was an example of this. The Taena Community was a group of Oblates[7] begun by George Ireson living close to Prinknash, and Eularia camped there. Her description of them is evocative and provides the groundwork for the painting:

---

7   A layperson who chooses to follow the same Rule of Order as Monks and is usually affiliated with an Abbey or Monastery.

'...altar, stalls of rough boards on the remaining long and two short sides, rough floor of worn and broken boards, tiny cobwebby windows, hills and trees, evening sky. A tractor-driver type, heavy in dirty working clothes, and an old white-haired lady lead the office, there were several adults, a girl in jeans, several young men. When we sang the Salve, a man lit the two candles in front of the lovely wooden carved Madonna.'

Oblates at Compline, Taena Community (1961)

In the painting we see Eularia capturing this moment when the candles are lit and it is possible to identify the characters that she lists here. It is a window on a moment in time and a dying one as the Taena Community was disbanded not long after this.

She travelled from Gloucester to Woodchester and what would be the subject of another painting, *Sunday Mass, Woodchester* (1961) depicting a group of people leaving the small chapel after Mass and gathering in the graveyard to chat. The men are smoking, nuns and Dominican friars mix with the parishioners, and children run and play around their feet. She gave it to Conrad Peplar and it hung in one of the bedrooms at Spode House until he retired in the late 1970s when he returned it to the family and the collection.

At this point Eularia, the new Catholic, was still experimenting and feeling her way. Her next painting, *Stations of the Cross, Holy Week* passed without mention in her diary but still demonstrates her fascination with the patterns of worship and ritual, the way people give expression to an inner experience of God, which had so spiked her curiosity as a child. One senses from these early paintings that she was still the observer, the outsider looking in. But as she became more familiar with being a Catholic she became all too aware of the very things that bothered Pat, David and those who desired to see change in the Church, the fact that most Catholics were simply doing things by rote, following learnt patterns out of habit, and it was for this reason that she often referred to them en masse as 'dull'. It was the lack of anything vivid or living in the ritual that spurred her on to express her own inner experience more directly.

Eularia was aware of this 'dullness' in herself and shortly after returning from Prinknash and Woodchester she assessed her own 'holiness' or lack of it, a list that is readily identifiable with:

'All around me are opportunities for holiness, and I don't take them because of 1) Laziness. 2) Suiting myself. 3) Wanting to be looked up to, and "on top". 4) Liking my comforts. 5) Living my own way. 6) Clinging to my possessions of all sorts, and also to my freedom. 7) Being unwilling to bother. 8) Liking my physical comforts. 9) Keeping free from people, especially ones I don't like. 10) Criticising hideously the people I do like.'

The beauty of this list is that it is so human. Eularia (regardless of whether she expected her diaries to one day be read by others or not) was always brutally honest with herself. Like many of us, she couldn't always do anything about it. She had far fewer resources as a means for transforming herself than we have available to us today. In some respects this made her choice simpler – it was a relationship with God or nothing. There were no gurus, no therapists, and no self-help books to fall back on.

In an attempt to dispel this lack of holiness and inconsistency, Eularia began to experiment. The business and distractions of summer 1961 reduced her intense experiences of God, so as soon as she was alone again in early September she settled down to give herself a three-day retreat at home, which included some rather dubious methods:

'I got into prayer and couldn't get out of it so started on nettles, which luckily hurt a lot because they are old. I don't quite know what to do about it all. I think I ought to starve a bit. I've put boards in the bed, but of *course* only under the mattress and partly owing to an article about slipped discs. Poems keep cropping up – that's four so far.'

In the early years of her conversion Eularia was not averse to using mortification in an attempt to improve her 'piety'. Mortification of the flesh is a curious spiritual practice not limited by any means to the Catholic Church, though early Catholics readily took to it as a way of identifying with the suffering of Christ. But the Church advises prudence in the use of mortification and severe forms should only be carried out under the guidance of a spiritual director.

The fact that Eularia was drawn towards mortification, which she would have read about, is not altogether surprising, given her poor self image and her constant need to try and improve herself. Angus had introduced her to the idea of finding joy in suffering, which, given her life to date, probably appealed as a way to give her suffering some meaning and some use. If she could offer it up then perhaps there might be joy in it, perhaps it could be transcended. She did not have a spiritual director at this point, nor did she inform any of her priest friends of what she was doing.

17

Going Public

From the first public showing of Eularia's work it caught people's attention. Around the time of her home retreat the *Catholic Herald* published an article by their art critic, Iris Conlay, about the paintings shown at the Bladon Gallery (*Palm Sunday, Lourdes, Touching the Walls* and *Stations of the Cross, Holy Week*):

'Have you ever noticed, as you kneel in church, what interesting patterns are made by the headscarves of the people in front of you? Have you ever watched the light flicker and illuminate the faces of candle-bearers in processions?

Have you observed the homely muddle of shopping baskets and music sheets and prayer books and gloves and rosaries that strew themselves over the benches as people drop into church at confession time? If you have been to Lourdes, do you remember the unearthly glow and heat of the candlelit grotto?

These are the human things about religion and the church that Eularia Clarke has observed so lovingly and has described so accurately and nostalgically in a series of paintings which have been recently exhibited in the Bladon Gallery in Andover.

Mrs Clarke's work echoes that of Stanley Spencer but without displaying any of Spencer's distortions. It may not partake of the intensity of Spencer's poetic vision but it has great qualities of feeling and rare humanity. It appeals where Spencer mystifies.'

It is in this interview with Iris Conlay that Eularia gives an insight into how she worked. She told her:

'I suppose they are all done from memory really; one mentally photographs a lot of people, etc., and they fit into the pattern as one goes along, or else one invents them as required.'

Eularia never painted any of her religious works using models, or from real life, they were always taken from her exceptionally good visual memory and imagination, sometimes with the aid of rough sketches of the locations.

Arising out of this review was the first intimation of a pattern that would ultimately completely undermine Eularia's relationship with Sidney Mullarkey and St Peter's:

'I... went to Mass with vague subconscious expectations of being received as a local success. Not a bit of it, not a single person either mentioned it (*the article*) or (apparently) had heard of me or the paintings. It's understandable because nobody knows I paint. And perhaps a good thing, they might think I'm laughing at the flock. But it's oddly hurtful to be so completely neglected.'

Eularia's biggest single bone of contention with her own parish at the time of her death was her belief that they never appreciated her or her paintings. Eularia did not help this by being a poor self-publicist, but the *Catholic Herald* article was an echo of things to come. She was saved from becoming too gloomy over it by the arrival of Michael Gedge, on his summer break from the Beda, who appreciated both the paintings and her poems: 'in his gruff way.'

Sidney Mullarkey and Michael Gedge were becoming the Cuthbert and Anthony characters in Eularia's mind. Sidney represented the paternal disapproval that she had laboured under for so long and Michael the bullying older brother. 'Michael gave me a tremendous tick off, and was a bit rude...' and yet it was often to Michael that she turned for advice, especially in the absence of Angus Mason.

David Mahy was having a much deeper effect on Eularia than Angus had, however. Angus had been very good at helping Eularia to feel better about herself. David did something else entirely:

'He (*David Mahy*) won't be disseminated, not an ounce of power or time or energy to anything else. Nothing else. It impresses me so powerfully that nothing else seems to have any value at all. My whole life looks silly. I can't do much about it except let it work in me as it does in him – and I'm right to have gone to him all this time in spite of hating it.'

Eularia was seeing in David Mahy a part of herself that yearned for God: the very part of her that she lost touch with at around his age through her marriage to Cyril. But, now that it was re-emerging, it was also a part of herself that she was afraid of giving in to, at odds with her love of the things in life that she judged to be silly. Yet it is that very element that can be so clearly seen in many of her later paintings where Christ holds a calm and clear space surrounded by people lost in their daily dramas. Eularia was to say of her Christ, who like Byzantine icons always appears the same, that he looked like her brother Anthony, which he did, but the way the energy flows around him in those paintings is much closer to her descriptions of how she experienced David Mahy as a young man. Much closer in fact to that part of herself that, no matter how much drama she was indulging in, always seemed to be untouched by it, holding a much deeper, stiller space.

Towards the end of the summer Pat Murphy-O'Connor finally shared with Eularia the circumstances of Angus Mason's leaving Winchester, probably because he feared (rightly) that it would soon become public knowledge and he preferred that she heard it from him. He had not told her before because he knew that it would upset her.

Angus had not been able to give up the nurse he had had an affair with and there was a child as a result. Eularia, who had done her best to help Angus through his trials over celibacy and who had felt that he was such a kindred spirit in the giving up of any hope of a physical relationship, was devastated. She was not at all consoled by the fact that Angus still wanted to remain a priest. Her faith wobbled, just as Pat had feared that it would.

Eularia, despite all her knowledge of theology and triumphing of the intellect, was essentially an emotional artist. The characters in her paintings are openly emotional people, showing their feelings upon their faces. The Christ figure encapsulates that strength of religion that holds us all. For most of her adult life Eularia had come up against the suppression of feeling in the typical English personality. Living in a small provincial town enhanced this, but it was at odds with her innate sense of feeling and emotion, which consistently felt stifled. Her feelings about Angus were a perfect example of this. Everything about the story was inverted, contained by a protective Church and she was asked not to share it. Once again it felt as if instead of being able to express herself openly she was being asked to draw herself in.

Pat, David Mahy, and Fr Robin Noel (who led her Newman Group) helped her through the Angus episode:

> 'One could feel the Church and the Catholic family closing round one, warming the heart, protecting one from too much hurt. But most supernatural of all, the three priests all making independent gestures of extra kindness and indulgence; it seems incredible after a lifetime of unconsoled griefs.'

Pat was the one who helped her most as he was the one who understood most clearly her feelings for Angus, having had so many heart-to-hearts with her about it. When she confided to Pat over coffee at Middle Road that she had lost her faith:

> '…he said it was about the best thing that could have happened to me, and that very few converts reach the depths of it like that.'

In every problem is a gift and Eularia's turning point came when she recognised how her need for drama was a driving force behind it all:

> 'I think probably what suits me about the Church is that one can only have the real spiritual dramas when there are hard laws and real difficulties, and drama I appear to need. As a free Protestant I couldn't disobey, I couldn't fight or rebel. There would be no lover's quarrels to make up, no striving and no relief, and no love, perhaps the Protestants find life easier because they are further from God.'

This realisation helped because the next day at Mass:

> 'I felt vulnerable and naked, but it was lovely… full of joy and peace… the cloud has lifted now, the real conflict has gone. I can't understand why it went, early this morning, when it did. It wasn't apparently due to any sacrament, it was suddenly realising what the quarrel was like.'

The 'Angus' episode served merely as a trigger for Eularia's own deeper issues, and it was these that really caused her crisis of Faith. The greatest insight into this comes in a letter from Robin Noel replying to one of hers that she wrote whilst in the depths of it all. It is an insightful and very sensible answer (four pages), which she greatly appreciated and helped her enormously. From it we are able to determine the legacy of her father's agnosticism and how her family's attitude to her faith was a continuing underlying problem. Robin said:

> 'As you say yourself, what really bothers you is the intellectual witness of intelligent members of your family, your Chestertonian Greats-at-Corpus father – but if it comes to siding with brains, St Thomas Aquinas was no fool, nor was Newman, or Chesterton, or Knox… It needs much more than

intelligence to arrive at the truth, especially religious truth and truths in the moral order – it also needs a great deal of humility; and I think it must be incredibly difficult to be intellectually humble if you have a lot of brains. This I suspect is why God has chosen the foolish things of the world to confound the wisdom of the wise... God has given you your mind and you must love Him and serve Him with that, as well as your heart and strength.'

The other thing he picked up on was her worry that her faith was a substitute for a relationship:

'People who tell you that you have invented God as an imaginary husband really don't deserve to be taken seriously – to me it looks rather like an impudent piece of innuendo. What proof do they produce? How *could* you prove such a thing? And even suppose the pain you have suffered over the lack of a loving husband *has* led you to find in God a loving Father – in what way does this prove He is imaginary? Please don't imagine that people who are cynical and criticise distinctively are necessarily showing mental vitality!'

A shift of focus in her work life was beginning to emerge. It would take a few years to fully form but a clue lies in the single word in her diary: 'PAINTINGS.' written very clearly at the end of a rather rambling list of potential self-improvements. Now that the children were off her hands and she was feeling more confident in her life as an unattached person she began to review her options for the future. This was partly prompted by a drop in the amount of music teaching she had and having paid for James' first car, so her financial reserves were low. But it also stemmed from a change of focus in her creativity. Music, whilst it was still very important to her, was beginning to take a more minor role and she was fed up with music teaching. Writing, as she told Alicia, was something she did when travelling and unable to paint. Gradually over the next two or three years painting would take centre stage.

In early 1962 she had two paintings, *Lourdes, Touching the Walls* and *Kissing the Cross, Good Friday*, accepted for the Wessex Artists show at the Southampton Art Gallery, which led to an interview on Southern Television. In a letter to Rachael she wrote:

'But I think I'm right to be showing these paintings, because they were beautifully hung, among the oils, in this very posh exhibition of local professionals and top amateurs... And one could see the young folk in duffel-coats going round, making a bee-line for the cubist painter just on top of mine, and then sliding their eyes downwards to these embarrassing pictures which roused their curiosity but couldn't be looked at openly because there was a possibility of religion owing to the crucifix. Pat is awfully pleased because he liked the Good Friday one ages before anyone saw it, and now he feels he's a good judge of religious art!!'

Of all the Winchester priests it was Pat Murphy-O'Connor who was most outwardly encouraging to Eularia over her paintings at this time. He had a meeting with Robin Noel and he told Eularia that they 'had decided to encourage me in lots of holy pictures!' which understandably gave her a big boost. Even Sidney Mullarkey encouraged her in his own way, although she later chose to forget this:

'I saw the Canon in the car park and told him about my paintings and he said, go ahead, you're on to a good thing.'

But Sidney Mullarkey had fallen foul of Eularia once again by employing another local artist, Mary Fairburn (who was living at the local convent) at £10 a week to paint a mural at St Peter's school. Mary's work was far more traditional and less provocative than Eularia's, and probably more to Sidney's taste. Once again it came between them. Eularia always believed that Sidney backed Mary over her.

One cannot blame Sidney if he found Eularia's paintings less to his liking than the more gentle and traditional work of Mary Fairburn. They did produce a 'Marmite' reaction in most people. It is symptomatic of the uneasy relationship Eularia had with Sidney. She simply couldn't relate to him in the way that she did to the younger priests. He would always remain a rather distant, authoritarian figure to her. The only reason that her relationship with Michael Gedge (similar in age to Sidney) was different was because Michael was not about to let any issues Eularia might have about authority figures stand in the way. He was unconventional enough to blast through all that.

Around this time Rachael had a suspected miscarriage and Eularia rushed up to Leeds. Fortunately all was well but Rachael was confined to bed for a few days, so Eularia held the fort while she recovered and found the inspiration for her next two paintings. Remembering how the priests had brought her Communion in hospital she asked the priest in Leeds to bring it for Rachael:

'He came – an elderly tall thin Scots in a black coat, at 7.45 am, in the dark, my candle blew out. He said peace to this house, and sent us out for confession, then he said prayers and Robert and I answered *firmly* Min (*me*) piping up. The sky out of the window was still dark blue with windows lit-up, as he held up the Host, and Alicia's candlesticks shone, and Robert's best linen handkerchief. He laid the pyx on Robert's handkerchief and said O' Sacrum Convivium, going off silently to the hospital after. It *was* exciting.'

This became *Priest Brings Communion* and the depth, sophistication and humour that can often be found in her later paintings is beginning to emerge. She set the scene in Robert and Rachael's flat with variations of her own and she was very pleased with the result, writing to Rachael:

'Needless to say, I've just done a really good painting (according to the Redrice art master) of the priest bringing communion, based roughly on Hyde Terrace but with everyone quite different except the eiderdown and the electric fire and the kettle. There are three children and a newborn baby in a cradle – that's Dominic Belfield (*her godson*) and the father is Mr Bogan (*headmaster at St Peter's school*) and the mother is Mary Kibble (*Kibblewhite, a friend*) only fatter, but the priest's Fr Murphy (*not Pat*), and Pat (*Murphy-O'Connor*) nearly wept out of professional fury, saying, "Oh, he *should* have taken off his coat, I know they sometimes don't in the North, but he *should* have taken it off, and it would have showed his cotta" – sigh, sigh, sigh!'

Pat, who had just spent an hour with Eularia bemoaning the morality of his Youth Club couples, loved *The Priest Brings Communion* however, and was very useful to Eularia in helping to get the little details right.

The second inspiration was while attending Mass at the local church with Robert:

'We went to St Augustine's Harehills in the car, and the lovely blue mosaic and the Ukrainian tenors and basses made me sing Byzantine hymns. Two christenings.'

This became *Winter Baptisms*, which is a more primitive and less developed work, but it was the first time she had painted a Christ figure since her teenage years and it foreshadowed the stillness of her later icon-like Jesus' figures.

Eularia's frames were always very simple, not so much from choice but from necessity. Framing paintings was as expensive then as it is now and she could really only afford the cheapest and simplest. She often made them herself, rather badly. It creates a dilemma over her work today as her frames do not do her work justice, but there is a body of opinion that maintains that the original frame that the artist intended should be kept.

Her diary suggests that if she had had the money she would have chosen much better frames and certainly those paintings that have been reframed have benefitted from it.

Eularia would always have ups and downs with the Catholic Church, but she had finally emerged from the devastation of Angus Mason's departure and her initial doubts about it all:

'On Sunday I realised that Mass is the best thing in life. High Mass becomes almost unbearably penetrating, I'm appalled to think of all those Sundays without it... Yet nothing could be more matter-of-fact – the boys with satchels, Mr Bogan and the deaf-aid man, the rows of women, and pious girls, the business-like priests. Yet the more ordinary it is, the plainer, the more I like it.... I'm healed from Angus's hurts, I start again and I'll never worry about set-backs again. Meeting happy sex *is* a cross, but it's easy to get over, and the feeling about God is better because it will go on after I'm dead, and I think it's more what I'm meant for, really. It seems always there, ready to sweep over me in spite of all my uncommonly wayward behaviour. I can get away from it, all right, by simply not turning to it, but I find myself choosing to put myself in touch with the means of grace, and that keeps me going.'

19

Singing a Different Tune

The Second Vatican Council was convened in October 1962 and rumours of more changes were already in the air in the spring of that year. Eularia heard about them from the priests but it was in the choir that Eularia first began to come across these in a practical sense. While Eularia was keen on the changes, most of the choir were very traditional and were not.

It wasn't just a few details that were going to change, but a centuries-old way of worshipping, a tradition that many of the choir had known from birth. By the time I was old enough to remember Mass it was in English but, coming from a musical Catholic family, I have had the experience of participating in the sung Latin version, the 'concert' Mass, and there is a profound and subtle difference in the atmosphere created by the two. They are not the same even though – in the sense of meaning – they are. There would be many who preferred the new vernacular version, but there were just as many who preferred the original. In some ways you could liken it to the difference between the Da Vinci painting of the Last Supper and the Eularia Clarke version, both are of the same subject and yet the experience of them is very different.

When Eularia arrived at the next choir practice, '... there was the Canon playing a tape of the People's Mass. He's going to put it on, my own doing.'

The People's Mass (by a Benedictine priest called Gregory Murray) had easier melodies for the congregational parts of the Mass, but was still in Latin. When they sang it on Sunday it went down like a lead balloon with the choir and Will Thomas blamed Eularia for its introduction. It was true,

Eularia had been partly responsible for the revival of this after the initial rather unsuccessful attempt made by Sidney Mullarkey a couple of years before, because she had urged Sidney to try again. It did not improve her popularity.

During all this she began *Ash Wednesday in the Wilderness* and once again had a powerful experience of God:

> 'I went hard at the Lent picture, with interruptions because of the love of God which seems to come so much with hunger, and discomfort, even cold.'

Ash Wednesday in the Wilderness is the first of Eularia's religious works in which it is possible to perceive influences of what was happening in her own life emotionally. After a series of paintings expressing her experience and observations of Catholic worship fairly faithfully, *Ash Wednesday* takes that subject right out of context by placing the worship in a desert. It is true that this was winter and Middle Road in February was Spartan to say the least, with no heating and a leaky roof. Eularia was also fasting for Lent, which may have contributed something to the barrenness of the setting. But the situation regarding the choir and the changes the priests were attempting to implement can be seen in the priest attempting to minister to a rather blue and sulky flock. Underneath this are Eularia's rather barren and blue feelings over Angus Mason. She wrote at this time, although not in connection with the painting, '...and I thought of Angus reading his breviary and saying his own Mass in the "desert"'.

Her own official caption for this painting states:

> 'The ceremony of Ashes, only set in the wilderness because it is connected with Christ's forty days. The blue is because of penitential gloom, also it is the time of east winds and coughs and colds.'

Eularia rarely wrote about any connection between what she was painting and her own life. She painted the images and visions that she had in her head and for her they were intimately connected with her expression of her faith and the Gospels, but it is impossible to create without putting something of yourself into the creation and increasingly, as Eularia became more fluent in her painting, this is true of her work.

Not all her work during the sixties was straight painting and the first influence for this is given in a letter to her daughter Rachael in May 1962. While collecting some paintings from Southampton she attended, '...a wonderful exhibition of Modern Spanish Art – paint, sand, leather, rusty iron, perforated zinc.'

Eularia's own collage work was never included in her collection of religious paintings as it was more usually done as gifts. Her first attempt was made shortly after seeing this exhibition, for Edgar Feuchtwanger as a present for his wedding. She would often experiment after this with other materials. To our knowledge only two survive now, a tissue paper collage of the Crucifixion and a fabric collage of St Cuthbert that she gave to her grandson.

Eularia also turned her artistic skills to 3D modelling. She made a crib for Rachael's family out of papier maché and plaster, which we still have, although it is sadly dilapidated as we used to love playing with it as children. She also made a Madonna (Our Lady of Middle Road) with baby Jesus, which sat on top of a bookshelf flanked by a couple of candles in bottles. She didn't always get her proportions right and the baby Jesus was too large so she made another which she described in the same letter to Rachael:

> 'I've made a new Baby, much smaller and not so nice – but it looks better for size, and the ex-baby is – of course, now St John B (*Baptist*), and is propped up under her (*Mary's*) cloak. Clerical jokes about my ending up with *all* the Holy Innocents all along the book-case top – are only what one expects.'

Despite the vagaries of Spo, Netley was a favourite place for a visit in the early 1960s. It was easy for her to reach, being just the other side of Southampton, and she had made friends with Fr Sutherland, the priest who was attached to the hospital there, another cleric from whom she occasionally sought advice:

> 'He told me to do nothing, not to multiply pieties, to rest, to accept life, to be calm, that I've improved the church music no end, and then we got on to prayer and meditation and I began to tell him about my fits of loving God. He said I'd reached a very high state of prayer, much higher than his, and would probably end up in a contemplative order.'

She found his advice very helpful (although not the prediction about joining an order, which made Pat Murphy-O'Connor laugh heartily when she told him). The clergy who knew about her experience of prayer always assumed that she was destined to become a nun and it played directly into Eularia's belief that laywomen were lesser beings in the eyes of the clergy, a belief that would come to define her relationship with the Church towards the end of her life.

From reading her diaries one gains the impression that Eularia's experience of prayer and of God was something the clergy she knew did not really know how to handle, especially as she was a laywoman and a new convert. Indeed most of them, like Fr Sutherland, freely admitted that they had never experienced such a deep state themselves. She would become much more vocal about this lack of support in the mid 1960s.

For now Eularia's persistence and discipline with her faith were working well for her. She finally had a network that she felt reasonably supported by, she had knowledgeable people that she could discuss theology with and who weren't boring about it, her painting was going well, she had time and space for her own contemplation and, despite the impact of Angus, she had not dipped and fallen out with the Church as she had in the past.

Then Rachael arrived with me in tow for three weeks over Easter (Robert joined us later due to work commitments). Rachael hadn't seen much of Eularia since the move to Leeds and had no family living anywhere near her. She was still in the early stages of her second pregnancy (not long over her miscarriage scare) probably looking forward to a cosy time with mum and relief from looking after me (Robert was never a hands-on father or house husband). School holidays had not yet begun, so Eularia was still teaching during the day and keeping up her rhythm of daily Mass attendance and Stations of the Cross as it was Lent. The upshot was that Rachael saw very little of mum and when she did Eularia was tired and not at her best. As Rachael could hardly complain about the teaching the Church got the blame:

'R burst out about not being welcome. She thinks I purposely make her and Robert feel guilty and I'm not a good grandmother, and don't welcome them or like having them. I go to Mass too much, and it tires me and is unnecessary, she says.'

Although Rachael had been the first of them to convert she had none of the piety and sense of drive over it that Eularia had and after a while really only kept it up for Robert's sake. It was a side of her mother that Rachael was never to really understand, or feel comfortable with. In some ways she felt that she lost her mother to the Church and religion. But Eularia would almost certainly have behaved in much the same way even without religion. Family gatherings for any length of time always tired her and left her feeling put upon. The teaching would still have been an issue and, like most artists, she liked her own space and quiet time. She did not understand why Rachael was so upset.

Rachael probably didn't know either; she was hormonal and tired, having to cope with a toddler and being pregnant with little help. Eularia did try to mollify her by cutting down on Mass, which only left her feeling depressed and tearful. So much so that after the Maundy Thursday service, which was full of the ceremonial trappings of worship that Eularia normally loved, she wrote in her diary:

> 'I don't like all this – the Bishop having his mitre taken off and put on, all the jewellery and drawing-room atmosphere. Christ hadn't got anybody taking off his hat, he put on a towel and washed all the chickens' mess and goats' mess and sheeps' dung off their feet. This is a Temptation Against the Church.'

This is the first evidence she gives of a deeper awareness growing in her about all the richness and rigidity of ceremony that, until now, had so inspired her. 1962 was the year that she would begin to paint Gospel scenes in modern day settings but, so far, all her paintings had been of Catholic ritual and worship. Her account of this particular Maundy service shows how she was beginning to sense the rift between what we do now and the reality of the original act, which she sought to overcome in her paintings. *Maundy Thursday* (1965) depicts exactly what was in her mind. Christ is stripped to the waist and wrapped in a towel washing St Peter's feet, which are exceptionally grubby.

Both Rachael and Eularia wished that they lived closer together. Eularia loved having her grandchildren but she couldn't cope with long stretches. Her ideal would have been to have Rachael near enough to drop grandchildren with her for an afternoon or overnight so that she could give her a break. She would have loved to be able to take us out for trips to the beach, returning us home afterwards. Robert did look at the possibility of work in the Southampton area and briefly considered the music master post at Redrice School, but he was never happy teaching children or teenagers. Students were his forte and in the end it was Leeds University, then York that gave him the work.

20

Pat

Pat Murphy-O'Connor brought his younger brother, Cormac (later Cardinal Cormac Murphy- O'Connor), for coffee at Middle Road. Eularia would come to think very highly of Cormac but her first impressions were not favourable:

> 'Pat came and asked me if he could bring his brother up to coffee – I suppose it's a compliment? He came – a shy silent simple (?) young priest, obviously good as gold, but no conversation at all.'

Pat, who was now Catholic chaplain to Winchester prison as well as his other parish duties, was putting his energy and passion into setting up a hostel for newly released prisoners. Had Pat not been a priest Eularia was of the opinion that he would have been a social worker. Newly released prisoners, especially young offenders, were in the habit of walking into town and knocking on the door of the presbytery because they often had no resources and nowhere else to go. This had inspired Pat to do something about it and the result was the Society of St Dismas[8], which operated from Southampton, providing them with a halfway house. He would often share his vision for this with Eularia who would ultimately give him two paintings for it:

> 'I was dreadfully rude to him. I said everyone loved him, though he wasn't worth tuppence to me, and only wasted my time in idle gossip. He told me he was getting a false reputation, that people were thinking he was marvellous

---

8 St Dismas was the thief on the cross next to Jesus who repented.

because of St. Dismas. I said you are becoming a popular saint? He said, well yes... I said it just reflected on the badness of Catholic priests that his work was so exceptional. I was hateful to him, but very lovingly, poor boy. He thinks he just does things on a human level.'

It's a wonderful tongue in cheek exchange, typical of the teasing that they both enjoyed. And it was because of this that Eularia never really considered Pat as a spiritual director even though she related to him far more closely than to David Mahy or Michael Gedge:

'Poor, poor Pat – he says he's sorry he can't be any use to me, in his stiff voice, so we talked about marrying James to his sister, which pleased him very much. But I'm troubled about him, he really is fond of me, and comes to see me in spite of being behind with his visiting, but I'm not good for him, or him for me. I'd never use bad language to the other priests, or discuss undone buttons etc. And I'm cruel to him, too. I wish I wasn't.'

By now Eularia was teaching extra Latin to the St Peter's choir boys and had also added guitar teaching at West Downs School and the newly opened Redrice School run by Adrian Stokes to her list:

'I now play the vi-olin (as John calls it when I play it) ... I have lovely duets with Pat, I play Careless Love and his Italian songs, and he strums, and it stops him going on about his shortcomings.'

Pat had really taken to the guitar since those early lessons with Eularia in 1958 and his visits to her often included some music making. It was Pat who was instrumental in inspiring Eularia to eventually compose her own church music.

The Stokes' and Redrice School were important early patrons of Eularia's religious work (if she can be said to have had patrons). Redrice was a Catholic boys school founded by Adrian Stokes and Richard Arnold Jones in 1961 and they borrowed some of Eularia's paintings to hang in their refectory. Ultimately Veronica Stokes (Adrian's wife) was the only person, besides the Methodist Art Collection, that Eularia ever sold any of her paintings to. Eularia wrote to her cousin Alicia in 1961:

'I'm not selling any, they are just done to impinge on folk who expect half guitars and three apples on a plate, and get excited by anything with people in it.'

But the more she painted the more she began to feel that she was creating something that should be seen as a whole and despite many offers refused to sell, preferring that the collection remain intact. Those she did sell she always made copies of for this reason.

Eularia's experiences of God continued to ebb and flow:

'Home, tea and lay in the sun, and read Dom Marmion[9], and bang, I was at it again, like lovers who keep on catching fire at all hours of the day and night. I said I didn't want anything else and I didn't want anything to come between, not sins or distractions, not pleasure or anything, I want only that, there is nothing comparable to it, and it will be for ever, it is a bit of reality. I can't exactly not believe in a thing when it blazes inside me and takes up the whole of me, everything I am, everything I feel and love. It went on and on, I couldn't bear it to stop, and it doesn't matter because it is there all the time, as I write, there is nothing in me except the feel of prayer... It now seems to be a goodish thing that I've no husband or lover, because what would I do? I'd be torn between two things.'

Unfortunately when it passed she was often left feeling low. Had she been able to turn to someone who really understood this kind of experience it might have helped her considerably, but there was no one, and Eularia was beginning to realise it. Instead she would lash out from her low place and this time she entered into a kind of war with the choir as a result, brought on largely by the feeling that she was the only one supporting the changes.

The summer of 1962 was a bleak time. She appreciated the continuing support of the curates and Fr Sutherland, the Stokes' and the Belfields but the rift with the choir at St Peter's continued to sour things for her. She wasn't immune to how they felt over the People's Mass, which turned out to be popular with the congregation, she regretted that there would be much less opportunity to sing polyphony, but she still felt it was the right direction to take.

It was the consistency of her friendship with the Murphy-O'Connors', David Mahy, David Whitehead (another priest friend), the Stokes' and the Belfields that really helped her through this period. Whilst she might have attempted to shut herself off they would not let her, and she did return to the choir after David Whitehead advised her not to take sides.

'It's odd how I felt so sure I was right, and now I'm not sure at all... I am puzzled about why I laid off so long, and I think it was mostly rebellion against religion itself... It was something to hit, and hurt, and destroy if possible.'

---

9   Blessed Columba Marmion, OSB. Abbott of Maredsous Benedictine Abbey, Belgium and a Catholic author. Died 1923.

Just as she was getting over this rather difficult period and beginning to feel the presence of God again she was unaccountably very hurtful to Pat in a way that she never had been before. It began when James took Pat for a ride in his MG and then went for a beer with him, something that James (when he was in Winchester) would often do with Pat, who he liked very much. The upshot was that James arrived home drunk, was sick and passed out, not unusual for a 21-year-old man fond of beer, but Eularia immediately went into a panic, 'I thought of Cyril and cursed Pat inwardly.'

The next day when Pat dropped in she began criticising him, but without ever mentioning the real reason – James, the events of the previous evening and her worry that he would end up like Cyril:

> 'I said how fond of him I was, and yet went on criticising him for not helping me spiritually... I said a lot of hateful things, esp. about how David (*Mahy*) was better at it, and all the mistakes he'd made with me, and how I'd got to learn, e.g. about sins. He looked *so* miserable, so when I asked point blank if David could see to me instead he went off and I begged him not to look so miserable, and said he'd done so much, and how grateful I was etc. etc., and he drove away, and I was full of remorse.'

This was Eularia at her worst. It was how she lost many friendships and probably went a long way towards souring her relationship with Cyril. You had to be very strong to take it. Once triggered into it she just couldn't stop herself and it was always those that she cared about most, and who were closest to her, who were on the receiving end:

> 'I damage people. In small doses I do them good and they welcome and like me. But when they come close I only damage them. My own unhappy temperament reacts on them, I want them to suffer with me, to assuage my own misery. And they do – John hasn't benefited a bit, nor Pat, nor Robert. James alone manages to cope. I don't know how to change!'

She was miserable about Pat because she knew how undeserved it was and, as Eularia left on a holiday the next day there was no chance of reconciliation for a few weeks. It left a sour note and caused much soul searching. She set off feeling low and with a headache, first to her cousin Catherine, then on to Canvey Island, with Spo being very unreliable all the way.

21

Painting the Gospel

Canvey Island provided the inspiration for a turning point in Eularia's painting that would define her future work. It was observing the crowds sitting and eating fish and chips on the grass there that inspired one of her most loved and best known paintings, and the first that depicted a gospel scene in modern day life, *The Five Thousand'* (Matthew 14:20). She began it as soon as she returned home and wrote to Rachael in August:

'I've stopped fussing about People's Masses and have done instead a big painting of the 5,000 on Canvey Island eating fish and chips on the grass. All those chips and newspapers took HOURS. In the corner is an ordinary pulpit with the hands and book and missal and stole ends of a priest who is preaching a sermon, the people are exactly like Catholics listening to a sermon, except for the fish and chips. Min is walking about just under the pulpit (rather nettle-y) holding a large fillet of fish, nice and greasy, and the new baby is right in the exact centre of the picture, wrapped up in a shawl on the grass, not belonging to any of the family groups, because − it's yours! James says it's the best so far − it's certainly got some very good bicycles lying on the grass − a real technical problem. Some folk are smoking or asleep, and one man is pumping a Primus, with a kettle, and there are thermoses, and blankets, and spinsters, and a carry-cot.'

In her diary she wrote:

'Instead of the idea of Christ going about today, it's the Church going around instead, linking the people with the gospel times and with them − that's where I'm different from S. Spencer.'

The Five Thousand (1962), from the Methodist Modern Art Collection,
© TMCP, used with permission.

She was later to say that at this point she didn't have the confidence to actually paint Christ so he became a priest instead. She sold this painting to the Methodist Art Collection a couple of years later, along with another, but made a copy for her own collection.

The obvious imagery in Eularia's *Five Thousand* is that of the gospel feeding people, which speaks to the influence of Pat Murphy-O'Connor and David Mahy and the desire to get back to the roots of the Church. It also hints at how, on the eve of the convening of Vatican II, the congregation (whilst still involved in their own personal activities during a service) are beginning to pay more attention to the priest. Even those physically turned away from him and eating have eyes that are turning towards the pulpit.

During August Robin Noel (the Chaplain at Southampton University), who was already a great fan of Eularia's work, asked her to paint him an altar back of the Last Supper that he could use to say Mass in front of at the Southampton Students Hostel. It was designed to be temporary, so that it could be taken down as needed:

> 'He really seemed to think I can understand and illustrate his more intellectual theological themes – I can't of course. But when I promised no HP sauce at the Last Supper, he said, no, put it in, put it *all* in.'

The Last Supper is arguably one of Eularia's finest early religious works. The tragedy is that it no longer survives and she did not make a copy. All we have is the photograph that Robin Noel gave to Eularia for her records. She painted it on rough canvas so that it could be rolled up and stored when not in use. By the time Southampton Chaplaincy moved to new premises in the early 1980s it was in such poor condition that no one felt it was worth keeping so it was thrown out.

Its genesis demonstrates just how cutting-edge Eularia was as an artist within the Catholic Church at the time. Most Catholics in the early 1960s were used to either classical, or the very traditional Victorian, images of Christ and the Gospels, which were, for the most part, very literal, unprovocative and placed the scenes in Biblical times. The reason Eularia was often likened to Spencer was that her scenes were set in the modern day, but Spencer was not a Catholic. The controversy that arose over *The Last Supper* illustrates very clearly, coming as it does right on the convening of the Second Vatican Council in October 1962, the divide between centuries of tradition and those who wanted something that would speak to modern day Catholics, and help bring the Gospel alive again.

The Last Supper was only the second Gospel scene that Eularia had attempted since her teenage years (following hot on the heals of *The Five Thousand*) and she didn't yet have the confidence that she later possessed in regard to her paintings. In fact the fuss over this painting also forced her to step into her role as an artist and stand up for her work.

Jesus and the disciples are pictured sitting at a corner table by the window in a café typical of the 1960s. The disciples are all in modern dress but Jesus, right from the first, takes on the icon-like role that he was always to assume in Eularia's paintings, wearing more neutral robes and having a gold halo (she bought some gold paint from Woolworth's which she always used for the purpose). A very young St John can be seen peeping out from under his robes and St Peter sits on his right. On the table are cups of coffee, sauce bottles, dirty plates and an ashtray under the hands of one of the disciples who is smoking. Another holds both a cup of coffee and a lit cigarette. Jesus is handing out hosts from a golden bowl and the golden chalice containing wine is in front of him on the table. To the right of the picture is Judas Iscariot turned away from the gathering with a little devil whispering in his ear, an image that was inspired by David Mahy having fallen asleep one evening at Compline in just such a pose. Eularia wrote to Rachael about the controversy. It is a more upbeat version than she gives in her diary but it summarises it well:

'He (*Fr. Noel*) rang up in the evening to say how thrilled he was about it, it's turned out exactly what he wanted! It's the Last Supper, with sauce bottles and ash-trays, 5ft by 3ft, and lots of mustard and lamp-shades. I got so shivery and neurotic about painting Christ that I nearly rang up to say I couldn't, only I thought I'll just have a bash, and when John (*Stallard*) comes he'll be frank, so I painted it in tears and terror, and ever since people have been so impressed by it that it's *well* worth all the upset. It's got a *slight* look of Christopher (*her brother*). John was knocked down completely by it... and Fr. Noel says he's going to show it around to everybody. Fr. Mahy says he doesn't mind the sauce-bottles but he *couldn't* say Mass on top of all those ash-trays, and St. Thomas is *smoking* over his coffee cup! And dear Pat (*Murphy-O'Connor*) clearly would prefer a few palm-trees, and ladies with jars on heads against the sunset, I expect − but they're all *very* nice about it, especially the lovely Woolworth gold paint, which produces the Byzantine look.'

In fact this was a culmination of a week of feeling caught between Robin Noel who, probably because he was in charge of students, was very progressive in his thinking, and the St Peter's priests who struggled with aspects of it, especially the smoking and the fact that it was set in a room with 'Café' and 'Way Out' emblazoned on the window. Eularia was so uncertain that she sponged out the ashtrays, cigarettes and the Judas figure (which she thought, wrongly, David Mahy didn't like) and wrote to Robin Noel to tell him what she'd done. Robin Noel's reply puts into words exactly what Eularia would later say her paintings were all about:

The Last Supper (1962)

'By removing the cigarettes and the Café and Way Out signs, you have removed just those things which will jerk the students into realising what a shocking thing the Incarnation is. You will also confirm them in their hunch that grace does not transform nature as it really is, but some imaginary ideal world of nature, which has little connection with our own – that real life as we have to live it, and religion cannot unite, but must be kept in separate compartments... It is you trying to say something important, but muzzled – like Galileo... Greater painters have had pressure put on them to paint drapery over the private parts of Christ on his throne of judgment, and have yielded – so I suppose I cannot condemn you. But apart from obedience, which will get you into Heaven, there is also integrity which is not altogether displeasing to Our Lord.'

Feeling confused and uncertain, in the end she asked Eversley Belfield's advice and he quite rightly pointed out that as it was Robin Noel who wanted the painting, he was responsible for it and she should do it his way. So, Eularia dutifully put it all back. But it wasn't the end of it as she wrote to Rachael a week later:

'We've had a quarrel over it – and I'm sure I'm right. He (*Robin Noel*) showed it to the students, and they were so pleased that the deplorable little drips began suggesting changes and improvements. One of their bright ideas was, that as the disciples are in modern clothes and therefore "representative modern Catholics" (*what* an idea!) and not, in fact, the disciples at all, would I put a girl in it, at the table, because of the new position of women these days? I'm afraid I exploded at that, mostly because a painting's a painting and comes out as a whole idea of patterns, and can't be adjusted to peoples wishes – but also because I'm afraid the *idea* of a Southampton University Catholic Female Student in MY PICTURE was not *at all* to my taste. That's what they wanted, all right! I'd have put Our Lady in with plates, but she wouldn't fit in the pattern, and anyhow, they didn't want her. I *was* cross. Poor Fr. N. – he sees my point but just *lives* for his Catholic Students, to encourage them and bring them out!! Well.'

The end result was that *The Last Supper* ended up as Eularia first conceived it. It was an important lesson for her, forcing her to step into her integrity as a modern religious artist and stand by her work.

Eularia used the gold paint she found in Woolworth's for all Christ's halos which does indeed add to the Byzantine iconic quality that the Christ figure expresses. She stumbled across the gold paint by accident while looking for another item:

'...two yards of chain that will just *stay there,* and remind me that I must be a bond slave and like it, I want never to take it off, and it will be just sufficiently uncomfortable to be always felt and disliked. It makes me happy for some odd reason, I feel the knots in my back and they fill me with love – perhaps it's all very dubious.'

This was a new phase of the mortification and without proper spiritual direction it was very dubious. The fact that she continued not to tell anyone about it, not even Pat Murphy-O'Connor or David Mahy, suggests that she knew this.

Towards the end of the summer Eularia drove over to South Wales, and it was here that she found inspiration for *Transfiguration in the Valley* as she watched the people leaving Chapels one Sunday in Ebbw Vale. Like *The Five Thousand* it depicts the modern practice of religion and a gospel scene coming together to illustrate something she observed; modern worship reflecting a gospel event, in this instance the Transfiguration. The people leaving Chapel populate the foreground but above them on the colliery slag heap in the background is a bright light and three figures lying face down representing the three apostles. She described the people leaving chapel as:

'...all looking transfigured... It happens to us all... extra shining and wonderful among the pitheads and coal-tips.'

All the detail and the reactions to the event are in the faces of those leaving Chapel and the actual event is relegated to the background. It was a device she was to use in her other Transfiguration painting *White and Dazzling* (1968) in which Christ is once again suggested by bright white light and the faces of the apostles show the event. But *Transfiguration in the Valley* places the focus firmly on the 'congregation' as having received the Gospel, rather than the historical figures of the disciples.

Not long after this trip Eularia finally gave up Spo, which had become increasingly unreliable, breaking down, stalling, and generally making driving it anywhere very stressful. Instead she bought a 'porridge coloured' Mini van and immediately decamped the mattress and cooking gear into the back. She could only afford the most basic model so the only seat in it was the driver's seat. Any passengers either had to bounce about on the mattress in the back or perch on the edge of it with their legs swinging over the hole where the passenger seat would have been.

1962 was another busy summer, rounded off by the birth of her first grandson, Cuthbert[10] (now Chris) which took her once again to Leeds. By the time autumn came, although she had seen Pat Murphy-O'Connor at Mass and they had chatted afterwards, he hadn't been to visit her at Middle Road. She missed him and began to fear that he had stopped coming for good.

Then there came a day in mid September when Eularia arrived for early Mass to find that Pat had no server, so she stood in:

'I felt remorse and shame, and couldn't answer with my usual aplomb, and I think he felt it, we were both outdoing each other in unworthiness.'

Eularia regretted her lack of appreciation of Pat more than anyone else she had fallen out with, and was overjoyed when shortly after this he arrived at Middle Road, returning to the 'Middle Road Curia', as he jokingly referred to it. It was a welcome reunion for both of them.

That autumn Eularia had three more paintings accepted by the Southampton Art Gallery: *Priest Brings Communion, Ash Wednesday in the Wilderness* and *The Five Thousand,* and painted a total of four paintings, larger than her Lourdes ones and more intricate. After a spring and summer without lifting a brush it was a real outpouring and she wrote in her diary:

'I don't want anyone or anything – but the painting is a great outlet, it's all about God, and the right thing to be doing... All day painting, painting, hungry, rather cold, hair shirt prickling on my back etc., sizzling with quiet ravishing love, every detail of the day lived only with and in the context of God, as near real steady happiness as I've ever known.'

Eularia was still experimenting with mortification (hair shirt) and sleeping on a board with just a thin blanket and sheet. She believed that it helped to keep her on track spiritually (it certainly seemed to be helping her with her art) but was afraid she was becoming too used to them. She finally admitted that she needed some advice and it was Michael Gedge that she turned to.

She attended his ordination as a sub-deacon in Portsmouth Catholic Cathedral on 29 September after which she asked him to be her spiritual director. In a letter a couple of days later Michael declined, feeling unable

---

10   Cuthbert became Chris after Eularia's death. Because she knew and referred to him as Cuthbert I have used that name for the purpose of the biography in order to avoid confusion.

to take the role on before he was fully ordained, but also pointing out that she had three perfectly good priests in her parish and accused her of 'shying off' from using them. He asked her if she had made it clear to them that she wanted instruction on what to do and if she was prepared to listen to them rather than just be listened to (Michael knew her well); he continued:

'...do try hard about this; I'm as much a talker as yourself; but one has to learn – while seeking spiritual direction – to shut up and listen, and above all obey.'

Of course she didn't want to shut up and obey, the rebel in her was far too strong for that, but on the other hand she did want someone to tell her what to do, to take responsibility for her, and she wanted a father figure. It was another rock and hard place between which she would always fall. As for going to her own priests, Pat and David were too young to qualify as father figures for her, and she didn't feel that Sidney Mullarkey understood her well enough.

Despite Michael turning her down he did offer guidance about the mortification:

'I really write this to say – most urgently – that *all* the spiritual authors agree that mortification should *only* be undertaken under the advice of a spiritual director; it is *most* dangerous, sometimes fatal, to ignore this... If you find that you can't bring yourself to speak to your director about this, that, too, is a sign of danger, and it would be better to mortify by *not* mortifying... until you can.'

To which Eularia only responded, 'He little realises my extreme timidity and self-love.'

Once she began painting the gospel scenes Eularia often received quite powerful images of what the next paintings would be. Her next two paintings were both conceived in this way.

Mass of the Circumcision is another of her paintings that was rarely shown, and Eularia withdrew it from her exhibition collection in 1968. The painting depicts the circumcision of Jesus by a white coated doctor standing over a howling and rather bloody baby Jesus while his anxious parents look on, with a procession of servers and a priest filing past in the background. Like *Transfiguration in the Valley* and *The Five Thousand* it is another transition painting between Catholic worship (a Mass celebrating the circumcision and naming of Jesus used to be celebrated on 1 January) and an original gospel event. Eularia later came to have much stronger feelings about blood and violence in visual art and regretted the earlier paintings she had done where she had been more explicit (some of her *Stations of the Cross* were the most bloody). Apart from the blood, *Mass of the Circumcision* is an interesting blend between the religious worship of Eularia's day and a much older Jewish ceremony belonging to the time of Jesus, once again bridging the gap between the past and the present.

Eularia settled down to a happy rhythm of painting and worship. She and Pat resumed their easy friendship and he loved her new work. Pat and David kept her updated about all the proposed changes for the parish as it began to respond to the new instructions from Rome. They undoubtedly enthused Eularia about them and they also helped her to realise that what she was doing was not out of sync with the way Church thinking was going.

Veronica Stokes gave Eularia the idea of doing a painting of St Joseph for Redrice School, which inspired *Buying Wood* (Luke 2:51). It is a lovely 'snapshot' of how Eularia felt Jesus' early life might have been. He is pictured as a young boy going to a local wood yard with his father. Both in shirts and jeans, Joseph gazes down on Jesus, whose face is hidden by the planks they are carrying. As Eularia said, Joseph knew that Jesus was special, but did not yet know how, so Jesus' face is hidden. The effect is gentle and charming, and speaks to the part of Eularia that wanted a father figure, a spiritual director, to guide her. In the end she did a different painting of St Joseph for Redrice a couple of years later and kept this one for her collection.

Eularia was very pleased with *Christmas Gospel* (Luke 2:7) when she completed it and wrote to Rachael:

> 'Cuthbert (*model for the baby Jesus*) has come out very nicely in the Nativity, with a huge Woolworth's gold halo, the picture is full of mangolds (*farm hands*) and Catholics, all indistinguishable from each other. A very nice donkey occupies the centre, asleep on the ground, and beyond a high wall of hay bales, Mass is being sung, the gospel is in full swing but the altar boys are straying vaguely round the hay wall – with candles and the boat – (the incense boy remains firmly at his post). They are not worshipping Mary and Jesus – they are looking at the men sweeping up manure and bringing in hay. The hay is carried on pitchforks exactly like processional banners. Joseph is asleep just like the donkey – same position. Mary is contentedly taking no notice of anybody, she's got as far as putting the bandage round His tummy.'

Again it is an intriguing mix of the gospel event and a modern day Mass, which do not seem to overlap. They occupy both the same space and time (as shown by the modern clothes) but the only Mass attendees that notice the actual nativity are the altar boys. The question is how aware Eularia was of the many levels of meaning that could be read into this, given the inspiration behind the newly convened Vatican Council and the influence of Pat Murphy-O'Connor and David Mahy who so wanted the Gospel to come alive again for the people. In Eularia's description to Rachael, even the altar boys are not paying much attention to Mary and Jesus; instead the minor players, the farm hands, are distracting them. It is as if everything is happening around the original inspiration of the Gospel, not because of it; although Mary and Jesus remain our focal point as observers of the scene, they are entirely unnoticed by any of the scene's players.

Christmas Gospel (1962)

Eularia began teaching guitar at West Downs Prep School for boys. It was the beginning of a long liaison between Eularia and West Downs where she would ultimately become the Art teacher. Her health was not so good, however. Despite being given the all clear from cancer she often complained of sick and painful stomachs during the early 1960s, and they dragged her down, plus it was the end of term and she was exhausted. Although it was rarely apparent to others, feeling unwell affected her mood and made her reluctant to socialise or even leave the house for Mass.

The winter of 1962/63 was a hard one and Winchester was snow-bound. The doctor signed Eularia off work with flu and a stomach ulcer, which was unfortunate because at least she would have been warm in the schools. Middle Road could be brutal in the winter. It had no heating except for one open fire and the cook-and-heat stove, no insulation, and by this stage the roof was no longer weatherproof. The pipes burst so she had no hot water and '...the soup in the kitchen had ice on it!' Eularia ended up living in one room, sleeping downstairs on the sofa in front of the cook-and-heat because it was so cold.

It was during this really bad freeze in January 1963 that she began *Across the Desert* (Matthew 2:14 and Matthew 2:21). (Eularia always gave the Gospel quotes where appropriate for her paintings and in some cases, as in this one, more than one reference is given, depending on which exhibition listings you are looking at). Perhaps it is not surprising, given the very cold conditions, that she chose to paint a desert.

She had some initial doubts about it:

'I looked at the crib (*at St Peter's*), the quiet pious figures, their holy faces, St. J (*Joseph*) like a radiantly nice French father. Then home and saw my young swarthy Jew, the unhappy dishevelled couple in the desert, am I right? One can't exactly *repose* in such a picture, such a conception. Yet it's so like real life! It's what I feel so often.'

In the foreground is her 'dishevelled' and exhausted holy family, baby Jesus wrapped in a red checked blanket being carried over Joseph's shoulder and only discernible by his halo. They are on foot in a gully and carry all their possessions with them – a basket of Joseph's carpentry tools, canvas bags, a blanket role and a tin water can with tin mug hanging from it in Mary's hand. They are dwarfed by rising cliffs of cracked desert giving the feeling of being very alone in a much larger landscape. In it can be discerned Eularia's own memories of constantly moving from place to place with her very young family, the loneliness of it and the exhaustion, constantly moving to where she could find work to feed them. Of all of her paintings so far it is the first in which we can really glimpse her own past as well as her experience of the Gospels:

'I imagined the Holy Family trudging over them (*sand dunes*) for weeks, with the new baby and the shortage of water and the thirstiness when one is breast feeding and the refugee feeling.'

It is a uniquely feminine view of the story; only someone with the experience of motherhood could have seen it like this. Her reference for the desert was the Severn Mudflats dried out by the summer heat.

She was beginning to recognise that her paintings:

'...are a witness to one sort of work to be done, they are work for God, only a bit complicated by the fame I get from them, which I enjoy very much. But I don't want to paint anything else.'

David Mahy refused to allow Eularia to fall into the Tomas Merton[11] idea that one shouldn't self-advertise (always a problem for her) and told her to do it for the glory of God. He and a friend, Mr Pave, were urging Eularia to put herself forward for a big exhibition of Religious Art that was due to take place in Bournemouth in the summer:

Despite not being very well she embarked on more mortification (she now refers to it as penance) and was deeply reluctant to confess it to David. Michael Gedge's warnings had not been lost on her and she worried about how to get permission: it made her feel rebellious. She divined, probably accurately, that David wouldn't give it. Instead she turned to Michael once again, who replied with possibly the longest letter he ever wrote to her, all typed in red:

'All authorities would agree I am sure, that when a soul is in fact suffering from unquestionable bodily illness, all corporal mortifications should cease forthwith. The first duty of every soul is to preserve its own spiritual and bodily life. The fact that you have got ill suggests that possibly you had undertaken too much in one way or another.'

He strongly urged Eularia to consult David Mahy once again and reminded her that obeying her spiritual director could be classed as mortification, if it is hard to do. He also advised her that mortification was not a substitute

---

11   Thomas Merton was an American Catholic writer and mystic.

for prayer. Eularia did go down to confession with the intention of telling David, but ended up with Sidney Mullarkey. As there was no way she was going to tell Sidney about it she backed out.

Michael was right in thinking that her desire for mortification did not come from entirely pure motives. Instead of seeing the love of God as a transcending force she associated it with the experiences she'd had of human love – vague and undemonstrative from her parents, judgemental from her aunt and grandmother, bullying and rough from her brothers, unsatisfying and even sometimes violent and frightening from Cyril – and so believed that the only way she could feel God's love was through pain and suffering. The transcendent nature of it was too remote for her to grasp. In short, if there was no conflict, no pull in the opposite direction, she found it hard to believe in. In fact it was when she stopped fighting it that she felt it most strongly, it was the conflicts that got in the way, but it was hard for her to let go of what she had known all her life and trust something so totally new and outside her experience.

This showed in her friendship with the priests too. Pat Murphy-O'Connor (who was friendly, congenial, chatty, openly loved her paintings, congratulated her and told her she ought to have an exhibition) she just couldn't take seriously as any kind of spiritual director. David Mahy, on the other hand, she found a real challenge and a test to her humility. Where Pat built her up, David always came across to her as non-committal. She felt that while Pat helped her to feel good about herself (a quality she placed little value on), David would teach her humility.

It was now that he relationship with John Stallard began to fade, partly thanks to advice from Michael Gedge. John and Eularia were both teaching at Redrice on Mondays, and Eularia had still been rushing back to Winchester to cook him supper, but Michael advised her that she might not be good for him. Eularia half-heartedly agreed because she wanted John to meet someone, marry and settle down. The upshot was that John ceased to come on Mondays and Eularia stayed on at Redrice for evening prayers after making friends with the new chaplain there, Fr Hugh Farmer.

22

Vision of Failure

Eularia began what she initially called her red painting in February 1963 and described it as a '...very *felt* picture.' *Gethsemane, Vision of Failure* (Matthew 26:39) reflects her on-going struggle with penitence and suffering, and she re-painted the Christ figure several times before she was happy with it. It corresponds with a dark night that Eularia herself was going through. She had been a Catholic for four years, the 'honeymoon' period was well and truly over and she was still suffering from her ulcer. So, once again, the priests at St Peter's and the Faith in general received the brunt of her ill humour and the Gethsemane painting reflects this. She set it in a London park and the perimeter of the painting is full of people leaving the figure of Christ alone in the centre. The three apostles are asleep on a bench and the only people looking at Christ in his hour of agony, and set apart from the everyone else, are two angels and two dogs: everyone else is turned away.

On a personal level the Christ figure can be seen as Eularia in her own internal agony and conflict, feeling as if no one is interested in her problems except God, who is represented by the angels and is insubstantial. This particular problem started with a bout of not feeling valued or important at St Peter's, brought on unwittingly by the Filippini Nuns from The White House in St Peter's Street. In the 1960s there were four of them under the care of Sister Mary Geraghty and they often attended early morning Mass at St Peter's.

Despite her rebelliousness and bouts of illness, Eularia still kept up near daily Mass attendance. She had resigned herself to being unusual in the Parish in this regard as, apart from another elderly lady, she was frequently the only member of the congregation (other than the nuns) who attended these early morning Masses. She never knew whose Mass she would be attending; it could be Sidney Mullarkey's, Pat Murphy-O'Connor's, David Mahy's or Raymond Lawrence's (the new Bishop's secretary). As there were rarely any men at that hour to act as servers for the priests she often took on the role, which she greatly enjoyed.

Gethsemane, Vision of Failure (1963)

Naturally enough the nuns, when they were there, often used to stand in as servers. Eularia hated this because it meant she didn't get to do it and had to be satisfied with being silent congregation. Consequently she took against the nuns. She was very honest about her motives. She knew that she liked to feel important and part of the show, and when the nuns were there she felt relegated to the role of unimportant lay female.

Of all the early morning Masses she liked David Mahy's the best, as, apparently, did the nuns. Eularia could be quite possessive about it, wanting him to herself, which meant that she got to ring the Offertory bell. One morning the nuns were there having just attended Mass and wondering whether to stay on to answer David's, 'However, she (*Sr Mary*) brought the bell and I pretended the usual disappointment.'

No wonder they didn't realise how much Eularia wanted to be valued, or to do these things. The nuns could hardly be expected to understand that she really liked answering David's Mass and ringing the bell if she gave them to believe that she didn't. It is impossible now to determine how much of Eularia's diary rantings about her interaction with St Peter's arose out of this simple habit of false modesty and misplaced manners, but some of it certainly did. Eularia was, all too often, the architect of her own frustrations and loathing, leaving everyone else to wonder what on earth the problem was.

One of Eularia's most enduring and sabotaging hang-ups was the need to feel appreciated and valued (a legacy of her youth). She considered it the height of bad manners when people didn't show appreciation for her work or her help and thank her for it. Having arrived for early Mass one day in March with a sick headache (not a good start), she found herself displaced by nuns and flew into an internal rage with it all. This was compounded by a Confession with poor David Mahy, where she maintained (untruthfully, but she was apt to forget when in a rage) that Sacraments never had any effect on her and she didn't believe in Absolution or the Resurrection. David, quite rightly, pointed out that it was a little tricky to give Absolution to someone who didn't want to receive it and so she settled for a blessing instead.

Eularia then developed a 'thing' about going to Confession and misinterpreted David's meaning in the most dramatic way possible – she decided that she had been excommunicated. For her no Absolution (which she had refused) meant no Communion and when she next attended Sidney Mullarkey's Mass she told the young lad serving that she wasn't having Communion and he told Sidney, so Sidney did not give it to her. She wrote:

> 'It caused no ripple, and why should it? The outcast was the only guest at the banquet, but no food, the food wasn't going to be given to the dogs, but carried to the children.'

This is Eularia at her most difficult and obtuse. Sidney was simply doing as she had asked, probably assuming that she hadn't managed the pre-Communion fast period, and had no idea that she had an issue with Confession or Absolution. To Eularia's mind this made it worse because it meant that they weren't discussing her cosily at the presbytery. She interpreted this to mean that she was, therefore, insignificant, just another parishioner.

Facts meant very little to Eularia when she was like this. The fact that David had honoured the sanctity of the Confessional by not saying anything to the other priests was immaterial. As Michael Gedge kept pointing out to her in his letters, if she wanted help she had to ask them for it and explain what the problem was, they were far too busy to second guess her or try and read her mind. But Eularia didn't want facts; she wanted to be commiserated with. Pat, who was the best candidate for this, was very busy with the St Dismas Society so she hadn't seen much of him and when she did she tended to listen to all his news rather than broach any of her own. She rarely saw John Stallard now, except occasionally when their paths crossed at Redrice, and David Mahy still confused her. That she should go to Sidney Mullarkey about any of it was never an option as far as she was concerned.

Consequently it was to Michael Gedge that she explained herself much more fully. He pulled her up on the Sacraments:

> 'And where, do you think, came those experiences of prayer which you recited to me a letter or two ago? From the very Lord Whom you had received in Communion. There is a direct connection: you could not have received one without the other – inside the Christian Church. And it is not true to say that Absolution doesn't give you grace: your own progress shows that: your paintings, your teachings, your self-knowledge and growing humility (!) all show that grace is being received and working. But of course God doesn't let you *feel* grace working – to teach you more humility...'

Michael refused to come between her and David and simply advised her to go back to him and explain herself more clearly:

'And don't forget that you are only excommunicated if

a) the priest explicitly tells you that you are.

b) You have *mortal* sins on your conscience. (These *could* include sins against the faith; but it's not for me to say whether they do. I think you should go back and clear *that* question up with Fr. Mahy – or some other priest... remember that it's his *business* to tell you what the Church says; not to pass on some more high-brow doctrine which "he thinks he feels"!)'

Michael had years of experience of handling difficult parishioners and it showed. Poor David had only been a priest for two and half years. That he persevered with Eularia when he could have passed her on to Pat, who knew her better, or Sidney Mullarkey who had so much more experience, was to his credit. She was never a normal parishioner.

Just as with Pat and John Stallard before him she began to give David a hard time. It almost seems to have been a test of friendship with her. If they could survive it she would trust them more but David never took her rudeness personally. In fact he probably didn't even recognise it. Like Michael, he was not affected by Eularia's fits of temper or snide attacks, as the more emotional Pat was. It left her less room to manoeuvre with him because she couldn't then dive into remorse and penitence. She had to take him or leave him as he was.

It is possible to see this Eularia in the Christ figure lying prostrate upon the red grass in *Gethsemane, Vision of Failure*. Like many artists, her temperament set her apart. It made it hard for her to be like other people, but it was the very thing that gave birth to the paintings. The child in her still could not understand why the priests treated her like all the other parishioners because deep down she knew she had to be different in order to do her work. But Pat and David did treat her differently. They were not in the habit of dropping in for coffee and cosy chats with other parishioners so regularly. They did not treat other parishioners as a confidante, but they were also part of a busy parish with many other duties and responsibilities.

Most of all, though, the painting speaks to the dark night of the senses and the soul, when faith is tested to its upmost and failure is foreseen as a possibility, and yet the world carries on regardless. In the painting the only concern comes from the dogs, and the angels (who stand by with mug, thermos and sandwich), still there, still watching, holding a quiet sacred space. Eularia wrote that a very holy man she observed in Church inspired the angel. She also wrote that:

> 'There is a theory that Christ's worst agony was his foreknowledge that we would go on being just as wicked as ever. It is the clergy's worry now so I put one in.'

She always said that she had to reference the other characters from gangster films, as she didn't know anyone wicked enough in Winchester. Of course there was an element in Eularia that perceived herself to be that constant failure, that she was the one who was not able to stop being wicked. On a personal level she becomes both the anguished Christ, suffering a dark night of the senses, and the wicked people surrounding him who will never turn from their evil ways.

Eularia's relationship with St Peter's continued to advance through a difficult year. What you gain from ceremony and the sacred reflects what you bring to it. Eularia had a subliminal understanding of this, but the rebel in her was stronger. The child who never felt appreciated or important continued to take centre stage and the priests weren't playing ball, which made them the enemy. Eularia was beginning to discover that no matter how long she kept up the tantrum, and even if she threw all her toys out of her pram, it didn't make any difference to them. They continued to treat her the same as they always had done, as a parishioner, and in the case of Pat and David, as a friend.

23

Blessing the Paintings

Spode Easter Music Week of 1963 was what turned things around for her this time. Once again she slept in the Mini van by the canal rather than in the house itself, despite rain, wet blankets and pillows. She brought her paintings with her, although she had given up hope of anyone taking any interest in them, when, just before she left, a Dominican called Fr Alberic arrived. She wrote to Alicia:

'Dominicans are *awfully* like Baines', I find; there was a painter – Dominican priest at Spode I talked and talked with; it's the first time anybody understood what I was after, because the art people don't understand about religion and the religious people don't know a *thing* about art, but Father Alberic was at the Ruskin, so we just fell on each other's spiritual necks.'

It was the first time Eularia gave a sense of just how alone she felt as an artist and why it was so challenging for her to fit in at St Peter's. It is one thing to have people admire your art, but to have someone who truly understands it opens doorways to a level of sharing which she longed for and so far had not found. Unfortunately Fr Alberic was at Blackfriars in Oxford, so once again regular contact was not easy.

Eularia did consider becoming a Dominican Tertiary but received what she described as a 'very sniffy' letter from Michael Gedge, who, whilst not being against the idea, pointed out that it may lead to spiritual pride as the Dominicans were seen as a select and intellectual body:

'...very much up in the world, which is rather what you want and like.'

Myself and two friends in the Mini van at Spode House: note the bedding
put out to dry after a damp night (1963)

Whilst it is unlikely that Eularia would have coped with the rigours of
a Rule of Order for long (she was too individual and creative), it would
have given her a more solid foundation with people who were perhaps
better able to give her the time and kind of support she needed, which
the busy parish priests were not able to do. It is possible that Michael did
her a disservice by discouraging her. Having the support of like-minded
people who understood art, spirituality and theology, was something she
always felt she never truly found.

She expressed her feelings about parish worship in her poem 'Walking
Along to Emmaus' which she wrote on her return from Spode:

> Walking along to Emmaus,
> Not in the hot pink dust, but depressingly
> Dark neo-gothic Monday, eight-o'clock Mass.
> Father O'Flanagan, bleary and tousled,
> Last night's whiskey, sick of the parish,
> Puts peoples' backs up, lost all his humour,
> Keeps going somehow.

Walking along to Emmaus,
Usual camphory felt-hatted faithful old ladies,
Broken-down man in a Macintosh serves at the altar,
One anaemic family, mother and children,
Two lovely girls come in late...
Mumbling of Gospel, yawning of Preface,
Heel-cracks and blisters, slithery ridges and cart-tracks
Sand in our gullets; what on earth are we here for?

Walking along to Emmaus,
Nearly there now; old Macintosh gropes for the bell.
Now we are out of the sunset, into the house with the table,-
Father O'Flanagan, bleary and tousled,
Made known in the breaking of bread.

The last couplet expresses in words exactly what Eularia sought to express through her painting, the idea that even in the most ordinary, mundane and unattractive of people and surroundings the Gospel still speaks.

Eularia replaced the mattress in the Mini van with boards and a sleeping bag and she was fasting. Once again she had not told anyone. It was a form of self-hate and self-harm which the priests would in no way have condoned and which did not conform to the reason for undertaking mortification as a penance.

In these dark periods she treated the Church in the same way, by 'punishing it' for not being what she wanted it to be:

'I choke off low people. All day I've wasted time hating the Church, planning to be away on all possible occasions, just hating, not even bothering to doubt; it is like last year. I don't even dislike the temptations, I give in to them and agree with them, I admit them. I want to hurt the Church because it hasn't valued me enough, I want it to suffer from my defection but I'm afraid it won't – more likely it's longing to be rid of me... and that's the heart of the matter – the Catholic failure to appreciate me, especially the Canon's.'

One might argue, as Michael Gedge almost certainly would have done had he known, that in order to feel appreciated one first has to appreciate oneself, and mortification when the body is unwell and you have been advised against it is not evidence of this. She was not entirely unaware of how ridiculous and ineffective her stance was. She knew that if she really didn't like the Church she could simply leave. She knew that her life flowed much more harmoniously when she didn't fight everything, that people were more open and friendly and helpful to her when she was open and friendly to them. It was an inner 'devil' that would dog her on and off until her death. Most of the time she was able to hide it from others, but on her own it had a habit of catching her unawares, fed by anger or frustration and the childhood sense of being at best unimportant and at worst just plain wrong.

She finished this polemic by asking herself:

'Supposing I give in, and went on steadily being generous and loyal to the Church, what would happen then? The priests would be smugger, but perhaps they might at least value me a bit and trust me.'

The priests would not have wasted time on being smug. They would just have continued to enjoy her company, as they already did.

During this period Eularia began *Supper at Emmaus* (Luke 24:30) which she described painting mostly with the canvas on the floor, or on chairs while she knelt or crouched (at this point she did not have a proper easel). Set in a pub, it shows the moment of Christ breaking bread (a bloomer with three pints on the table) and being recognised by the apostles. She used a subdued and rather dark palette in which the figures seem to emerge from a mist, mirroring her own sense of coming out of her gloom and back to the realisation of her faith. Only the head and hands of the Christ are clearly defined, a reflection of how she was experiencing Christ at the time – as less distinct but re-emerging. Along with the drinkers in the pub is a congregation in the foreground and an altar boy doing what Eularia herself loved to do, ringing the bell at the moment of Consecration.

A much calmer Eularia emerged for a while from this spell of angst:

'I find to my amazement that I don't lose my temper, I'm not angry, hardly ever, I don't want to say things against people, I don't mind failure and humiliation *nearly* as much. I don't want to interfere and boss and cause trouble. I want to be alone, probably too much. I want to keep other people out, I want peace and silence, work alternating with prayer and reading. I *love* the van, it's a cell I rush into, I creep into it at odd hours and read and meditate and think up pics.'

Eularia had been asked to exhibit a painting at the Bournemouth Art Gallery for the Biblical Art Exhibition (*Christmas Gospel*), and with this began a practice that was to remain until nearly the end of Eularia's life:

'I asked Fr. M (*Mahy*) if I should have the Bournemouth pic. blessed, and he said at once that he'd come and do it.'

After this blessing the paintings became standard procedure for David Mahy and all but the very last few were blessed by him on completion.

This was the beginning of a new relationship with David. Because he was not of a very demonstrative disposition, Eularia had never been quite sure what David thought of her paintings. The fact that he came up to Middle Road to bless the painting the very same day left her in no doubt.

Eularia found the inspiration for her next painting and another poem[12] at Glastonbury during the annual procession of crosses from St Louis Convent to the Catholic Church. *Glastonbury, Taking up the Crosses* (Matthew 16:25-6) shows the moment just as the procession began in the convent field with the Tor in the background. From a point of view of perspective the painting is intriguing, as the men hauling the crosses upright are much larger than the crowds, no matter where they stand. It is as if the masses are diminishing, leaving the focus on the central players, reflecting, perhaps, Eularia's current battle of always wanting to be centre stage.

With the exception of Confession, her relationship with the Sacraments was undergoing a change:

'Communion is a meeting of love in complete deep darkness. Such darkness that only the unknown bit of one does the meeting at all. One's conscious mind gives consent and goes through the necessary motions – and somewhere deep in the darkness and invisibility and silence a meeting takes place, of so much love and so much intimate closeness that even the remote reverberation of it is enough to bring one to it with daily hunger. Nothing is felt, He is completely remote, there is only the horrid visible Church, there *too* close, repulsive and annoying, even hostile. But yet the thought of meeting in the darkness is enough to grip the heart with unbearable emotion, a sorrow that has joy underneath it, so much joy that one clings to the sorrow, wants more and more sorrow, more suffering, more repulsiveness and annoyance. There is never any doubt about the touch of God, it is only difficult to think of because other things must be chased away.'

---

12   "Glastonbury Pilgrimage", 1963.

24

Oils

The Second Vatican Council had only been in session for seven months of its three years when Pope John (the inspiration behind it) died on 3 June 1963. His death would have a profound effect on the course of the changes being discussed. The new Pope, Paul VI (elected at the end of June), vowed to carry on the work but was not able to hold back the conservative influence in the Church. Many liberals ended up feeling that the reforms were watered down and that Pope Paul was weak. It gave a platform for the conservative voice and effectively created a polarisation in the Church, which still exits today. It would also become increasingly frustrating to Eularia who, on the whole, tended to side with the liberals.

Shortly after this Eularia went to Bournemouth to see her painting hanging in the Biblical Art exhibition:

'The exhibition was fun, me underneath Blake and next to Holman Hunt and Burne-Jones (Miss Tarrant opposite, alas!!) and the curator taking me round and asking me if I was pleased with my hanging. I was – but it was a bad pic. More devout than most, which were very humanistic, almost non-religious, but I decided OILS.'

This is the only indication we have that until this point Eularia was not using oil paints but probably a mixture of size and pigment.

As luck would have it, her son James arrived on a rare visit. She had not seen much of him since his move to Norfolk. He was very much in love with a young Norwegian girl called Marit Aamodt (known as Marita), but she was not ready to move to England and settle down. This meant that he spent much of his free time going to Norway so, when he came to stay with Eularia that summer, he took her into Southampton and bought her oil paint and brushes as a compensation present.

Summer 1963 found Eularia in a calmer, more reflective state of mind. Aunt Margaret and Trixl died within three weeks of each other and she began to review her life in a different light:

'I've had the three bouts of loving, the three Johns who opened my heart and two of them insisted on my love and took it greedily and didn't give me what I wanted, the gesture of wanting *me*. They only did the opening-up, and got me ready for the job of pursuing a dark and fugitive love. Sometimes this isn't dark or fugitive, and it's a love that *does* want me, and insists on having me, even against my will. It does nourish me, it does teach me and lead me and control me, occasionally it delights me, and inspires me. But here under Axe Edge I know what has happened, the truth about me and my life.'

Michael Gedge added weight to this when he returned from the Beda as a fully ordained priest attached to the Portsmouth diocese, where he was assigned to Fareham with Cormac Murphy-O'Connor under Fr Joe Rea. Now that he was more local he was much better able to observe Eularia's actual behaviour (he was very stern with her about gossip) and her painting. He drew attention to a purpose for it:

'It is to preach sermons to people who would find ordinary sermons not much help, and in a language which many outside the Church can appreciate. One is told these days that all the best religious art is being done by agnostics – but I doubt it; with them art is a real (and so far as it goes true) substitute for religion. i.e. they get as near God as they can *by that way*; but it isn't the best religious art, for the latter would surely bring people to God in Christ and the Church?'

September 1963 was when Eularia first wrote about painting her religious works in oils:

'…and several times I simply had to stop trying to paint, because the paralysing power came over me and I was engulfed, no good trying to resist it. The joy was very great, and as always I wanted it to last forever, but of course it never goes on for more than a few moments, and when it has gone away it is a very forlorn feeling. That's when mortification begins; a sort of bribe I suppose.'

She made a real attempt to remain in tune with God, despite distractions, although she found it hard, especially when other people were involved:

'I... received Communion in the middle of a tremendous effort of will, and it was like standing still in a stormy sea, and everything else disappeared and I concentrated on just one single thing, and it was about as much as I could do, and the priest put the wafer on my tongue and I drew my whole self and all my powers round just that one fact, and I felt it with every sense, and received Christ with all I had, really receiving, a real act, as real as the act of love, not passive, hoping for the best, but active, and it was different from all the other times.'

The sense of standing still in a stormy sea presaged her next painting *Storm Over the Lake* (Matthew 8:26). She began this painting as her career took a decisive step that would completely change the focus of her teaching. Before the end of the summer term Jerry Cornes, the headmaster of West Downs School, had asked her to take over the Art Department. Arthur Newton, music master at Winchester County Secondary School for boys on Romsey Road, also asked her to do an evening a week of guitars. It was to be a busy autumn.

She began *Storm Over the Lake* just as she started the new term and it was a real shock to the system. Up to this point she had either been a supply teacher or a peripatetic music teacher, which meant that her classes were extra-curricular and it therefore didn't matter so much if they didn't happen. Becoming Art Mistress at West Downs completely changed this. Now she was expected to be at the school from Monday to Thursday. At the same time she still had her music classes at Medecroft and Redrice, her new class at Romsey Road and assorted private pupils.

She found the older boys at West Downs very challenging to begin with, although she loved working with boys again, especially the younger ones, '...tiny little boys with damp trousers and scared eyes, the good old smell of small boy, which warmed my heart.'

After years of being fairly casual about her classes she had to be disciplined and follow a strict timetable, but she loved the boys and they were from upper class families, which she felt were her kind of people.

Being surrounded once again by people she felt were her type on a daily basis caused her relationship with St Peter's to nose-dive. In fact everything was suffering: housework, correspondence, painting, shopping, sewing. After years of making do with the solid fuel cook-and-heat stove she finally decided to invest in a proper gas cooker as she explained to Rachael:

'A new white miniature one which lights itself, so now I can at *last* commit suicide whenever I like, as well as cook proper food.'

But what she really loved was teaching something she actually felt qualified to teach:

'I now see how it was always a *bit* nerve-racking, knowing no piano or harmony; whereas if I've got to *draw* a horse or a clenched fist I can *do* it!... And teaching Art is very good for one's technique – it makes one think about it more.'

Eularia teaching art at West Downs (mid 1960s)

She didn't have the energy or motivation to keep up daily Mass attendance and turned it into a crisis of faith. Instead of simply relaxing it all somewhat and expressing her faith in other ways through her work (a concept that seem to completely pass her by in anything other than painting), she, once again, turned on the Church as if it was the Church's fault:

'The odd thing is that I have to protest so much – instead of just leaving it, I have to quarrel with it and hurt it if possible.'

It is an unrelenting theme. Whenever life was stressful she lashed out at those nearest to her, and in the absence of any closer relations the clergy and the Church became the focus. Underlying it was the deep frustration of being a talented woman and craving acceptance in a man's world, where the ideal for women was to be passive and meek. It would become increasingly irksome to her as the sixties progressed and feminist voices began to emerge.

This angst may have been why she listened to James when he advised her that she should be selling her paintings, not giving them away, and she decided to do a few 'pot boiler' landscapes while she was painting *Storm Over the Lake*, but she knew something was missing. They did not hold her attention or satisfy her as the religious painting did. There are only five surviving landscapes in oils or pigment by her, which are not dated and which, judging by style, were not all painted at the same time. It is possible that three of them come from this period. Any others must have been painted over, as she never sold any landscapes in the 1960s. The jolly, surface part of her, which had to cope with day-to-day teaching at West Downs and which was attempting to be practical and do paintings that people would want to buy, seems very insubstantial and rather fake:

'How can you practice the faith? Once you begin, it gets you and you are fighting towards practicing it wholly. You can't do this *and* earn money, and teach successfully. So you drop it entirely, and somewhere your soul bleeds, you want people and events to pull you back to it again. Otherwise I suppose you just go on with nothing.'

Storm Over the Lake reflects much of this internal conflict. It depicts the miracle of Jesus beginning to calm the waters just as the boat is going to sink. In her painting the boat, full of disciples, is tossed and almost completely submerged by rough black and green water. The disciples cling on frantically, pleading and praying, and at the front in the bottom left hand corner of the painting the calm figure of Jesus holds his hand over the water and we see that underneath it is still.
Eularia said of it:

'I was thinking about drowning people, how they clutch at absolutely anything; a bit of rope, a person's hair, clothes, anything. There is a lot of cruelty, they hurt each other, but help each other if they can. If you are clinging to the gunwale, people with nothing to hold on to will soon start clutching at you, this often happens over religion. But the main thing in the picture is the power of Christ's calming, which is a common experience.'

Pat Murphy-O'Connor loved *Storm Over the Lake* and she poured out all her woes to him, which must have inevitably included her sense of being on her own. He sent her a genuinely beautiful letter, which she deeply appreciated:

'Please don't think that nobody cares. It may not be obvious but there are many who do care for you and respect you more than you can think. I am one of those. I didn't use the word love because it's so meaningless these days, but that too.'

Fr Hugh Farmer, at Redrice, also divined some of Eularia's problem and wrote:

'Surely the point is that you have to keep that inner citadel of your soul for God alone, even while you serve Him with energy and devotion in the souls of the boys you teach. He's in *them* too, though he certainly hides himself!'

Storm Over the Lake (1963) from the Methodist Modern Art Collection,
© TMCP, used with permission.

In November Eularia received a cheque for £30 from Veronica Stokes for the purchase of *Lourdes, Grotto from Outside, Lourdes, Way of the Cross* and *Priest Brings Communion,* all of which she copied for her own collection. They were the first of her religious paintings to be sold and almost the last. It is likely that, if James hadn't been pressuring her to stop giving her paintings and time away, she would never have sold any. Eularia was never a businesswoman, but more than that, the purpose of her religious work was never about profit.

In December she began *Blessing the Babies* (Mark 10:13). She wrote to Rachael that:

'Cuthbert is in the picture of the Blessing of the Babies (he is in a nappy, and being carried dangerously by a boy in jeans of course – but he's making it, and you can tell him by his feet). It's not a very nice picture, everyone's being turned away except one mother who's too distracted to notice that no. 2 is being blessed, and a young father with a pint-sized new-born baby. There are tarts and remand-home babies, and one paralysed one, and many babies brought by children, or fathers and blocks of flats and terylene curtains and push-chairs and prams etc. etc. and the idea is that babies are not always a sentimental pastime, as the Victorian artists thought. People with babies need blessing – babies can be hell!'

Blessing the Babies was one of Eularia's more popular early works and was exhibited often. It is a classic example of a painting full of action and emotion being held together by the calm and iconic Christ who is dressed, as he frequently is in her paintings from now on, in a red kaftan. In some respects many of Eularia's paintings owe as much to Brueghel as to Stanley Spencer, especially in the way that she paints her emotive people and shows them in their everyday lives. They are always busy, always engaged. Compared to Eularia's, Spencer's figures seem almost emotionless and still by comparison.

In her caption for this painting she said:

'This is a council flat estate in East London, near the docks. It was a hot evening, parents looked exhausted and I thought of the long strain of bringing up babies, especially if they are delicate or defective, and how Christ knew this, and blessed them at the end of his own exhausting "out-giving" day.'

The navy blue woolly jumpers that the apostles often wear from this time on are inspired by the jumpers worn by the West Down boys after swimming.

Blessing the Babies (1963)

Pat Murphy-O'Connor inspired another idea in Eularia that was to become a fundamental part of her collection. It was just before Christmas and she had been shopping when she came across Pat on his bike in the churchyard:

'...he said he wanted something but didn't know whether he ought to ask it....I begged him to ask, and he went round and round on his bike, the east wind made his face purple and pink, he wanted one of the pictures. I'm not certain if he meant give, or what....When I got home, I realised how pleased I was. I wrote offering to lend them all as if I was a library – to Fr. M (*Mahy*) as well.'

To lend the paintings gave Eularia far more pleasure than selling them and it was later to become much more important to her. Pat chose *Storm Over the Lake* and it stayed with him until she exhibited it in 1964, when it was purchased for the Methodist Collection of Modern Art.

Eularia left for Christmas in Leeds fortified by an odd cocktail of cold coffee, whisky (a Christmas present) and cold milk. Good relations with son-in-law Robert were helped by the fact that she did not stay long. The fear of leaving the house too long (and returning to find it all frozen up) and the drive back meant that she left at 4am on the day after Boxing Day.

One of my enduring memories of Eularia was that I never saw her for long enough and it began with this Christmas. I remember vividly waking up to find her gone. She was so unlike every other adult I knew: much more tactile than the other grown-ups around me and very happy to play rough and tumble with me. We children teased her mercilessly in a way that we never did with other adults and she took it all in good part. To me she was the only adult that did not feel rigid in some way. She still possessed that wild sense of creativity that children have, full of imagination and with fewer boundaries about what is possible, and she encouraged it in us.

Part 4

A Teacher of Art

1964 – 1967

25

A Sense of Vocation

'This life is married life, only so invisibly. There are quarrels. The prayer is like the homecomings and embraces, the reading is the conversation, the official prayer, the concentration, the painting etc. is the ordinary marriage routine, the continual production of offspring, cooking, scrubbing... And Mass is the marriage act of the soul, I suppose, a cold act at the worst time of day. But one that produces the union and the fruit.'

In January 1964 Eularia began what she originally referred to as 'the Nettles pic or the Precious Blood pic.' eventually called the *The Vinegar Bottle* (Mark 15:36 and John 19:29). In the foreground to the left we see a man in the act of fixing the sponge to the stick, in a weedy place full of rubbish and surrounded by youths smoking and jeering and others praying. It is an early example of Eularia painting from an unusual perspective. We appear to be looking down on the group standing around the cross as they look up, but we can only see the bottom part of the cross, which sits in a clump of nettles. Out of this clump a pair of ghostly hands emerge holding a chalice in which the blood of Christ is being caught as it runs down the cross. Eularia told Rachel that it was set in:

'...the dump in Bartlett's field (*Great Rissington*), complete with nettles, rusty junk, St. John and Mary, man with vinegar bottle and sponge, puzzled rifleman, lots of Romsey Road boys sitting smoking and scoffing, and the bottom of the cross with blood running down it on to the nettles. The junk has been done *so* carefully, you can recognise each object, and the nettles were done out of Granny's botany book – as all nettles are dead now.'

The captions that Eularia wrote for the paintings come mostly from her one-woman exhibitions from the mid 1960s onwards and (in the case of these early works) were written some time after she completed them, but through them it is possible to gain an insight into her own intention for the painting and how she used her paintings to express her sometimes rather idiosyncratic theology. This is the one for *The Vinegar Bottle*:

> 'This is the rubbish dump I remember outside our village in Gloucestershire. The crucifixion seems to have been such a noisy and undignified business with a lot of insults flying about; a crucifix is a quiet respectable thing lifted right out of it all, so perhaps we forget. I thought the vinegar man ought to be remembered, because he seems to have been the only person who actually tried to help. Perhaps he was English.'

There is a bleak darkness in *The Vinegar Bottle*. Eularia's palette veered towards sludgy browns, blues and greens at this time, which almost certainly reflected her own tiredness and inner bleakness. She looked forward to 1964 with trepidation. She was teaching at four schools – one Art, three Music – and Rachael was expecting her third child in the summer. She was reluctant to begin another painting from sheer exhaustion.

The Vinegar Bottle was in process at a time when more changes were in the air for the Church. By this time divisions were emerging between the traditionalist and progressive factions, and Eularia complained that everyone was very fed up with the bishops. Once again the choir proved to be the barometer for the greater Church. Just after Epiphany she attended a Sunday Mass at St Peter's, after which Sidney Mullarkey played a tape of American Laymen doing a vernacular Mass (English) unaccompanied which strongly divided the choir. Eularia liked it but many hated it. Scenes like this were being played out all over England, indeed probably everywhere in the world there was a Catholic community.

Another new innovation, which Eularia was originally dubious about, but attended because David Mahy encouraged her, was the first parish ecumenical service held at Weeke which David presided at. This followed the Decree on Ecumenism from the Vatican Council and opened the way for much greater ecumenical relations between the Christian faiths. Eularia enjoyed it very much and was quite proud of David. But her willingness to side with innovation was once again undermining her relationship with the more traditional flock at St Peter's, especially the choir.

Despite her workload she began experimenting with icons and made a head and shoulders copy of the Christ figure from Fr Noel's *The Last Supper*. She began a proper icon of *St Joseph* for Redrice School, although it would take her several months to complete.

Michael Gedge had finally given in and agreed to be her Spiritual Director:

> 'He says my religion is too much "people" – he's right – all people, people, people, and that in the night of the soul one doesn't grumble. One hates what one is, because it's incompatible with God.'

Michael was correct, but it was Eularia's feeling for and attachment to people that brought her paintings alive, uniquely so in religious art, perhaps. The idea that the Gospels come alive in the people rather than the other way around is the theme that runs through all her work. Several times we see examples of Gospel scenes playing out alongside religious ceremony, *Bent Woman Straightened* (1970), *Coming up from the Water* (1965), and the laity, the 'people' are regarding the Gospel rather than the ceremony.

She caught a bad bronchial flu just before Easter, which she struggled to shake off, so still wasn't feeling well when Robert, Rachael and we grandchildren arrived. Typically she said nothing, so Robert and Rachael took her up on her offer to look after Cuthbert and me while they took a short break. By the time Rachael and Robert arrived back Eularia was too tired and unwell to cope. Rachael was now nearly seven months pregnant with Austin and once again more emotional than normal. Again she blamed her mother's exhaustion on religion, which was unfair. Eularia had dropped daily Mass during busy term times, she was tired because she hadn't been able to shake the flu bug due to the teaching. It is also ironic that, despite having a strong need to be needed, when Eularia met situations where she was needed, as with the family, she either shied away from it or couldn't cope with it.

As her Spiritual Director Michael Gedge told her:

> 'You MUST – repeat – MUST – get a week, if possible, or as many days less than a week which you can extract, clear away from everything and everybody, before next term begins. It is not sensible to exhaust yourself, and your daughter is in principle quite right. There is certainly no substitute for God: but your first duty is to preserve yourself in reasonable health.'

Michael had more foresight here than he could ever have known. Ultimately it was Eularia's health that would prove to be her undoing, but at this stage she still believed that she had the same strong constitution that she had had as a child, despite the health scares.

She did follow this advice, however. She took off in the van for Lyme Regis in the pouring rain (not perhaps quite what Michael had in mind) and spent the first night stuck, wet through, in a lonely and isolated lane, which made her very anxious, but by the time she reached Lyme the sun was out and her mood was improving. It wasn't until she was camping on the Cobb at Lyme with the back doors of the Mini van opening onto the waves that she began to reconnect with her experience of God.

This trip provided the setting for her next painting, *Rescuing Sheep* (Matthew 12:11 and John 10:28). Both the Bible references she gave for this painting speak to her own sense of feeling in need of rescuing. The dull palette of rusts and greens and rather dingy browns persist and the Christ figure, despite a strong pair of arms doing the rescuing, is otherwise insubstantial as if emerging from a mist.

Eularia wrote in her caption for this painting that the cliff fall she used was near Lyme and in fact it is part of the Jurassic Coast near Charmouth, which she described in her diary:

'At Black Ven, the huge towering black shaley cliffs tower up, with falls of black and grey mud, all very villainous, shiny and cracked – ominous cracks and falls, Coltsfoot and rough grass.'

In her caption for the painting she said:

'This is a terrifying place, where the cliffs have fallen, beyond Lyme Regis, leaving huge deep chasms. I was thinking about the parable and how most sheep don't want to be rescued, and the strength of Christ both as a carpenter, and far more as we know him now. I have mixed up sheep and people, but you can spot a prison chaplain and a hospital chaplain.'

The prison and hospital chaplains are not obvious, although they are probably the two figures reaching down into the chasm (one has hold of a hospital bed) and, without doubt, refer to Pat and David respectively. In her diary it is clear that Eularia wanted to be rescued again by the love of God. Her exhaustion and upset had cut her off.

She returned to Middle Road to a request from Adrian Stokes to take over the Redrice Art for the summer term (their Art Master having left suddenly). Despite knowing how pushed she already was, she agreed to take this on.

Michael Gedge now really came into his own, taking his role as her spiritual director very seriously. He warned her about taking on too much and told her not to try and fit daily Mass in as well, but gave her a way to make an act of spiritual communion instead that she could do herself. He pointed out:

'You rather pile on the agony by an almost daily pessimistic appraisal. I think it would be much better if you gave God what you can for *His* sake, and stopped worrying about how awful it all is.'

But the fact was that she now had two Art departments and three sets of music classes to fit in and she found it completely exhausting, what she called 'black tiredness'. Despite this she followed Michael's advice about spiritual communion and found that it worked. The presence of God came back strongly for her. Once again she associated it with the pain, suffering and tiredness. Rachael's anti-religion stance with Eularia may have had more to do with this than anything else. They made up rather uneasily by letter and Eularia wrote:

'I quite agree about too much religion, but I can't do much about it – you should be thankful I at least shut it out for the 1937 – 1957 period when conducting motherhood – *what* a mess your childhoods might have been!'

Rachael's, and James', problem was that the more secular mother they knew was only a small part of the real Eularia who had done what she needed to do to survive. While she did convert to Catholicism, she didn't suddenly acquire God. That aspect of her faith, her art, her core self, had always been there, even up to the time when she and Cyril were courting. The disappointment with Cyril and years of being a single parent had simply pushed it underground. In fact, expecting Eularia to stop being spiritual and involved with God was like expecting the proverbial leopard to change her spots:

'They all say the same, that God's intention is clear with some people, and Michael has always thought so, and goodness gracious, don't I know it! Who else do I seek the company of? Who else do I read about and think about and talk to? Who else do I love and keep seeking? Who do I hold fast to? Who do I thank, who do I call on in trouble? Only God, because in fact there is nothing else. Only God melts my heart and sets it on fire and engulfs me in force and waves and joy, and more joy, joy to the point of anguish. I must try never to forget these things.'

26

Half a Century

Eularia turned fifty in May 1964 and the experience of God continued:

'But what does this mean? *This is twelve days* – far, far the longest, this isn't just a glimpse of light, a short refreshment. This goes on; I am praying *always* with one bit of my mind – I wake up, knowing that the praying part of me wasn't asleep even, it was going on, apparently, all the time.'

The experience carried her through the first very difficult part of term when she was adjusting to the new intensity of working, and coping with young boys. Even after it was gone she noticed how much more tolerant, cheerful and loving she was with them, calling it the '...new calm of the soul. No more wish to dominate, only to enthuse, help, encourage, love, sympathise.'

Michael Gedge continued to be very supportive, especially over her problems with the family:

'I don't need to tell you again that you are, for better or worse, called to the life of a saint, quite literally! We are all so called; but most of us give it up and become hopeless sinners who may *just* scrape into purgatory.

'It is not so with you. And you know also that the life to which you are called will be and is one of suffering. It is your own family who turn against you first; well that's a common experience of saints. It's true that the family come round in the end, as Pat says: that is when the darling girl starts doing miracles and the cult begins. But not *yet!* There's no kudos to be had out of you at the moment.

'It seems a horrible life doesn't it? But you know it's the only life for you.'

But the dynamic between the solitary path as a Religious Artist and her desire for popularity and acceptance, for some kind of grail that she considered normality to be, would always turn on a pinhead, triggered by the slightest thing. Ultimately it was never an external issue but an internal one. Eularia would never accept her path with joy. She was never able to fully embrace it with generosity of spirit in a way that could be shared. The two warring parts of her were both too strong. The best that she could hope for was to have periods of truce between them.

The work of Jean Nicolas Grou were a particular influence on Eularia during this period, as was that of Evelyn Underhill, an Anglo-Catholic mystic who wrote many works on religion and spiritual practice. Eularia read widely when it came to theology, religious and spiritual practice, and mysticism. If they influenced her painting it was through the support that these authors gave to her own spiritual practice and sense of spiritual and religious self. She was attempting to make sense of her deep experiences of God and prayer. She found it hard to bridge the chasm between these high states of meditative prayer and the day-to-day reality of dealing with boys and the frustrations it caused.

By the summer of 1964 Eularia's relationship with Michael Gedge began to deteriorate again. She visited Fareham a number of times and although she spoke to Cormac Murphy-O'Connor, Michael seemed to ignore her. Her immediate reaction was that he was fed up with her. From the surviving correspondence what becomes evident is that she really didn't know what she wanted in terms of a director, or confessor; she was confused. Part of her wanted the kind of gentle, light hearted, compassionate acceptance and friendliness of Pat Murphy-O'Connor, but another part insisted on having a much rougher, harder, taskmaster and she remained caught between the two.

To a man as single-minded as Michael undoubtedly was, this made their interactions with him very unclear. Whatever qualities he possessed, subtlety was not one of them. Eularia's rather dithering timidity when faced with situations where she had to ask for something simply passed him by. Michael urged Eularia not to mix up social and spiritual visits:

> 'I always make a point *not* to assume that, every time I see you, you are there because you want direction: that every time you are praying in Church you are waiting for *me*. After all, you might be there for God.... But you do make a point of being obscure or allusive.'

For all Michael's urging, Eularia found it very difficult to be up front and decisive over her needs. Being Mistress of an Art Department challenged her to do it and she managed it enough to make a reasonable fist of it, but beyond that she was much less organised, more chaotic and, when it came to asking for things, timid. She would write reams in her diary about how no one ever gave her any gratitude, appreciation, notice or care; about how she was always the one left out, but when it came down to it she was terrible at making her needs known.

Although the summer term's teaching was a massive load, in the end Eularia enjoyed it, but she finally gave her notice at Medecroft. She realised that the kind of teaching she loved most would always be among boys and men and Medecroft was all girls. It was a wise choice. She did excel with boys and Medecroft was simply too much on top of her other commitments. Added to the Art at West Downs in the autumn there were recorders, and although Redrice had a new Art master she still kept up the guitars there.

During the summer term she had had very little time to paint, but over the summer holidays she completed the *St Joseph* icon for Redrice, but Eularia was disappointed that they weren't going to hang it in the chapel as she wrote to Rachael:

'Father Hugh has turned down my icon of St. Joseph – the reason is that it can't be combined with the "Our Lady" installed by Fr. Bushell. She's 18[th]C. Italian, in pale blue velvet ball-gown, glass eyes, real hair, and both hands on one shoulder – so naturally one can't give her a rough peasant husband!'

As the autumn term contained less teaching, she finished *Rescuing Sheep* and began two for the St Dismas society, requested by Pat Murphy-O'Connor. The first of these was *The Penitent Thief*, a portrait of St Dismas (Luke 23:43). St Dismas was the thief who repented on the cross next to Jesus. Eularia's official caption reads:

'St Dismas became a saint so quickly, he hadn't time to start looking like a stained glass window, he went to Paradise just as he was. After a life of crime, too. It makes me feel very fond of him, and also it seems high time we commemorated a man who spoke up for Christ at that unlikely moment, and when he himself must have been in agonising pain.'

Again the perspective is interesting. We are on a level with St Dismas as he hangs high above the crowd, a sea of grey faces emerging from the darkness below. On the left, one nailed and bloody wrist of Jesus can be seen as St Dismas looks towards him in a kind of harrowed, resigned amazement. She captures the lengthy agony of what St Dismas has been through perfectly in his features. Here is man at the end of his endurance, and yet he can still look up to the man on the cross next to him. It is a powerful piece of work and, according to Pat, was much loved by the men at the hostel of St Dismas.

The Penitent Thief (1964)

The other painting that Pat requested was one of Jesus as a young man. St Dismas was a hostel for young men, so this made sense. He wanted them to have a 'Jesus' they could relate to. This inspired *Chairs to Mend* (Matthew 13:55). Eularia's official caption of this tells us:

'What was Christ's life like, as a young man? I thought of little towns in the Midlands, say Staffordshire, where there are a lot of small family workshops and businesses, and of Christ working hard at repairing jobs, helping Joseph. Gradually the idea came, of Christ in Nazareth mending up the broken bits of people's lives. Later he would bring them the "more abundant life".

She shows Jesus in a street (she referred to it as Tamworth, but it was probably inspired by the town rather than an actual representation of it) of small redbrick shops surrounded by people bringing broken items to him to mend including chairs, farming implements, hutches, even a guitar. Given its intended audience, it is a powerful image of a young man who has not yet walked out fully into his path in life, which is foreshadowed only by his halo (much less dense than in the paintings of him during his ministry). She copied both these paintings, which is fortunate, as the originals appear to be lost.

Her choice of Tamworth as a location is also intriguing as Tamworth belonged to her pre-painting and Catholic years when she was considering moving in order to be nearer John Hough – an element of her own life pre-ministry, perhaps.

Pat Murphy-O'Connor and Eularia always enjoyed sharing their music-making and Eularia's music teaching was becoming influenced by her Faith. She continued with the more informal music at West Downs and had a band which, among other things, performed a Beatles version of the *Old Hundredth*.

She also wrote a blues version of the Catholic hymn *Hail Holy Queen* for the Romsey Road and Redrice boys. Music was fast becoming another area where Eularia was very much keeping pace with the prevailing winds, even running ahead of them.

It was Pat who inspired another creative endeavour that was to consume much of 1965. He asked her to write some simple music for a Mass for the inmates at Winchester Prison. This would become *The Prisoners' Mass*, a simple setting of the Latin text for unison voices and guitar and included the Kyrie, Gloria, Sanctus and Agnus Dei.

Towards the end of 1964 Eularia also helped to organise a new singing group for the Catholic Women's League, to learn the *Grail Psalms*. In 1963 a new English translation of *The Book of Psalms* was published following the school of Fr Joseph Gelineau. Gelineau was a French Jesuit who developed a method of singing the psalms in 1953, which involved a regular metre and the congregation singing a simple repeated response (a chorus) with a cantor or choir singing the verses.

The Prisoners' Mass was a natural progression for Eularia musically, and the *Grail Psalms* added weight by showing her that simple settings of the Mass were going to be needed. In the autumn of 1964 the priests at St Peter's began saying Mass in English, facing the congregation. Eularia loved it and needed little persuading from Pat to set the Mass (even though it was still the Latin version). Pat and the prisoners enjoyed it and it prompted her to do much more throughout 1965, even writing her own hymns. Sadly these are now lost, although I have vivid memories of her sitting with us in the garden at Middle Road and teaching us *Bread From Heaven* (one of hers) and *Judas and Mary* (Sydney Carter), accompanying us on her guitar.

Eularia knew what her own emotional pathologies were, but seemed helpless to act on them or change them. She was known, when the doorbell rang, to pretend she was not home in order to avoid visitors. She longed to be accepted and yet did her best to avoid people. When people who cared came too close, like the priests, she would often back away. She often referred to herself as a snob, and others have agreed with this, but this was a protection. She used her frankly not very high upbringing as an excuse for not mixing with people. When the family attempted to include her, or had her to stay, she struggled not to take everything personally and end up in rows, and then when they did not contact her she complained. Reality so often did not measure up to her expectations.

During the summer of 1964 she was beset by jealousy, which caused her to explode at people. She exploded at her brother, Christopher, for wanting to tell her about his honeymoon trip to the Rockies, she refused to listen to David Mahy when he wanted to tell her about his trip to Rome. In anguish she wrote in her diary, 'Why am I like this? Why do I hate so much, get so bitter and black and jealous?' But then, when she was trying to explain about Christ to me (aged four):

'I was trying to tell Min about Christ, and she kept asking WHY they hated him? And I knew – I often hate the priests.'

She knew what it came from:

'I know the reasons *so* well by now – jealousy of the privileges of the priests... resentment of the too low place assigned to me, among the pious illiterate crones, or unappreciated in a bad, bad choir.'

Like many women, Eularia was finding that there was no real place for her spirituality within the Church other than as a submissive female, and this was not what she was called to. It wasn't the priests who had a problem with it though, but Eularia herself. There was still a part of her that was attempting to fit in with the accepted role of women in society because when she didn't she felt outcast, but as she said herself, 'What's the good of my screaming for equality for the sexes, when people would just say I've failed with men?'

Once again she was ahead of her time: an unwilling pioneer when it came to the equality of women, without the confidence of the Germaine Greers of this world. The Catholic Church led her back to her relationship with God, but she would never find a real home there because, like her family, it was far too male centric.

A large proportion of Eularia's diaries are devoted to these inner struggles, alternately railing against herself or against some aspect of the world for dealing harshly with her; it would be pointless to keep referring to it because it never really changed, the themes remained the same. There were periods when it receded and her experience of God was much stronger, and times when she would fall back into it again. Like many creatives she was a mystic, a visionary and a troubled personality.

In September she painted the first version she made of the calling of James and John, *Weighing the Catch* (Matthew 4:21). Her official caption reads:

'Fleet Ferry is a wild and lonely place, and inland sea with hills all round, not a house in sight. The men from Chickerell and Langton Herring go out in beautiful black boats, and come rowing in after dark; the lorry from Weymouth comes backing down the landing-stage, and the mackerel are weighed and packed into boxes. I thought of the calling of the first disciples, and wondered if it was in a setting like this, quite unexpected, everybody hard at work.'

This expedition to Fleet is one of the few examples she gives of actively going out to paint in a specific place for one of her religious paintings. That she used real locations is certain, but often they were done from memory, or from sketches and notes she had made at an earlier time. She had visited Fleet the year before and had made preparatory notes on details, many of which end up in this painting:

'Then boats came in, and were pulled up the shore, oars and the curious punting pole with a fish-tail. The nets were in sacks already, the fish, silver one side, blue and green checks the other, were in baskets, boxes and buckets, curved and shining.... They lifted the fish from the boats, carried them to the weighing-machine, weighed them in boxes, and put the baskets and buckets and nets and oars in a shed, then hung about and mostly went home, the boats were roped to posts. The men wore, old jackets, navy trousers or jeans, gumboots, turned down (one sea-boots) caps (peaked) or pom-pom caps, or nothing and zipper (young) or shirt, or dark sweater, *not* navy, or sweater round neck. After dark (they sweetly moved me out of harm's way) the lorry came down and they loaded the boxes from the drop-side, and the bicycle, and all was quiet.'

Weighing the Catch (1964)

Despite her concerns over 'blowing her own trumpet' she began to write to various clerics about her work. To her surprise Sidney Mullarkey came up to visit and greatly enjoyed looking at all the paintings, and David Mahy particularly loved the *St. Joseph* icon.

At this time Eularia had a number of wooden Galt toys at Middle Road that she had ordered as Christmas presents for the grandchildren. She wrote to Rachael:

> 'I'm having a lovely time playing with the screw toy, but it's too difficult for Fr Pat, he prefers the Pop-up (*a kind of jack-in-the-box*) while cursing Heenan – (no not him, someone else – I get so *muddled* about bishops, don't you?) They'll miss Cuthbert's toys a lot.'

The image of priests playing with wooden toys whilst discussing Church politics is a riveting one, but it is clear from what Eularia says that Pat, at least, was longing for the changes to be accepted, and was finding the uncertainty trying.

Michael Gedge was not so keen on the *St. Joseph* icon, however:

> '... (*he*) said it wasn't an icon, icons were done by conventions and regulations and all the faces were the same – unlike portraits. He's right, they don't look like people, no naturalism like in Roman or Greek sculpture. Whereas my St J. is exactly like a person – an imaginative portrait imagined by me.'

Feeling rather disappointed in Michael as a Spiritual Director, she picked up a book about Christian yoga from the library and found that the deep breathing exercises helped her to calm down and she made herself some 'yogi trousers from blue jeans stuff.' The whole concept had a familiar appeal to her as she wrote:

> 'I was thinking about yoga, and how all my life I have pursued the same things, outdoor life and simplicity, poverty, Cardew, austerity and artisticness, with the religious angle cropping up now and then. The yogi book makes it seem as if these things went with religious dedication. I rather wonder, when I think of Spartans, and Hitler etc. But it's a way of thinking and living that's always called me.'

As a leaving present for Medecroft she did a painting of Christ's entry into Jerusalem called *Hosanna*. It is unlikely that she ever gave them this painting. Her diaries suggest that she later improved it and it became *She-Ass and her Colt* in 1969. She wrote to Rachael:

'I did them a painting of the children of the Hebrews chopping branches off trees and casting zippers and table-cloths and eiderdowns and coats and bath-towels all over the road, and a discreet donkey's head appearing through a Benidorm-type arch. They also play mouth-organs, and Cuthbert and Austin are in the middle of the road sitting on bath-mats waving branches of pussy-willow, all very Tweet.'

With her teaching jobs bringing in much more money Eularia finally began to envision a much needed remodelling of Middle Road, so she devised a plan one night while suffering from flu:

'Yes, roof off, top storey off, new cheap roofing over the whole area, including new patio, studio... then I'll live downstairs, sleep in living room in winter, studio in summer.'

While she never did have the top storey removed this plan gave birth to considerable change at Middle Road. It arose out of her concern about the current state of affairs being less than salubrious:

'If I can *hide* sordidly, I'll become sordid forever, so I must frill myself for public living. Simplify possessions, have washable surfaces and more room, have real beauty, simplicity, originality, convenience though *not* luxury or even too much comfort. But so good to spend on such a sensible thing, and how my prayer is answered, the plan has come from God, and the courage and the cash, too. No more leaking roof, spongy floors, sagging cardboard, up and down stairs, draughts and open windows, dark corners and dirty surfaces... my flu is better.'

Eularia had an enquiry from the Methodists about her paintings, which left her uncertain what to do. She now had photographs of the paintings and had been leaning towards giving some of them to her priest friends (she gave the *Palm Sunday* painting to Sidney Mullarkey). She was already intending to give *The Penitent Thief* to Pat and she had decided to give him *Storm Over the Lake*, which he loved so much, but as it was now part of the selection being considered by the Methodists she couldn't. She mentioned this to the Stokes' and Adrian sowed a germ of an idea when he told her that:

'...he'd have the paintings in a tin hut, on the road, all together.'

It would never materialise, but it began to crystallise for Eularia the idea of keeping the collection intact and all visible in one exhibition place.

But Eularia approached the end of the year still feeling caught between the different aspects of her life:

'What do I really want? The sense of God never goes, and I suppose that alone holds the promise of fulfilment, the fullness is there, beyond the muddle of different religions.'

With a touch of serendipity Robin Noel contacted Eularia to tell her that *The Last Supper* was now permanently installed in the new Chaplaincy at Southampton University so she went to see it:

'Inside the door, a room on the right, Catholic Chaplain, and on the wall facing the window was the 'Last Supper', hung in exactly the right light, with the sacking edges, so that it looked a bit like the miraculous Guadalupe cloak. The Christ blazed in gold paint and really looked far better than I ever saw it. It was quiet, I was alone in the room and I saw what I exist for. These conceptions painted.'

27

The Pops

Christmas 1964 was remarkably successful by Eularia's standards. Once again she made the long drive to Leeds and was joined at Rachael's by James. Now with three grandchildren she had her hands full but, as always, enjoyed us and managed not to fall out with Robert who, most importantly for Eularia, made a tape-recording of them singing and playing *The Prisoners' Mass*.

Now that she had a recording of *The Prisoners' Mass* (also referred to by her as the *Blue* or *Guitar Mass*) she began playing it to everyone she could think of who had a tape recorder. Pat Murphy-O'Connor, she already knew, loved it and Sidney Mullarkey seemed quite pleased with it too:

> 'Apparently guitar masses are not allowed, but "one can get permission from the bishop of the diocese" says Pat wickedly. So I'm to start a break-through.'

She then took it over to Fareham and, as Michael Gedge was out, played and sang it live to Cormac Murphy-O'Connor:

> 'He sang with gusto, and we talked, and Michael came in and I played it to him. He wants it for the convent, Cormac for the Youth Club.'

The 'Pops', as she termed her Mass and subsequent hymns, were absorbing much of her time and creativity, so there was little painting. She hawked it around to whoever would listen, including the Reverend Mother at the Zion convent opposite Cheppers and Robin Noel at the Catholic Chaplaincy at Southampton, where she gave them a live demonstration, which they all joined in. Eularia is possibly the first person to have composed a guitar congregational Mass and the first half of 1965 was all about publicising it with a confidence that she always failed to adopt when publicising her paintings. It was so completely new that no one had heard anything like it before.

It was Cormac who saw clearly where it would be most appreciated, and he would be proved right. He wrote to Eularia:

'As you say, I don't think it would do for nuns; not quite their style. What I will do if possible, is teach it during the vocations retreat at Highcliffe; the boys will love it, I'm sure.'

Cormac was right, it was the boys Youth Clubs, Eularia's guitar classes and young seminarians who really related to her Mass. Given that it was written for male prisoners this is perhaps not surprising, but it shows how well Eularia fulfilled the brief that Pat had given her.

She struggled to have it taken up by any serious publisher however, because: 'the future of Latin music is so uncertain.' In fact, rather like *The People's Mass*, Eularia's Mass bridged the gap between the old Latin and the new, more popular, vernacular and was ideal for its time, however fleeting. What it did, which until this point had been so rare, was directly appeal to the man on the street. It was written by a layperson, very experienced at keeping pace with musical trends especially when it came to boys, hence her understanding of just how popular the guitar would become. The fact that she was able to blend this with the old style Mass speaks to her skill. Who else could have a room full of teenage boys all playing the guitar and singing a Latin Mass at the tops of their voices? That young seminarians might pick this up is not surprising, but that prisoners and Winchester youths might is astounding, given how hard it can be to engage these areas of society even today.

The Rev Douglas Wollen, who was making the selection of works for the Methodist Collection of Modern Art (which was to become the second biggest collection of Christian art outside the Vatican) finally offered Eularia £25 each for *The Five-Thousand* and *Storm Over the Lake*. She began a copy of *The Five Thousand* for her own collection (in oils rather than the original pigment and size), but was determined that Pat should keep the *Storm Over the Lake*. These were the last of her religious works that she would ever agree to sell. Her concern was always that these paintings would end up on private walls hidden away from view. But she strongly agreed with the aims of the Methodist Art Collection and without them she would have disappeared from view as an artist entirely after her death.

Now that she was painting in oils she made oil copies of some of her other earlier works including *Candlemas* and *Lourdes: Communion of the Sick*, and she began *The Lepers* (Luke 17:12). Eularia was later to dismiss this painting as a kind of cartoon strip. It has a sickly yellow palate and the lepers are pictured in a pool of bandages as Christ heals them. The influence of teaching boys can be seen as it is cruder and less detailed than the work she had been doing. In her diary she wrote:

'Pat... looked at the Lepers and was rather doubtful! He may be right – is it *too* schoolboy?'

Iris Conlay, the Art Critic for the *Catholic Herald* who had written the article about her back in 1961 (now also working for a publishing firm called Geoffrey Bles), suggested that Eularia might like to illustrate stories from the Gospels, translated by J. B. Phillips and aimed at teenagers. Iris was prepared to put Eularia forward, but it would be a big job. It was also suggested that she contact Geoffrey Chapman about having her paintings reproduced in book form, which she did. To have a 'coffee table' style book of her paintings remained an enduring dream for Eularia. In the event none of these projects came to fruition and, after other later attempts at illustration, Eularia was quite pleased about not getting the Bles one, as she found book illustration too restricting for her style.

Once again Eularia fell out with Michael Gedge, who was not very well at the time, and answered one of her naval-gazing letters by telling her to stop analysing herself because it didn't do any good. Eularia disagreed quite strongly with this point of view and chose to interpret it, once again, as an indication that he couldn't be bothered with her anymore.

It was David Mahy who helped her to see this, not Michael. She said of David when he came round to hear the recordings she had of the *Grail Psalms*:

'I was listening and watching the peacefully contented young man – everything seems well with him, he expects little, doesn't mind things, not much ambition, nor self-love nor fancy ideas, modest, good-humoured, good-natured. And beyond it the real purity and goodness and dedicated holiness. Not emotional holiness, not self-regarding, certainly no fancy mysticism, but the real mature sort, which makes me see myself as I am – a tense frustrated self-absorbed woman, tiresome, often boastful, often eccentric and arty – all this gets shown up. Possibly I'm really grateful for the showing-up. There is much to be grateful for. I can't be like him, ever, that's a sorrow to be lived with.'

With Michael she simply fought back, but the same qualities that she perceived in David often irritated her just as easily. She judged them to be lacking in emotion and difficult to engage. She could be as rude about him as she was about any of her other friends, but David, for all his faults, was able to show her something of herself that she seemed unable to see in any other way.

Eularia was writing more 'Pops' during this time, spurred on by the success of *The Prisoners' Mass*. She wrote versions of *Hail, Holy Queen* (Salve Regina), *Anima Christi* and *Our Father* and then branched out into her own hymns, *No Other Tree*, *Bread From Heaven* and *Tell us Mary*, her enthusiasm only being slightly dented when she discovered Sidney Carter's *Judas and Mary*, which she considered to be infinitely superior.

During Lent 1965 Archbishop John Henry King died. It was the end of an era for Winchester as the new Bishop took up residence in Portsmouth and the administrative centre of the diocese moved back there, but it also meant the loss of a man who had been at the heart of the parish for as long as Eularia had been alive. At Sidney Mullarkey's request Eularia made five chalk and pastel sketches of John Henry in his coffin.

As soon as the schools broke up for Easter Eularia took off in the Mini van and ended up overlooking Swanage bay where she found inspiration for her next painting:

'...the huge green seas and sheer cliffs and rocks, the cave – exactly right for the resurrection.'

This was Tilly Wim's cave; a large sea cave near Swanage and it became the setting for *Cave, Shroud and Angels* (Luke 24:4 and John 20:12). The choice of the Resurrection as a subject, following hot on the heels as it did from the death of the Archbishop and with Easter fast approaching, is not surprising, but it also reflects Eularia's more up-beat mood.

Cave, Shroud and Angels is an interesting interpretation of the angelic. She said that as the angels were only described as wearing white garments she didn't bother with nightgowns. Instead she painted them as angelic versions of the boys she was so familiar with, in white jeans and jerseys. The angels are showing the two women (shown by their shadows falling across the floor) the empty shroud which she based on the shroud at

Turin, and the hand of Christ can be seen on a rock on the far left of the painting. After the rather sickly yellow of her *Lepers* painting, *Cave, Shroud and Angels* reflects the more golden glow of early morning sunlight and possesses a calm assurance. It is a deeply meditative picture, almost the opposite of the more cartoony *Lepers*.

Cave, Shroud and Angels (1965)

For the first time Eularia wrote in her diary about something that was beginning to go through the minds of other Catholics who had previously been keen on reform and, once again, it involved the choir and music. New people were attracted to the choir by the changes but it had lost many of its original members, most of them men. She said of one such practice in the run up to Easter:

'Big hymn sheets of hymns nobody knew, Mr T very depressed, all v. sad and I realised that the nuns were running the music in St. Peter's, and they may possibly be said to have earned it... yet when I think of Will, and all those men, and the lovely music there used to be. I wonder why I was so keen on the "people singing"?... Now I regret it all, the music there used to be.'

Nowhere were the Vatican II changes felt more keenly than in Church music. Some of the most beautiful choral music ever written was inspired by the old Latin Mass and the desire to praise God. The young composers who were beginning to set the English Mass found it a very hard act to follow, not least because the English words did not lend themselves to the music in the way that the Latin had. Eularia's son-in-law Robert was one of these composers, setting the new Mass several times, and yet he too came to regret the loss of the Latin and gradually reverted to interest in Plain Chant and the music of the Orthodox Church, which had remained unchanged.

At Spode Music Week Eularia and a band of Dominican lay brothers performed her Mass at the Members Concert at the end of the week amidst Mozart, Schubert and Telemann:

'The brothers came up from the back, primed with beer, carrying their guitars and the drums, we sat on the stairs, Peter Paul Nash fixed the music, we let fly. After the delicate professional music, it sounded so different, so emotional, so human and uninhibited.'

It was a great success and a photograph still exists of Eularia and the lay brothers gathered together as a band outside Spode House.

Most of the composers at Spode were very worthy and serious, but Eularia always had the common touch. She was able to reach across the divide that she herself felt so stuck behind (intellectual and high-minded) and scoop up those that she herself often discounted (the less well educated, the less refined, the youth, the masses) and provide them with music and art that they could relate to. It is no coincidence that one of her most appreciative audiences when it came to her art was young people. She was a pioneer at the very forefront of a wave that was sweeping through not just the Catholic Church but the whole of Western spirituality. From the 1970s onwards the young would increasingly look for new ways to express their faith and spirituality, through enquiry, through art, through music. That Eularia didn't live long enough to see it perhaps speaks to the part of her that still felt very stuck in the old. That her art has spent so long hidden away, and much of her music is now lost, speaks to her intellectual family's inability to cope with just how 'out there' she was, just how moved by God and the spiritual.

Eularia's band of lay-brothers (Spode House, Easter 1965)

She had the ability to span worlds, to keep one foot (even if rather unsteadily) in the world of spirit and the other in the world of matter and express this through her creativity. This is the act of a shamanic artist. It is not a word or a description that Eularia would have recognised and yet it is one that is recognised in the modern world of today. Those who are called to this path know how uncomfortable it can be, because it can be difficult to feel wholly part of either world, and it is a singular (and often lonely) path that can only be walked by the individual. The fact that Eularia often felt unsupported by those around her only demonstrates how hard it is for anyone not walking this path to understand it, or to know how to support it.

28

Going Solo

Eularia returned from Spode to what would be her first solo exhibition – at St Swithun's in a newly decorated studio. Consequently she began to claim back the various paintings she had lent out. She now had nearly 40 canvasses.

Eularia considered the exhibition to be a flop because the people she most wanted to see it were the priests, but in typical Eularia fashion she didn't produce a poster or any clear instructions about it, she just dropped vague hints that something was going on and they didn't show. As David Mahy told her after it was finished:

'...apparently he hadn't realised about it, none of them had mentioned it to each other at all or known what it was about – he would have loved to have seen them!'

The exhibition wasn't a flop. People had gone to see it, the girls from St Swithun's and their parents, and many friends of Eularia's, the Belfields, the Brookes' and Douglas Wollen (she finally agreed to sell him *Storm Over the Lake*) whose letter had prompted a very favourable review in the Hampshire Chronicle. But it was the support of her own clergy that she needed more than anything else, just as it had been the support of her father so many years before:

'Pat (*Murphy-O'Connor*) came along to congratulate me on the article. I told him I was going to burn all the Catholic ones because people didn't understand them and Catholic's weren't interested, he said, but *we* understand them... I only wanted a pat on the back from the Canon (*Sidney Mullarkey*).

He said, the fact is none of us are much good at that sort of thing... but it doesn't mean we don't appreciate you... He has a delightful way of stopping my self-pity at once, and cheering me up.'

Eularia came out of the experience wiser:

'The moral is, don't expect people to do as you imagine. They'll act according to certain laws, which include my own reluctance to publicise. Somewhere among all this the will of God works invisibly, unexpectedly, contrary to what one wants and expects, painfully for me. Yet it does work, and the main thing is to go on painting as long as the inspiration goes on.'

Hugh Farmer (Chaplain at Redrice) replied to a letter she had written, just after the exhibition:

'Now about the Art Exhibition. Artists are notoriously touchy, I know!! *But* you mustn't expect the clergy to fall over themselves with unqualified approval. And I might as well warn you that you're doomed to a series of disappointments if you expect it. So – much better to expect to be ploughing a lonely furrow.'

But Eularia really did feel that she needed her clergy's support and that she would continue to need it. Her close friendships with Angus Mason, Pat Murphy-O'Connor and subsequently with David Mahy had led her to depend upon the clergy in a way that, without those friendships, she might not have. They had become her family because her own brothers now felt so distant. The lonely furrow was to become her abiding theme and it appears in 1969 in a painting that is perhaps the closest to a self portrait that Eularia ever made (although it was not her intention that it should be). The lone ploughman in *Not Looking Back* is the perfect image of how Eularia experienced her life.

Self-publicising was always an issue for Eularia. Some of our most successful artists today are largely so because they are also brilliant self-publicists. This exhibition had been her first lesson in this, and she would become better at it, but it always produced a paradox for her. As a painter of religion, to be a self-publicist seemed to negate everything she was representing. This was why she wanted the clergy to back her. She wanted her friends and supporters to get behind her and do the publicising for her, thus removing the confusion of the paradox. But priests, by their nature, are unworldly, and where they are worldly they tend to focus on worthy causes, such as Pat's prisoners. That Eularia might need such backing probably never crossed their minds.

In Britain today Art is often used in Churches as a way of supporting the Christian message. In the mid 1960s there was still too much confusion around the changes being brought about by Vatican II and effort going into implementing them in parishes for there to much energy left over to give Art any real consideration. Once again Eularia was ahead of her time. But David Mahy did, in the late 1960s, use several of Eularia's paintings as a support for his sermons.

The clergy at St Peter's were not only dealing with all the new changes but profound changes of their own brought about by the death of Archbishop John Henry King. Pat Murphy-O'Connor was expecting to be moved in the near future, so was Raymond Lawrence, perhaps even Sidney Mullarkey. But it rankled with Eularia that Sidney seemed to be so much more prepared to support Mary Fairburn's work. Mary was given an exhibition at St Peter's School (the parish school) and it hurt.

Now that Douglas Wollen had bought *Storm Over the Lake* Eularia began to make a copy and it was the first time one of her copies was not almost exact: called *Storm on the Lake* the waves are far more turbulent and the emotions on the faces of the drowning disciples much more intense.

At the same time as making this copy she began *Picnic on the Shore* (John 21:9), which must surely rank among Eularia's finest works. It is set at Charmouth at sunrise and in it we see a fire with the fish on skewers, behind which the figure of Christ hands out bread. The wispy blue smoke that rises in front of him lends him the unworldliness of the risen Christ, and around him the apostles stare in love and amazement as they sit around the fire, drying themselves and relaxing in his company. Once again there is something slightly off balancing about the perspective. It is as if Christ and the apostles are not quite in the same picture as each other, which lends a sense of unworldliness to the person of Christ having risen from the dead. It is the solidity of the food that he is cooking and handing out that bridges the gap, a reference to the Sacrament of Communion.

Eularia was very pleased with *Picnic on the Shore* and it is now that she painted *Maundy Thursday* (John 13:4-5). This was the scene that Eularia had envisaged when watching the Archbishop in his finery dispensing the Maundy oils a couple of years before. It depicts Christ stripped to the waist with the towel wrapped around him, on his knees, head down over a pair of very grubby feet immersed in a chipped enamel bowl, with a large block of Lifebuoy soap in its newspaper wrapping next to him. There is no gentle symbolic washing of feet here. Christ is laying into them with a scrubbing brush because, as Eularia said:

> 'I have seen very clean and tidy paintings of this, with no hint of what feet get like with only dirt roads, and the livestock running about and not much washing. This is how people washed in older cottages before the war, it seemed nearer to the story and shows what Christ did; not a fancy job at all.'

David Mahy saw these new paintings first, '…and remarked that Christ was always the same in all the pictures, which I hadn't noticed.' The iconic quality of Eularia's Christ had developed without her even being aware of it, and yet it is clearly there.

Picnic on the Shore (1965)

St Swithun's was the first exhibition for which Eularia typed out captions for her paintings giving the Bible references, an idea that she had pinched from something David Mahy had done. Despite her issues with St Peter's she had come to appreciate her friendship with David, and he once again reminded her that he would love to have the *St Joseph* icon (currently at Redrice) for his own church when he had one. Eularia was not to forget this:

'I said that like all converts I was still trying to get into the Church! He said, long after you're dead, it will be in your biography that you were a Catholic!'

How right he was.

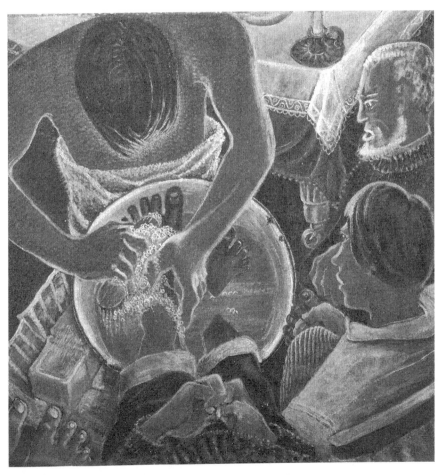

Maundy Thursday (1965)

29

Flames on Their Heads

On visiting Fareham (by appointment; she had learnt that lesson) Michael Gedge requested not one painting but two for a chapel that he had a particular link with, having helped create it in his Anglican days. Eularia refers to it as Horseshoe, but I have been unable to trace where this chapel actually was.

Unfortunately the manner in which Michael asked for them seems to have been particularly tactless which enraged Eularia, but in the end she gave in and painted *Flames on their Heads* (Acts 2:3). It is the only painting that Eularia made based on a story from the Acts of the Apostles and she made two versions of it, almost identical, at the same time. She set it in 'One of those dreary public rooms, looking worse than ever on a Sunday morning.'

It shows Christ hovering over the disciples releasing a dove shape. Their hair is red and standing on end and they have looks of elation and surprise on their faces. Some of them appear even to be levitating and the Holy Ghost is shown as curious white bird-like shapes flying above them, like paper airplanes. The yearning and thrilling experience of Eularia's own experiences of God can be glimpsed here, although she did say that all the disciples looked like Cyril. Part of the inspiration for it had come from a day spent at Brownwich Farm Gap:

'It was a wild place, oat fields with pale blue stalks, and the trees bent sideways by the wind – I thought how the H.G. (*Holy Ghost*) is a wind, and a holy person would be bent a bit out of shape by its breath.'

Flames on Their Heads (1965)

Eularia was becoming increasingly aware of the restriction on women in the Church and wondered whether '…they (*the clergy*) resent the lay-people's qualities of apostleship?' Whether this was true at the time is not for me to say, but it would fit with the history of Catholicism in England. For centuries the laity in the Catholic Church could not speak its language (Latin) and therefore relied on the clergy as intermediaries. In the Middle Ages only the very rich, or the clergy, learnt to read and write at all. In more recent times the Church had established education at a basic level in some of the poorest parts of the world but Latin (which was still the language of the Church itself) was only taught to those seeking to be priests, or to the privileged. In England this was different as, post

Reformation, they had been largely cut off from the mainstream Catholic Church. When Catholicism did begin to become 'legal' again it was picked up and popularised by intellectuals who understood Latin and who were educated at a university level, very much Eularia's kind of person. This was contrasted by an influx of Irish Catholics, most of whom had received a much more ordinary and less privileged education and were used to a more continental form of Catholicism, having never suffered the schism of the Reformation.

What Vatican II did was open out the ability of the laity to become more involved in the spiritual life of the Church everywhere, by using their own languages instead of Latin. Thus the clergy were now in a position of opening the doorway onto this new world (even if reluctantly in some cases) instead of simply mediating it. But English intellectuals like Eularia were already familiar with it and already had a tendency to feel side-lined because they were laity, even though they were as educated and as knowledgeable (more so in many cases) as their parish priests who did not need to have a university education.

David Mahy, to this day, credits Eularia with teaching him much of his Theology and through this example it is possible to understand some of Eularia's frustration with the local Catholic Church. She knew more Theology and Latin than most people there. Her spiritual experiences and her experiences of prayer were beyond anything that most of the laity, or even the priests, experienced. It could be said that she was an adept seeking a master among servants. The problem lay, not in the fact that the local Catholics and clergy could not accommodate her, but in that she refused to accept this about herself, insisting instead that she should be recognised by others and included as part of a flock that still did not know how to include her, as much as they might want to. Humility was not a quality that she ever mastered.

In some ways Eularia was the Tracey Emin of her day: she was colourful, outrageous, unconventional, outspoken and eccentric. Had she had more self-confidence, a good publicist (or been good at it herself) and lived longer, she would probably have rocketed to fame on her character alone.

She copied *Chairs to Mend* in order to give the original to Pat Murphy-O'Connor for the St Dismas Society, but with a heavy heart. She was caught in a dilemma. In her heart she didn't want to receive anything for the paintings but the more worldly part of her felt the lack of appreciation, and doubted that, whilst Pat would appreciate her painting, anyone else would, or that it would be hung in a way that did it justice. She was right. Pat, wonderful as he was, was no interior decorator, and didn't understand about good lighting and visibility. *The Penitent Thief* had been hung in a very dark room at the hostel and she feared that the same thing would happen to *Chairs to Mend*.

Her fears were not without justification, as the history of the paintings show since her death. Poor storage and lack of care has meant that many of them have deteriorated and need restoration. It has also meant that few have seen them.

The transformation of Middle Road began, giving it a new roof and the conservatory, which would become her bedroom, although it caused major disruptions for her right through the winter of 1965 and well into 1966. The builders arrived, the scaffolding went up and Eularia found prayer and contemplation all but impossible, never mind painting. She lent most of her paintings out to friends, largely as a way of keeping them out of the 'builders-yard'.

The building work gave Eularia more time to focus on the choir (never a good move) and once again there were rows. The choir at this point was something of a tinderbox anyway. The changes had hit hard and it appeared to be suffering an identity crisis which no one really knew how to sort out. When everyone was supposed to be singing the Mass why would you even need a choir? And because they were no longer set apart in the organ loft they were consigned to the back of the congregation. Members had stopped coming to practices and poor old Will Thomas, the organist, was caught in the middle of it all.

Things were very different in Fareham and Cormac informed Eularia that his Youth Club were going to perform *No Other Tree* at their concert. Eularia's music was popular elsewhere, but she was such a bad self-publicist that very few people realised that she was the composer. She used to copy her music out by hand but never wrote her name on it, which is why most of it was mistakenly thrown away. No one realised she had written it. It was the same with her paintings. She never signed a single one.

The vivid image of the replacement of her kitchen roof was to provide inspiration for one of her 1966 works, *Hole in the Roof* (Mark 2:4-5). Eularia said of this painting:

'The builders were taking off my rusty kitchen roof, and I looked up and saw them looking down through the gap, and this is the result. The palsied man needed a lot of help and ingenuity from his friends and I also put in praying people – monks and nuns pray for us all. I was also thinking of Confession, which is why Christ, as he forgives the man's sins, makes the gesture of a priest giving absolution in confession, and why the invalid has as much face as you can see of your own face.'

Again the perspective is unusual as we look down the stretcher from the eyes of the man lying on it and up towards the Christ and the others in

Hole in the Roof (1966)

the room, and ultimately to those 'builders' on the tin roof lowering the stretcher down. And yet the focus of the painting is very much around the body on the stretcher and the action of Christ. In her own notes Eularia said:

'The Ropes (*her nickname for it*) has a funny twist – I didn't notice that in the gospel, the house was full of Scribes and Pharisees. I put, instead, very catholic Catholics, with habits and medals etc. I just didn't realise, or was I expressing my subconscious resentment at the black wall of sisters (*nuns at St Peter's*) in the Church? There is perhaps something in it – I don't know.'

Once the roof was finished Eularia was able to move into the old attic above the stable that had been James' room and which now had a skylight in it, so it became her living space and studio while the builders knocked the rest of the house about. She loved this new space and began *Coming up from the Water* (Colossians 2:12), which is the only painting she ever referenced from the Epistles of St Paul. Essentially this is a painting about Baptism and Eularia wrote of it:

'I used to be very frightened of canal bridge-holes when I was a child; I thought they were bottomless. So I used this as a symbol of dark unfathomable mystery. Baptism is so mysterious, so much more than white-iced cake, a child introduced to the community. It is called a death to pagan life, a rising up into Christ's life...what does it mean? We shall know when fewer and fewer babies are christened, I suppose; or when christening becomes a cosy social function only, no exorcism, nothing serious. The people on the towpath are at the Easter Vigil, which is all about baptism and light-after-darkness and of course the resurrection after the dark sepulchre. It all fits.'

Christ stands waist deep in murky water just in front of a canal bridge and the dark shadow it casts, with a queue of people waiting for baptism. Under the bridge, in the darkness on the opposite bank, are the people at the Easter Vigil holding their lighted candles. On a simple level Eularia's feeling of having a light studio to paint in comes through here, but on a deeper level are her questions about what the paintings are for? There is a sense of holding a light in the darkness. Once again we are the observer, looking on from the opposite bank: the recurring theme of the outsider looking on at something she does not feel truly a part of. Once again Christ stands between the Catholic activity and us. Those attending the Easter Vigil service seem to be barely aware of him. Those emerging from the darkness of the bridge hole are moving towards Christ and away from the service.

What is interesting about this painting is that Christ is not part of the Easter Vigil service, indeed those coming to be baptised from the darkness of the bridge hole are leaving the service to come to him. But there was no intention on her part to suggest a move away from the Church at this time. It is more likely that, as the observer, she is reflecting her inability to fit in with the flock and the clergy. Whilst Eularia undoubtedly had spiritual experiences during her Church worship, her most powerful ones were when she was alone, at home, in contemplation or while painting. There is a sense that the act of painting, the very nature of the art, kept her separate from the community that she wanted to be part of and a perceived lack of response on the part of those she shared it with seemed to confirm this for her:

'I pour them out and somehow nothing comes. It makes one waver a bit in one's faith, what's it all *for*? However, time will show.'

Eularia began another painting at around this time, although she gives it almost no mention and never assigned a Gospel reference to it. *I Say Unto You* is a generic illustration of Christ preaching. Her own description states:

'The disciples are being taught, and the bread is ready for supper afterwards. The other people are half listening; people who take their dogs or families out to quiet wild places for a nice quiet ramble often have a look about them which suggests the kingdom of God. I suppose it's the un-best clothes and courage about weather and not needing lush entertainment and giving the dogs what they really enjoy.'

It was set in the New Forest and is evocative of her many outings there, especially in the period when the builders took over Middle Road and she did her best to escape to somewhere peaceful.

Eularia had begun to suspect that her mission lay outside the Church in what she called 'the region of doubts and cynicism.'

'I am interested in the way the soul is supported, the sheer strength of the invisible master. No other joy, no other interest, no other world. It isn't unpleasant, one knows it's all right. I do no good works and the peace is entirely a gift – yet I know I am made into a sort of entrance channel of God's love in the ordinary world. I can't imagine God loving me – but I can imagine Him working through me, as I never really knew what I wanted, never had any sort of direction – a vague plastic person.'

Her doubts about the purpose of her paintings were reinforced by her son James who, being young and at the beginning of his career, tended to see success in terms of money and renown, which he believed meant selling the paintings: 'but it's not what I want.' was consistently what Eularia's wrote in response to this, even when she felt like giving in. In her heart she did not want to sell.

30

The Passing of the Curia

In January 1966 Eularia was recovering from another bout of flu when she heard the news that Pat Murphy-O'Connor had finally been given his own parish at St Michael and All Angels, Leigh Park in Portsmouth and was leaving:

'Pat came in, out of the sun, very tall and cheerful, off to live among the scum from the slums of Portsmouth. I loved him so much, and said so with the happiest spontaneity, not a cloud in it, not a scratch, just love. As he went he thanked me for all I'd done for him. I laughed about that, and said he'd put up with so much – and I'd just taught him his chords. He said no, he wasn't thinking of that, and he was driving down to hear Confessions and was in the car, and I was holding on to the window of the car so as not to let him go. And that was the real heart, not the upper tides of nerves and tumult; the real genuine feeling I have for him, not even wanting it to make any demands on him, not wanting him to be any different from what he is. I shan't see him anymore, possibly – nine years in and out, smoking, joking, being himself. I told him about the memories of the days when I got the altar things for him, and I became almost like a church hassock, and he laughed... Well, that's nine years ago when he first came, and I pressed his fingers over D7, the shy young priest, always asking if he could smoke? I see now that there is nobody to take his place, nobody like him, and I so often let my hateful prejudices come between me and appreciating him. Yet, in spite of everything, he thinks I have done things for him... that's a wonderful thing to hear though, as C.S.L (*Lewis*) would say, holy people – you *think* you're being kind to them, when they're being kind to you. Pat thinks I've done things for him, but really he's just put up with me.'

With Pat leaving, Eularia's links with St Peter's began to shift and loosen, imperceptibly at first, but Pat was really the only person there who understood Eularia and her vulnerability as an artist, even if he didn't always manage to be the active support that she wanted. She would never have another friend like Pat. With John Stallard having faded into the background, Pat had been the one consistent person who she could rely on to listen to her grumbles and concerns and who invariably brought her out of her gloom. While her friendship with David Mahy continued it had always been on a different footing than her friendship with Pat, the proxy brother. The days of the Middle Road Curia were passing.

Around Easter Eularia began her next painting, *Miracle at Gadara* (Mark 5:15 and Luke 8:27). It was an interesting subject to choose, possibly a swipe at the 'swine' critics hanging onto the old ways of doing things in the Church and the poor soul who had been sent mad by it all, possessed by it, being held gently by Christ and the disciples. In contrast to the previous paintings it is bright and sunny, giving a strong contrast to the black cloud of red-eyed devils on the right of the picture, and it depicts the moment (despite the second Bible reference that she gives) when the trauma is over. The devils have been expelled and the swine are about to run headlong over their cliff:

'It is very difficult about the herd of swine – everyone feels a bit RSPCA about it. It is also a very mysterious business when one comes to think about what the incident implies, about unclean spirits, and how He was the only person who knew just what was going on. I have suggested without any authority, that the swine were eating corpses out of the tombs – a rather nasty idea which would explain why they did as refuse bins for the devils. And here again is the pattern of people helping – somebody must have helped with putting on his clothes, even finding clothes for him, I mean the Lunatic Boy. I was also thinking about people coming out of mental hospitals, feeling rather unsure and frightened. The place is by Durdle Dore, Lulworth in Dorset where there is a sheer drop and a steep run down.'

She found that she painted much more 'restfully' when the weather was bad. Eularia never coped very well with hot weather and her painting output often dropped in the summer months, partly because she became much more absorbed in her garden, but also because she found it hard to work in the heat.

Once the sun came though, just as her father had before her, she found a whole new joy in concrete and hard landscaping. Initially she used what the builders had left behind. 12 Middle Road, being an old muse cottage and stable, fronted straight onto the street but at the rear it had a long, narrow garden, which dropped down the hill at the bottom of which was the old Bramley apple tree. By 1966 it had been allowed to run wild and the builders hadn't helped, but with the discovery of cement, sea glass and shells, local flint and the eventual completion of the 'greenhouse' on the back of the parlour, she found a renewed enthusiasm for the garden and gradually completely landscaped it with an eccentricity that only Eularia could muster.

She was very pleased that the house was finally finished. The back wall of what had been the old stable (the parlour) had been removed and a conservatory added. From now on this was where Eularia slept and did a great deal of her painting. Even in the depths of winter she would sleep in her greenhouse (she refused to call it a conservatory), often with the doors open. She loved watching the wildlife around her and seeing the birds hopping along the grass roof as she lay in bed. Much to her joy she had even acquired a frog in her sink-pond, to go with the newts and snails, whom she christened Erk.

Before the summer heat arrived she began two new paintings, *Walking on Water* (Matthew 14:25) and *Village at Sunset* (Mark 1:32:).

Walking on Water once again uses a perspective from above so we only see the lower half of a very luminous Jesus walking towards the boat in the foreground full of amazed apostles above whom seagulls fly – reminiscent of the mysterious flying shapes of the Holy Ghost in *Flames on their Heads*. Eularia's caption of this painting says:

'Anybody who thinks Christ was just a good man, a healer and a great moral teacher, should try walking on the water in a storm, in the middle of the night, and then come home and preach materialism… The disciples were terrified and thought he was a ghost, but St. Peter is about to jump overboard. Meanwhile the passengers are complaining about the rumpus. Possibly it is a great limitation to be unconcerned and contemptuous about the supernatural, even if it looks like courage.'

Village at Sunset is set in a Cotswold village like Great Rissington and shows the sick arriving in the last of the daylight. It is an unusual shape for Eularia, being small and slim in width. Most of her paintings were much better proportioned. Eularia's caption for this painting says:

Walking on Water (1966)

'They brought their sick and crippled friends. It must have taken a lot of helpers and a lot of muscles; it takes a lot of people to bring about the turning-point, whether it's illness or religion. All forms of conveyance, including doctors, nurses, casual acquaintances, odd experiences. The village is a Cotswold one, but there is also the pattern of communicants.'

Both these paintings return to her dark palette of reds, greens and browns. Compared to the light and colourful *Miracle at Gadara* they are quite sombre. *Village at Sunset* was rarely shown and it isn't Eularia at her best.

At West Downs a new young teacher, called Timothy Russ, arrived for a term. He was a devout Catholic with ambitions towards the priesthood and he and Eularia clicked straight away. Russ became a regular attendee at St Peter's:

> 'I chatted with Timothy in the corner... Then I suddenly explained: "I get so bored with anything unless it's about God". And the lad nearly dropped his glass, and said "*SO DO I.*"'

This new friendship came at a time when, due to the on-going choir troubles, St Peter's was feeling very unattractive to Eularia, but it gave her an incentive to go. It was for Tim Russ's birthday that Eularia painted the last of her private (gift) works, referred to by her as the *One True Vine*. Quite by chance a friend of mine was a parishioner of Tim's once he became a priest and attended his memorial service in 2013. She showed me the card that had been printed for it because she recognised the name of the artist whose illustration they used on the front. It was Eularia's *One True Vine*.

It was around this time that Eularia heard a sermon by a visiting priest at St Peter's on the Hole in the Roof, which was what prompted her to paint it. Tim Russ was very keen on Eularia's paintings and thought them 'truly apostolic'. Eularia, of course, always responded well to having a positive supportive male around and this showed in the quality of *Hole in the Roof* compared with *Village at Sunset*. In it we gain a sense, perhaps, of Eularia's own inner paralysis dissolving. She noted while she was painting it that '...they (*the other figures*) all started to pray with Christ.' It wasn't the first time that Eularia would say that her paintings took on a life of their own as she was painting them, the people themselves deciding how and where they wanted to be.

Tim Russ became a substitute for James for a while (being of a similar age). Eularia saw very little of James while he was in Norfolk. It was a long and difficult journey and James was a young man with a career to build and a woman to pursue so perhaps can be forgiven for not being over keen on visiting or calling 'Mum'. Nevertheless Eularia missed him.

With Tim Russ's friendship Eularia's vision of what her paintings were about began to become clearer to her:

> 'The paintings...are of Sacraments, large and clear... The paintings are of Christ's hands, and His gifts, and His sufferings and His Humiliations.'

She began what she described at the time as 'the most difficult pic. of all.' And doubted that she could pull it off. Indeed it is questionable whether she did. *Water from the Rock* (John 4:15) depicts the incident where Jesus

Water From the Rock (1966)

meets the Samaritan woman at the well and Jesus tells her that he will give her living water, and thus the Samaritan woman sees Christ.

Jesus talks with high symbolism throughout this passage. It is one of the more complex theological passages in the Gospels and if Eularia was to even attempt to portray what Jesus is actually conveying through painting, then it is impossible to do it as a straight illustration. None of the important subtext comes across in simply seeing Jesus talking to a Samaritan woman by the well.

It was on a day out that Eularia found the solution for it:

> 'I drove to the canal bridge, walked along, and found the waterfall, the whole Itchen canal pouring out of one small opening into the decayed lock. It was so hot, I got in – the waterfall was in the dark of the trees, slightly frightening because of my early terror of locks – and the force of the water tremendous. I sat under it on a shifting bed of bricks and ironwork, remaining stationary by inertia. The water consisted of white cold sparkling threads. I suddenly saw how to do the Well picture.'

Eularia's version shows Jesus as the eternal spring, the rock from which the water gushes into the well itself. To the left the (rather brassy) astonished Samaritan woman looks on and beside her is the tip of a bloody spear, a foreshadowing of the spear that pierced Jesus' side at his crucifixion – the inference perhaps being that this is what pierced the rock and allowed the water to flow.

Eularia's caption states:

> 'The Samaritan woman at the well, at the moment of her conversion, suddenly seeing what it is all about, the Rock that is Christ, the rock which Moses struck and water gushed out of the cleft; the spear which will strike Christ on the cross, and the promise of living water with no more thirst. The deer walking round the rock is thirsting for the running water-brooks in the psalm.'

It is the first of Eularia's Gospel paintings that relies heavily on symbolism and it has always received mixed reactions. Although the palette is light and colourful, the execution lacks subtlety. She painted the gushing water with Magicote Emulsion.

31

Er-Prayer

Tim Russ was responsible for bringing out in Eularia another strand that she had wanted to express: prayer and her experience of it:

'Most of all I enjoyed his quick understanding of my wild conversation and muddled logic, and the absence of barriers of language and nuance... and each time he referred to "Er-prayer".'

This led Eularia to write a long article (she referred to it as a sermon) entitled ''Er-prayer' – a case for encouraging, understanding and helping passive prayer in laity'. She began the article by saying:

"Er-prayer' is my word for passive prayer, the sort that is operated by God, not by us. It is very difficult to write or talk about; that is why I call it 'er-prayer' in the embarrassed English manner.'

Water from the Rock is a painting that comes close to illustrating Eularia's own experience of God, and her article on 'Er-prayer' the culmination of what she had drawn from it. In it she highlighted with pinpoint accuracy an issue that is still current today. She lists a number of 'snags' to prayer:

'Snag one is that a lot of holy people and saints have been given it (er-prayer) and written books about it, so people assume – quite against logic – that anybody who has this gift must be either vaguely holy or else pretending to be; whereas I've been told (much to my relief) that lots of frightful people – actually living in the world – are given this passive prayer regardless of their unholiness. So no need to be quite as cagey as we are.

'Snag two is the common idea that this sort of gift is a sign of God's special love. This would be a big worry if true, because none of us could really believe ourselves specially loved; it's difficult to believe that he manages to love us at all, knowing what we are like. I was very worried and puzzled about this until I came to the conclusion that in some cases er-prayer is given for a useful purpose, to supply a need, to make some job possible. I know for instance how important it is for a painter of religion to have this extra certainty and force which er-prayer gives; and perhaps there are other jobs which lay-people do, needing this strong conviction. If they ask for er-prayer and He gives it to them, this must be all to the good, especially in these days when witness is badly needed. But who is to encourage and foster this growth when the seed is sown? The man who wrote to the C. Herald recently asking for advice about it was fobbed off with silly patronising jokes till some kind spinster sent in a list of useful books. But what then? Books are too expensive to buy usually, you can get some from the Public Library, but who is going to have the face to keep on borrowing those books with such appallingly holy titles? And if there is a milling family around at home, it must be difficult to read books on prayer and the Interior Life at all. Much less embarrassing to read pornography in these days. Retreats are tricky except for certain types, and more and more retreat-givers are concentrating on aspects far removed from er-prayer. Who is to help?

'Priests? It isn't easy to find a priest who knows about er-prayer. One hears that seminary students don't often study the subject much; perhaps they haven't the time. Priests give one the important things, sacraments, the inspiring example of dedicated life, their increasing knowledge of one's sins and shortcomings through Confession, preaching, teaching etc. But just occasionally, in times of darkness and doubt and depression, I have wondered how many people, less toughened by life than me, might get completely discouraged and give up because the priest in the box does not understand what is going on and cannot help with a bit of constructive advice or even simple encouragement. Each failure must mean the loss of a strongly convinced witness to the Faith, for the lay person has really no backing, no holy framework to support him, no religious community or rule; he is at the mercy of moods and circumstances, and subject to continual temptation against even practicing his religion more than the minimum. Yet his witness stands right out in the danger-zone where it is so badly needed. If er-prayer can make his witness really powerful, shouldn't the priest perhaps help him a bit, by knowing roughly the course which er-prayer takes, so that he can advise?'

She did her best to get clergy to read this (she sent it to the Bishop) which shows just how much she was prepared to use that snobbish elitism to cut through the tendency towards embarrassment that still prevails over religious belief, or spiritual matters. Today thousands of people have moved away from Christianity because it does not seem to answer the need for support at the very level Eularia refers to. Prayer is the active relationship and conversation with God and it is always personal. Eularia was speaking from experience but when she sent this 'sermon' to Derek Worlock, the new Bishop of Portsmouth, she felt that he missed her point. She continued with a second part, 'Er-Prayer, a Digest for Busy and Overworked Parish Clergy':

'The first turning to God is, I suppose, the same in all cases; - whether it is a religious vocation, or a reforming of a sinful life, or just the vague idea that He is calling one in some unknown direction. Life begins to narrow down; obstacles and distractions are dealt with, many things, interests and activities for instance, are gradually thrown out if irrelevant, thought becomes concentrated, reading exclusive in range, religious practice becomes somehow obsessive and all-important, though one can't think why. I believe these conversion patterns are apt to follow certain crises such as bereavement, serious illness or danger, adolescence, advancing age suddenly noticed, conversion to the Church, career failure, marriage failure, or some powerful person encountered etc. This shedding–off of superfluous bits of one's life goes along with self-knowledge and repentance and forms the "purgative way", and eventually the time of Beginners' Consolation begins. This can be very intense and physical, it can contain elements such as intoxication, electric shock, and semi honeymoon sensations; one is perfectly aware that all this is being done by some Person who is very strongly present and out to wean one away from any other desires. One does in fact lose the taste for anything else (night of the senses) and begins to pursue God quite selfishly.

'Then the big Let-Down begins, sometimes years of it, often only a short stretch or patches. The happiness and sunshine goes, all physical feelings stop; (one wonders dismally if they were only the projection of one's emotional needs?) – faith goes dark and a general malaise sets in. Probably it's partly sheer reaction after the strong responses of the nervous system to the divine action. Things all go wrong, temptations against faith crop up continually, quarrels with the Church, difficulties with fellow-Catholics, and in addition a sort of "bad luck" hangs over life; things just tend to go wrong, such as health, work, money, personal relationships. Religion gets utterly distasteful, prayer goes dead, God has disappeared. But the odd thing is that nothing else will do instead; it seems vaguely all right although things go all wrong. The obsession with God can be somehow felt underneath it all, and the books say He is very close to one at this stage, testing to see if one can keep going under defeating circumstances. Most people must feel a longing to pull out of the whole thing. For instance, one snag is that during the "honeymoon phase" one needed solitariness and silence, and it's very tempting during the dark time, to go back to any sort of activity or interest to deaden the pain of being deserted by God.

'I think priests could be very helpful at this stage; one does tend to confide in them and turn to them as the next thing to God. If they were to watch out for those people who seem to be attracted to daily Communion without any obvious reason (such as belonging to a priest-fringe family, or holding some office in the parish), then they would know who might be expected to run into those rough seas and they could help and explain. It would be very cheering and strengthening to learn in Confession that God sends the darkness on purpose, to see if you can hold out. During this time, non-lay people are told to Meditate. Lay-people usually aren't, they just do it at random so their course is different. Meditation is supposed to produce resolutions and "affections", but the darkness stops this, so lay-people at least are let off the frustration of dry meditation, they just get *nothing* – except sad memories of what has gone. The accepted thing next on the list is the Prayer of Forced Acts, which at the time is a rather horrible affair. You tell God that you love Him, which feels false and contrary to your true self. Something nags "Hypocrite – telling lies – you don't mean it" etc. Yet the fact that one sticks at it, and forces out Forced Acts is very curious, and strong evidence that He means business – how else could one do it? Forced Acts are astonishing, looking back.

'At this time the Illuminative Way develops, but in ordinary people this simply means that with our attention held firmly by God, everything becomes a source of light to our minds; not only liturgy and reading but all the contacts and happenings of everyday life. We talk and think automatically about religion, our minds continually relate everything to the supernatural. Then the prayer of Forced Acts softens up a bit, and Affective Acts start on their own; the sort of wordless talking becomes a prayer of feeling – (no longer physical though) with odd words here and there. The funny thing is that when word and prayer becomes a matter of the heart, one's heart really does swell up, like a balloon, I suppose owing to a psycho-somatic relationship like car-sickness or concert nerves. A sort of electric toaster switches itself on full of light and heat, and things seem unreal and far away, and after a time this state, having one's attention held, becomes semi-permanent like a compass needle pointing north. You just notice, often as a surprise, that you are praying, even while driving in the Leicester Inner Ring Road for example... or waking up at night, or in Sainsbury's.

'It would be difficult for an amateur to sort out when the Prayer of Quiet begins, but some of the symptoms are all too obvious. Even tough monks get a lot of minor illness; laypeople may get careless and unambitious at work, housework may be neglected, no keeping up with the Joneses, and there is a disastrous insulation from social demands or even conventions too. God will dominate the subconscious and sometimes envelope the conscious as well; something seems to struggle like a chicken hatching, then it gets out into a sort of sea of emotion which makes human romance seem like a bad film... by the way, an awkward hunger to do things for the Church may at this stage cause embarrassment to the parish organisations; perhaps priests should know this and direct it tactfully! A more useful result is perhaps the certainty and conviction about religious truths, and much more courage in expressing them. Of course the books have whole chapters on stages beyond the Prayer of Quiet, which is only the beginning of passive prayer, but the snag is that you can't advance any further without getting perfect first. So this is where I must end my Digest.'

This 'sermon' is the clearest and most lucid piece of writing that exists by Eularia about her personal spiritual journey up to 1966. For the first time she hints at what it was she was hoping to find in the way of support from the clergy, coupled with her understanding that most clergy were not equipped to provide it.

But it also speaks to a greater evolution of spirit that was emerging in the late 1960s through an increasing interest in other forms of mysticism. The Christian Church was not, and, for the most part, is still not (in the author's opinion) addressing what Eularia so clearly described – the personal spiritual experience as felt by laymen. Here Eularia gives her own experience within the context of what she had learnt in an attempt to find answers. It is a Catholic framework and what she described may be familiar to many even if the context is not. Although it might be argued that today the Church is doing what it can to address this issue, it inevitably comes up against the paradox of balancing individual calling against a set of rules laid down by an organisation, which by its very nature is not individual.

Inevitably there is a clash, a line of tension, which creates conflict between any religion that lays laws for how spirituality should be followed and how the laity should behave, as opposed to the inner experience, the personal experience of God and how we feel called to express it. Sadly, organised religion often lacks the flexibility to cope with the personal experience and so those who feel a strong call are left no choice but to it seek elsewhere, some with success, some not.

The fact that her words fell on relatively stony ground (because the clergy she spoke to did not understand it, or had no personal experience to match hers) demonstrates why our organised religions have becomes so undermined, either by those leaving them or those turning to the extremes of fundamentalism. As human beings we are naturally spiritual as well as rational. If that spirituality is not addressed at the fundamental personal level then those experiencing it will seek an outlet, a framework in which they can express it – whether fundamentalist or New Age, it will stand outside the mainstream, because the mainstream has failed it.

Eularia felt increasingly strongly about this. But like so many she did not know where to go with it. She feared an increasingly secular society because she understood at a fundamental level how impoverished it would leave us, and how unable we would be to meet the challenges that the world presents us with. This, more than anything, was why she clung to her Catholic faith. She felt that without it there would be nothing.

32

Stations of the Cross

Eularia finally gave up guitar teaching after twelve years, leaving her with only the Art at West Downs. If she could have afforded to give that up and paint full time she would have and, for a while anyway, she believed she had found a way to achieve this, thanks to Michael Gedge.

He offered her the possibility of a commission to do a set of Stations of the Cross for the new church of St Margaret Mary at Park Gate, Southampton. Fareham, a large parish, had more than one church in its care and Michael was in charge of this one although Fr Joe Rea remained the overall parish priest, essentially his immediate boss.

Eularia was very excited by this and began to see herself as being a properly commissioned Church artist, providing Stations and other works. This would have been a valuable source of income for her, had it come off, allowing her more flexibility to continue her other religious painting without the need to teach.

The Catholic Church has been more responsible than any other for bringing about the extraordinary richness of Sacred Art that we have in the Western world. The first authoritative document issued from the Second Vatican Council in 1963 was 'The Constitution on the Liturgy' and Chapter 7 was entitled 'Sacred Art and Furnishing':

'The art of our own days, coming from every race and region, shall also be given free scope in the Church, provided that it adorns the sacred buildings and holy rites with due honour and reverence.'

After the Council there was an upsurge in the building of new Catholic

Churches and a need in the old ones to re-organise their layout to accommodate the new direction to say Mass facing the people. The decorating of Churches, which included sacred images and the Stations of the Cross (the fourteen illustrations of Christ's passion hung around the nave in order that they can be followed and meditated upon and which are a feature of all Catholic Churches) was and still is given plenty of scope by the bishops and is left for the local parish to choose or commission in line with their tastes, provided it conforms to the Vatican II guidelines. As a new church, Park Gate was starting from scratch, but while Michael was keen to have Eularia's work, she also had to convince Joe Rea and the architect that it was appropriate for the building. She was one of only a number of possible artists under consideration.

She duly went to see the new church at Park Gate and was immediately concerned. 'My heart sank when I thought of my art on those austere columns! It would look all wrong.'

Despite this intuition she painted five of the fourteen Stations as samples, 18 inch square, based on the *Way of the Cross* meditations by St Alphonso Maria de' Liguori, which were, and still are, the ones most commonly used by the Catholic Church for Lenten Devotions. These were *Jesus is Condemned to Death*, *Veronica Wipes Jesus' Face*, *Jesus Falls for the Second Time*, *Jesus' Clothes are Taken Away* and *Jesus is Nailed to the Cross*.

Most Stations of the Cross, even today, are quite sedate affairs, usually painted plaques, or sculptured reliefs, sometimes a simple cross and a number: tending towards the emotionless and serene. What they are not is graphic. The Passion of Christ was a tortuous and bloody event (crucifixion was not known for being humane) and most artists choose to play down that side of it. Given that the Stations are used for meditation purposes and are prominently placed around the main body of the church, one can perhaps see their reasoning. But Eularia found it impossible not to express the suffering and bloody aspects of what Christ went through, which makes her Stations, perhaps uniquely so, very vivid, graphic, gory and quite alarming. Her ability to paint emotion shows clearly in the tortured face of Christ and those around him. Initially she wrote of them as she contemplated the job:

'Pain, blood, sacrifice when the blood "bedewed the ground" in Station XII (*Jesus Dies on the Cross*). Blood fertilising, as in the propitiatory sacrifices, the libations, making the ground fertile and making up for sins. The cries of the animals having their throats cut. And interwoven with the theme of blood, fertility and sacrifice, is the lunar withdrawal into solitude, when the heart is at its most tender.'

But as she immersed herself in them and began the work she later wrote:
'As for the stations, I'm full of doubts – the actual paint isn't good, some of it is dragged on, it has got dry in between work. But the designs are good. The snag is, I suppose, that I don't really like Stations - I like expressing Christ doing wonderful, powerful things, healing and making everything all right. I hate all this concentration on his degradation, it is as if I were in it too, which I am, and I hate having to think of it.'

Jesus' Clothes are Taken Away: Station 10 (1966, 18-inch version)

In the end she never enjoyed painting the Stations. She undertook them because she saw it as a way of breaking into Church Art and being paid, but she found the work repetitive and depressing compared with her other painting. Not surprisingly, Joe Rea did not take to Eularia's version of the Stations and she later regretted using the Liguori meditation's as her source rather than simply doing a set of 'ordinary' ones. They are by no means her best work and they were undoubtedly far too rough and raw emotionally for priests and parishioners who had been used to the gentle and quiet vision of Victorian Art. The architect did not like them either and instead chose some suitably demure reliefs made of bronze. Joe Rea supported this and so the 18-inch Stations were never completed beyond the five that she had already done.

While she was painting the Stations Eularia entered a deep phase of Er-prayer:

'Yesterday, clearing out the garage, their seemed to be a sort of Cup Final crowd inside me, shouting, yelling after God, the urgency of it was enough to blot out all thought, and it was continual. As if the whole powers of the soul were rising up, concentrating on the Sacred Heart and the Stations, this went on and on.

'I went down to buy my fish, and came home in the dark and ate them, and went to bed in the rain, and the powers of my soul reared up almost painfully, and then the presence of God began – like that first time in 1961, the electrocutions, one after the other, each lasting a long time and causing joy, dizziness, faintness, longing, and a sort of drunken stupor. And behind this was the perception of a love, so much love that we could all be loved enough, and more, to fill all our emptiness, to stop suicides, breakdowns, wars, broken marriages, crime – all this love going free, and people would need or want nothing more.'

These experiences continued:

'I knew my arms and hands were there but I couldn't feel them, still less move them, the rest was like paralysis. And soon something mounted in waves, higher and higher waves, taking my non-body with it while my eyes could still see the sycamore tree waving in the wind. My non-body was plunged and swimming in some sort of tangy sea, it was plunging up and down in such joy and so free, being itself and so happy because the sea was God felt as pure love. And my body, though it was helpless and left out of this, was somehow pulled and lifted, not physically but yet clearly felt, it somehow partook of this glorious swimming although it wasn't doing it, it was radiated through and through by the experience going on.'

There is no rational explanation for spiritual experience and it is challenging to put into words. It was exactly what she meant by passive prayer, some might call it a form of ecstatic prayer, and it is not surprising that the rather staid British clergy did not really know what to do with it:

'Now I can only greet death with increasing joy, because I know I shall eventually be plunging in that sparkling tangy sea where I am free and at home and don't have my self to bother about, to shelter and protect and champion all the time.'

On a more sombre note she received news that Robin Noel had died suddenly on a trip to Yugoslavia. Another priest friend gone and she knew she would miss him.

With Middle Road now looking so clean and fresh she decided to hold an exhibition of her own using the stable end as a gallery, and she began reclaiming the various paintings she had lent out during the building work. She was very unimpressed when she arrived at Horseshoe to swap *Flames on their Heads* for the *Hosanna* painting only to find it standing on the floor. Because of this neither copy of *Flames on Their Heads* was returned to Horseshoe after the exhibition.

Nowadays thousands of artists' studios and houses are open annually all over the country for Artweeks-style exhibitions and are widely publicised. Eularia must have been one of the first to do it and needless to say the exhibition didn't go quite as she hoped, but this time the St Peter's clergy supported her because she told them about it, asking Sidney Mullarkey to come and bless her new extension on the first morning of the exhibition, as she wrote to Rachael:

'Yesterday Canon said he'd come up and bless the "new Premises" – and see the paintings – and to my astonishment, more and *more* black figures got out of the car, Canon, Fr. Mahy, the new senior curate (*Fr. Bennett*), and "our deacon" who is still at St. Sulpice but here for a month to help. They all four came in and all blessed the exhibition with holy water and lots of prayers, and whenever the priests chipped in with the priests bits, the Canon said, "Shut up, you're all the Congregation now!" So they had to say "and with you" like me!

'Now they are spreading the exhibition around and people are beginning to trickle in through the garage....You'll laugh, my "public" are *not* keen on R.C art, they come either 1. To admire my pot-plants and ask for cuttings – which is fair enough as most of them *are* cuttings, cadged! 2. To admire the beach-glass and find out how it's done 3. To pick free apples... 4. To tell me about some friend of theirs who is a "Roman Catholic". 5. To tell me about other things. 6. To have a nice sit down on the "lawn". 7. To poke for the frog, who has wisely decamped elsewhere etc. etc.'

Even Michael Gedge was very complimentary. It was the first time he had seen all the paintings together, properly hung, and he returned a few days later with Joe Rea and Fr Faulkner, who borrowed several to show at an exhibition in Fareham.

This prompted her to return to the idea of having a library of paintings lent at a charge of £1 a year:

'This would mean a small but useful income and solve the problem of selling them, and probably "do good" – spread them around and get people used to the idea. I don't think they should be just stored under dust-sheets.'

Just after her exhibition she began painting *A Boy Here* (John 6:9). When it came to exhibitions this was one of Eularia's most popular paintings and the only one that she painted on stretched canvas rather than her usual canvas sized onto board. Again the viewpoint is unusual. We are looking at the torso of the boy from the adult's eye line while he holds the loaves and fish in suitably grubby hands. We do not see his face, the attention clearly being directed to the loaves and the fish. In this manner he becomes a sort of 'every boy' clothed in the usual navy knitted sweater and rolled up jeans, with the hand of St Andrew indicating him. Behind and below him, as if he is standing on the edge of a cliff top, is a small rowing boat suffused in a sunset pink sea. What is startling about this painting is how the characters speak without us ever seeing their faces. It is all in the body language and the way our eyes are directed by the hand of St Andrew, the awkwardness of a boy singled out and the accusatory, rather dismissive motion of St Andrew's hand over such a meagre offering.

Eularia's choice of reading material began taking her in a more feminine direction, theologically speaking. She read about Astarte and Isis and felt very reassured by it, finding more clues about her experience of Er-Prayer:

'Apparently the upsurge of emotion is just a part of the earthy nature, and there is even something right and suitable about the introversion and withdrawal at the times of sickness, and we are supposed to have magic powers then, and so are taboo, and keep away from men, and there is fear of us. Is this

A Boy Here (1966)

fear because in our solitude we are in a state of heiro-gamos (*holy marriage*)? God is with us, only Him. This may either cause the love, or else the love rising up powerfully finds Him ready to master – He made us. And in Christianity there is the blood and pain, and the efforts of men to stimulate this in scourging etc., whereas to us it just comes.'

Here we see what Eularia had taken from her years of experimenting with mortification, the final realisation that, as a woman, she did not need it. Eularia was following a path that so many have followed. With no real answer to her questions about her spiritual experiences (her passive prayer) she was beginning to look beyond Christianity. She was a part of the first trickle that would become an avalanche as my generation and those beyond, especially women, found that no matter how much they might want it to, the male-centric Christian church did not hold explanations or answers for their questions and experiences. Women were no longer intellectually ignorant and were able to begin investigating for themselves. In the Church of England it would ultimately give us female Bishops, in the Catholic Church such change is yet to be seen (although I understand that it is common for spiritual counsellors to be women these days), but it has also given us the foundation of our 'New Age' movement which places so much more emphasis on the value of the feminine. It is tempting to say that the Church has missed a trick here. It was inevitable that women would begin to walk this path at some point. What is certain is that Eularia would never have wanted to be the kind of priest that men were, and nor would most women. They have a different experience, one that is uniquely feminine. It is not that of a nun, it is something far less submissive and it could stand in partnership with the male version. Perhaps one day it will.

Eularia often wrote letters to the *Catholic Herald*, which she read regularly. She wrote one such letter in October 1966 as a result of a piece she had read there about divorced parents. She challenged the idea that a deserted wife is a failed wife, another pro-woman stance, and concluded:

'Might there not be some point in the exceptionally rigorous training which a deserted wife is forced to undergo? The life is so isolated, so bitter, so frightening, even with the help one gets. One doesn't choose it, there is no warning, no vocation, no pre-training for nightmare years of stumbling along under impossible burdens – yet it may provide a formation for purpose, some work lying ahead. Once in the Church, I returned to my childhood plan to be a religious painter, and now I see that I needed all the tough training I got. Perhaps many women are trained and destined in this way, it is worth thinking about. As for the Church's attitude, I have had nothing but kindness and help from priests all along; they know a thing or two about hard training themselves.'

For Eularia feminine spirituality would become increasingly important. Her portrayal of the Gospels is uniquely feminine, she paints in a way that a man never would. The little details of life, the way she sees women, mothers, children; her understanding of dealing with young boys as a mother figure and teacher; her knowledge of the trials of young men, especially those following a spiritual path; her connection with landscape in such a visceral way, all are there to be seen and she never flinched from depicting raw emotion in favour of some more refined masculine ideal.

Her *Stations of the Cross* are a prime example of this. There is a Buddhist mediation that takes place in charnel houses, where the bodies of the dead reside, in order that through the practice of mediation the young monk might overcome his fears of death. Eularia gives us this with her *Stations,* a chance to journey and meditate upon the physical and emotional suffering of walking this path and overcoming it. It is raw and more challenging than the ethereal and refined versions. It does not hold much meaning when walked through as a ritual often repeated with set prayers, but as a direct meditation of learning to transcend the emotions of suffering and pain it speaks volumes. You have to have courage to travel in Eularia's hands.

Eularia undoubtedly found painting the *Stations* challenging and it caused her to think about Religious Art which helped refine her view of her own place within it. One day she was looking at books on Icons, and Italian and Spanish paintings of the Passion in a local bookshop:

'...and I realised what the problem is – first He was just God, a shepherd, He didn't suffer. Then the Passion "came in" – about 1000 (AD), and the Italians and Spanish went emotional and operatic over it, but their painting was primitive and they still felt in tremendous awe of the Pancrator, the Christ in Glory. Then anatomy, flesh, muscle, operatic terror, grief, noble suffering. Then just theatre. I'm to produce something new, the Christ in Glory on the way to the cross. I am the synthesis, the culmination. I shall be one of those big "oversize" library books, and much more.'

It was a big ambition. Did she succeed? Not in the way she envisaged here, or even perhaps in the way that she intended. At the time of writing there is still no "oversize" library book and Religious Art has had no great revival in the mainstream Art world. But increasingly for Eularia, who had for so much of her life been the robust one, it would be a case of the spirit being willing but the flesh being weak. Almost straight after this entry in her diary she described another bout of illness. These were occurring more frequently, especially with her stomach and the migraines. As the next year would show, her health was on a downward slide. She described her diet for overcoming her bouts of sickness as, '...rest and Complan and eggs and sponge cake and tea and bread and butter.' It would have given any nutritionist a heart attack!

Hole in the Roof was printed with a review of the Southampton Painter's Progress exhibition in the Evening Echo much to Eularia's amazement:

'How could I have been so silly, all these years, not to see my destination? Yet I needed all the toughening, the independence, the loneliness of my desertion. Cyril was right, he knew I was a painter, not a musician, hardly even a mother, never a lover. And all those years of side-track.'

Eularia's early desire to be a religious painter had come full circle:

'Peace descends – peace is nothing to do with outside things, it's to do with one's attitude to them, one's confidence, one's ability to cope.'

33

Sacred Heart

It would be easy to think, given the very illustrative style of Eularia's paintings, that book illustration would come easily to her, but this was not the case. In late 1966 she submitted rough illustrations for an Old Testament story (she doesn't say which) written for children by Rosemary Haughton for Dove Books. In the end artist and writer did not see eye to eye enough for Eularia to illustrate her work, and much as she might have liked to be paid to illustrate books, she never did consider herself to be an illustrator. She found it hard work and felt that she would have to evolve a new technique.

Eularia clearly did not consider that what she was doing was simply illustrating gospel stories. Later, in her gloomier moments she dismissed her paintings as mere illustrations more than once, but in each case this can be put down to her state of mind at the time. Had she been a good illustrator then the Dove Books project would have been more successful and she would not have struggled so much over the Stations of the Cross. Eularia's art was never about just supplying a visual representation of a text, but something much deeper and less tangible.

Fr Agnellus Andrew O.F.M, who, in 1966, was in charge of all Catholic broadcasts in Britain, contacted Eularia about doing something with her paintings for the television. Eularia wasn't quite sure what to make of it initially. She had seen television at our house and had a son working in broadcasting but had no television of her own, so until now it had not figured very large in her world.

As a result, just before Christmas 1966, John Brode and a BBC cameraman came to Middle Road to see the paintings and Eularia duly joined him at the BBC Studio in Southampton the following day for the interview. She wrote to Rachael about it:

'Grandmother is a T.V. star, by the way ... I didn't realise until the next day that I'd been just after the 6 o'clock news, (with a lady icing cakes and a Nutritional expert just before me) and so was seen by the whole less-cultured South! All my early recorder-kids fetched their mums from kitchens to see me on the telly, even Alison Poole (*a cousin*) saw it! You'll be glad to hear I combed my hair, and it didn't come down, (because the Canon was praying for me) – and I'd made a lovely Lapp shirt out of rough off-white hairy wool and lots of patterned braid and a big collar, and Mrs Gladwell (*a friend*) said it looked just right. I asked not to be made up and they said Mai Zetterling is *never* made up either (!!!).'

Eularia greatly enjoyed her television appearance, and it would not be her last. Much to her delight, many friends and fellow Catholics had watched it. With the illustrations and renewed interest from Chapmans' over the 'Pops' she really felt as if she was on the crest of a wave.

'The year ends with endless undeserved success, risks taken, praise received, talents recognised, confidence after fifty years, my promises of youth fulfilled, and now freedom to go ahead and do more and better. Yet the only certainty is God. God has directed me, laid down the path even in small details like funny clothes and no make-up and ignorance of TV.'

She spent Christmas quietly at Middle Road with James as it was to be his last one as a bachelor (Marita having finally agreed to marry him), and just after it began *Sacred Heart Devotion,* her first painting not based on a Gospel story for a long time and one that she would always consider to be among her best. Her caption for it is one of her longest:

'The Sacred Heart is one of those Catholic things that sets many people's teeth on edge. Those statues and pictures, in churches or homes or convents, on sale at Southsea Funfair, are all apt to be sentimental and very effeminate. Apparently even Catholics are beginning to wonder if that curly beard, weak blue eyes and limp hands could have much connection with Christ, who was a strong, open-air preacher ex-carpenter son of a Jewish peasant girl.

'The nun in the 17th century who saw the visions which began the cult, certainly wasn't to blame, she seems to have seen something rather different and much less "visual". No details, no sentimentality, no curly beard or such, only a powerful impression of Christ calling people, and this extraordinary vision of the heart giving out rays of light and heat. This painting is simply the result of thinking about what St. Margaret Mary wrote about her visions, and the words she heard spoken; the fussy decorations of the convent of those days, and the present distaste for the cult among modern minds, and the overpowering truth at the depths. We may, perhaps, depend too much on human hearts and human love and need to know about a much more powerful and dependable sort of heart, which the Christian religion and the Gospels and the Church etc. are really about.'

In her diary she wrote, 'The *Sacred Heart* is good. The Christ *is* beautiful, a broody, concerned, careful Red Indian.'

The painting shows the upper half of the figure of Christ with the traditional open chest to reveal the heart. Christ wears the wounds of his suffering but there is a peace about him as he gathers the masses to him into the cave of his chest where a heart of white light is suspended. All the figures are blue except for one haloed nun, St Margaret Mary. Around the outside are other blue figures jeering or turning away in doubt. In the background are two altars and in the foreground two incense burners, reminding us that this is a Catholic cult and closely associated with the Church. She knew that this painting was unlikely to be appreciated by anyone except Catholics but she loved painting it, and she always considered it to be much closer to what she felt her painting was about than some of the more obvious Gospel illustrations.

Consequently her next subject seemed tame to her at the time, but again she would later rank it among one of her best works. She said of it, 'My next will be fairly easy Oxfam stuff – Martha and Mary.'

Martha and Mary (Luke 10:38) shows a harassed Martha, carrying a pile of plates, being comforted by Jesus and in the foreground an entranced Mary dropping the cutlery as she listens to Jesus' words. Eularia's caption tells us:

'Mary is no good at laying the table; she is too busy listening to Christ. The child in red, in front, is a Mongol (*the common term for Downs Syndrome in the 1960s*); people used to say that Mongol children know a lot about supernatural things. All the people are slightly hypnotised, except poor Martha who is having to concentrate on the job or there won't be any supper.'

It is an image that Eularia could easily identify with, having had to be Mum for so many years, doing the chores while everyone else enjoyed themselves.

Sacred Heart Devotion (1967)

Martha and Mary (1967)

Having ended 1966 on such a high, she began 1967 with a corresponding low and indigestion was a problem. Term began again and she found teaching increasingly tiring. She took to painting in bed in the greenhouse with the canvas propped up on a pillow.

Earlier in the year she had taken the photos of her paintings 'en spec' to Corpus Christi College in London, then a relatively new institute for teaching Catachetics and situated just round the corner from Cheppers. They were impressed enough to ask her for a few paintings to show, so she took them *Picnic on the Shore, Maundy Thursday, Coming up from the Water, Miracle at Gadara, Hole in the Roof, Rescuing Sheep, Water From the Rock* and *Sacred Heart Devotion,* and was comforted when the young priest said that they were the best religious paintings he had ever seen. Her paintings were going to be shown to Cardinal Heenan, which, of course, made her day. Whether they actually were is uncertain.

Shortly afterwards, while she was working on the Stations, Pat and Cormac Murphy-O'Connor arrived. It was the first time she had seen Pat for nearly twelve months and she readily agreed to his request to supply a set of *Stations* for his own new church.

But another infection followed hard on the heels of the first and for the first time Eularia really felt fear over her health:

> 'But as it grew dark, at 5pm, I grew lonely and afraid – what about tonight and tomorrow? How bad will I get?'

Gone is the coping Eularia who blazed through her mastectomy. After a year of frequent infections, increased migraines and gut trouble she was beginning to feel vulnerable and far less confident of her health.

When she recovered she went to Park Gate to see the new brass Stations of the Cross in situ:

> 'They were very good Stations, but all unreal and "artistic". A boy was there, we said how good they were, and he said he hadn't liked "those pictures that were here" – I asked why. He said they were "too rough" – people acting rough and cruel.'

This made Eularia think. It began a train of thought that would take a while to mature but would later lead to her decision to stop showing the bloodier of her paintings, especially the *Stations*. But Park Gate taught Eularia that:

> 'Craftsmanship fits with architecture. Art is different, it dominates, distracts, gets the attention; the building becomes just a frame. No wonder cast bronze is the stuff.'

She was right. Paintings, by their very nature, draw people to them. Place a painting in the middle of a wall and it is the painting you see: the wall simply becomes the frame that holds it.

Sidney Mullarkey (encouraged by David Mahy) had asked Eularia to paint a set of *Stations* for a new chapel at Weeke in the middle of 1966. One can only assume that he hadn't seen the samples she did for Park

Gate and, unsurprisingly, the set of *6-inch Stations* she produced for him didn't meet with unqualified approval, so Pat's request for a slightly larger set was very welcome. Eularia was cross with Sidney about this. It had been a lot of work for no result, but Sidney redeemed himself to a certain degree by liking *Sacred Heart Devotion*:

'He wasn't a bit shocked at the S.H. – he said Burnes-Oates don't offend, don't shock, but don't *say* anything. Yours say something and so they might shock.'

Then in February she heard news that really rocked her and which would ultimately change her relationship with St Peter's entirely:

'Today to Mass in frost, Fr. M (*Mahy*) with cold as usual and looking ghastly, and at the end I was wiping the windscreen when he came out – I said how sorry I was and he mustn't stand in the freezing cold chatting to parishioners. He said he wouldn't be able to do that much longer as he was leaving in a fortnight. The shock was so great that for a moment I could only gasp with the pain of it. I asked where, he said Portsmouth as I'd predicted. I couldn't do anything, I found I was waffling towards the car, but I turned round to smile at him and saw him standing watching as he waved.

'It is a sunny cheerful morning, and now that the first shock is over I am getting balanced again. At first I realised that I was losing my closest and most stable personal relationship – probably of my whole life. The seven years of Fr. Mahy have been years of love such as I am capable of – love of man, son, brother, father, who has always been there, always at the centre of religion and also immensely attractive and charming as a man, and stable as a friend. I never tried to get to know him further, like Pat, because my love for him was real and live, and I know from experience how easily I become demanding and cruel and jealous. I have never done this. Other men, from Cyril onwards, have taught me little by little how to get over my hunger and greed, and I've learnt the lesson, Angus was my last possessive relationship. This young priest has been the flower of all the training, the reward of the effort and suffering.

'But when I look into the future I see great darkness. I know that God will strip me of everything, and I know it's good and right, my strength will increase, I must love Him and not his creatures. I must plough a *real* lonely furrow. How will I stick to Mass going, Devotions, even painting? What will life be?'

David Mahy had been appointed as an assistant priest at St John's Cathedral in Portsmouth and six months later was appointed Administrator there, which was the old term for the Parish priest in charge of the cathedral (this has now been changed to "Dean" as at Anglican Cathedrals). He would remain in this post until 1975 when he became island Dean in Jersey. David's move to Portsmouth was to prove decisive for Eularia's painting, even if she did not yet know it. It would open up her options in a way that she had yet to experience, but on that cold, sunny day in February she had yet to see this.

Eularia went to Redrice to reclaim the *St Joseph* icon that David had loved so much, which she found hidden away in a cupboard. She, therefore, had no qualms about reclaiming it and duly presented it to David as a leaving present. Of all the paintings she gave as presents, it is one of the few that we know survive. David kept it with him throughout his life as a priest, taking it with him to his various parishes until he finally left it hanging in the presbytery of St Joseph's at Aldershot when he retired. He felt that it was an appropriate resting place for it.

Eularia continued to have health problems throughout the spring. Since her bout of flu her chest had not improved and she found herself very wheezy and under the weather. For the second year running she just couldn't shake off the bug. This time she couldn't put it down to a busy schedule, as she was now only teaching at West Downs and the workload was not nearly as stressful as it had been. It irritated her because it affected her ability to paint.

She wondered again if, by not selling her paintings, she was making herself too cheap. This was reinforced by another visit to Horseshoe only to find her *Hosanna* painting sitting on the floor on its side. This, on top of finding her *St Joseph* icon consigned to a cupboard at Redrice, acted as a warning that giving away the paintings led them to be less valued. She also worried that by not selling she was indulging in self-glory and acting as if she was above money.

The bigger picture also troubled her:

'It seems such a tiny thing, to be a Christian Catholic painter, "revealing too much" as Michael says... revealing my own thoughts and feelings, which may soon be so irrelevant. Will religion soon be out of date, Sacraments just quaint survivals? Yet what else is there? What else can ordinary people live by? Am I just in the grip of a violent enthusiasm, or craze?'

She went to visit Pat Murphy-O'Connor in his new parish at St Michael and all Angels, Leigh Park in order to see where his set of *Stations* would be hung:

'*What* a place to find! At last I located the brick hut in a patch of rubble opposite the Tampax factory (it would be) – the posh ecumenical church up the hill had, of course, everything. I never saw a shabbier church, odd pews and chairs jumbled, a pathetic attempt at being ecclesiastical, no modern tendencies, everything True Church, on the poorest level, I warmed to it.... (*I*) was asked up to the "Council house" presbytery, up-to-the-minute but so poor, so splendidly uncultured, and I saw how even a bit of uphill walking made Pat breathe heavily, his colour was bad – but he's very happy and fulfilled in this poor place.'

Pat wanted some pictorial Stations, especially for the children, which appealed to Eularia. She made an *8-inch set* for Leigh Park, which hung there (especially low on the wall for the children according to Pat), at least for a while. Whether they made it into the new church, completed in 1970, is uncertain. If they did they would certainly have been lost in the subsequent fire in 2001 following a lightening strike, which destroyed the church.

There are no surviving images of this set of *Stations*. The *8-inch set* that does survive (a 'sample' set in a ring binder) may be copies, we cannot be sure, but all the surviving *Stations* that we have are very similar in design, regardless of size, so it is probable that the Leigh Park set were very similar.

Intriguingly neither of the two sets of *Stations* that survive, the *6-inch set* (the Weeke one) and the 'sample' *8-inch set* include Station twelve, 'Jesus Dies on the Cross'. Why this should be missing is not explained. The *6-inch set* includes a prepared plaque for it but it remains blank. As a whole Eularia was never really happy with her Stations and after completing Pat's, she abandoned painting them as a subject.

Eularia saw David Mahy's departure as the end of an episode, which left her in a temporary limbo artistically:

'I see that the last ten years have been one long round of Fr. This and Fr. That. Several visits a week, long intimate congenial conversations, chance contacts, closer and closer friendships, and my own response expressed in poetry, music and art. Now it is all over. Angus went, Fr. L (*Lawrence*) went, Fr. N (*Noel*) died, Pat (*Murphy-O'Connor*) went, Fr. M. (*Mahy*) went, and my response has just dried up.'

It was, without a doubt, these friendships that did more than anything else to help Eularia realise her childhood ambition to be a Religious Artist. Whilst her experience of God and prayer spurred her on and inspired her, these priests (along with Michael Gedge) had, each in their own way, been her muses and her Greek chorus, unfailingly cheering her on and encouraging her to believe in herself and her talent. Now that influence would be more distant. She and Pat continued to correspond, but she saw much less of him. David, on the other hand, would become more influential for a while once he had taken up his role as Administrator at St John's Cathedral. But this was six months away and 1967 was to prove a year that would turn Eularia's life upside down.

At first she suffered her usual backlash at feeling deserted and complained that the paintings were just a sop to the clergy. But this was just her habitual fit of temper, her worst side, which insisted that the clergy had just been a family substitute. If it had been true she would have had no incentive to pick up a paintbrush again, let alone continue with her religious painting, and in the next three and half years she would produce almost half of her catalogue of religious works, over forty paintings.

News arrived about the success of the Corpus Christi College exhibition in London. When she went up to collect her paintings Desmond Brennan, who was in charge of the Audio Visual side of things there, told her that '…at present I'm the only *English* religious "artist" in Holy Church.' and she was asked to give a one-woman exhibition there later in the year: a good incentive to carry on.

34

Preaching

1967 was turning into a year of disappearing friends. After Easter she once again attended Spode Music Week and was dismayed to find how many of the Dominican brothers that she knew had left Holy orders, and indeed Hawkesyard Priory itself would cease to take novice monks only a couple of years later due to lack of vocations.

Hawkesyard was not alone as the waves created by Vatican II began to make themselves felt: many were questioning their vocations, the Church was in the grip of profound change and was beginning to feel like a ship floundering in a stormy sea. Things would get worse before they began to improve, too. It was a challenging time for Eularia to have lost the Middle Road Curia.

Like many Catholics at the time, Eularia was becoming disillusioned with the practical results of the Vatican II changes. The priesthood as a vocation was becoming unpopular, the number of new priests was dropping and Eularia was concerned that there was a growing swell of opinion against a personal relationship between the soul and God, which was, of course, her main thing:

'...the private devotion, the private mass, mystics never mentioned, saints wiped out; – but will it work? What is the liturgy without any prayer or love?'

Given that much of Eularia's own experience of God and Faith had risen from precisely this personal relationship, she was well placed to be concerned about it, and she was not alone. Eularia cited the writings of Fr Francis X. Murphy, who, under the pseudonym Xavier Rynne, attended and reported on Vatican II as a journalist and was credited with seeding the view that it was Liberal versus Conservative. But the popularist idea that Vatican II was a split of this kind is misleading. Many who were branded conservative, whilst they may have felt strongly about losing their old rituals and the Latin, also, perhaps, understood that something deeper and more spiritual was in danger of being lost, that making everything readily accessible to the laity also removed the mystery. This perhaps led to the decline in the Church today as younger generations look elsewhere for that relationship between soul and God. There is always the danger, when such major changes sweep through an organisation, that the baby will be thrown out with the bathwater. Sometimes the voice of caution is too easily dismissed as conservatism.

Eularia's own paintings were a testament to the power of the relationship between the soul and God:

> 'I know that each time I look at the S. H. (*Sacred Heart Devotion*) I am looking at the expression of something real and powerful.'

All this was a sobering backdrop for the start of her next painting, which, again, was not a Gospel illustration. Instead Eularia returned to Mass and Catholic festivals, choosing the Easter Vigil as her subject. *Easter Candles* is far from being a repeat of her earlier paintings of Catholic worship. Instead of orderly rows of Congregation we see an Icon of Christ, in front of which is the priest holding the Paschal candle and altar boys reaching up to light tapers from it. A sea of chaotic humanity of every kind surrounds them; indeed the sea itself is present on the right of the painting. Eularia's caption is again one of her longest but necessary in order to understand the abundant symbolism within the painting:

> 'At 11.30 at night on the eve of Easter, they light the new fire – they used to light it with flint in a big cauldron just outside the church door until just lately when they went modern. But they still light the huge Paschal Candle from the new fire and carry it up the church chanting "Lumen Christi" (*Light of Christ*) and the people answering "Deo Gratias" (*Thanks be to God*) and the altar servers light long tapers from it, and each person has a candle, so as the candles are lit from the taper, and from the paschal Candle all over the church.
>
> 'The ritual comes from dark pagan ceremonies, it has been transformed by Christians into a Resurrection celebration and there is a lot more to it, we don't get home till after one o' clock usually. The rest of the painting is imaginary of course; we go home with our candles and that's that. But as all

Easter Candles (1967)

do-gooding really comes from God, and Christ commanded it, and started it all by the Resurrection anyway, do-gooding is lit from the Paschal Candle in a roundabout sort of way. It couldn't be lit from anything else.

'The do-gooding is: – Top left going round clockwise, a lonely old person; missionaries going overseas; people in a mental home; prisoners; the "potholer" is a person who can't communicate with anybody, the do-gooder can't see where the candle is, so he just has to push his one down in the ground and hope for the best. The next is an unmarried mother in her private hell, the nun works in a home for mothers and babies. The kind boy at the old lady's bedside... well, she knitted him that sweater and he rather hopes for another from great-granny; the next bed is a car-crash. The Dominican friar is praying, as they do, for the dead; above him the social misfits hold out their candles for lighting. "Joe" doesn't want light, only lots of candles. I don't yet know what he's there for or what he represents, though I have my suspicions.'

Sacred Heart Devotion and *Easter Candles* represent something of a departure from Eularia's usual style as neither are direct Gospel illustrations nor are they simple depictions of worship. Eularia was very pleased with them both although she realised, correctly, that they would not be as popular with her public who tended to prefer the Gospel illustrations like *A Boy Here, Christmas Gospel, Buying Wood* and *Maundy Thursday*. It was the clergy who really understood and appreciated *Sacred Heart Devotion* (it was Sidney Mullarkey's favourite), and yet it was the Catholic Community that inspired *Easter Candles*:

'I look at the Paschal Candle (*'Easter Candles'*) and think, this painting is inspired by my close contact and strife with the Catholic Flock. Much of my best work is about Mr Thomas, Ron, Julie, Gilbert, Mary Bristow, Mary Downie, M Zollo (*the choir*) – but most of all Mr T (*Will Thomas*) – the Catholic who is in the Church without any assent to religion, any religious act. Lights our candles from his own lighter, has none of his own, doesn't do that sort of thing and laughs at the Paschal Candle – dislikes his choir to kiss the Cross but doesn't approach it, or the ashes, himself. This is the only Church which can contain other than the devout, the only Church for all the people And I've been to the bottom and come up again, I've not rejected the close contact and experience of the Church via the choir, because of various factors, Brookses (*friends*), love of singing, even loneliness. Result – I can express this very picturesque thing – an ideal subject. That's why Canon likes my S. (*Sacred*) H (*Heart*) painting – it expresses what he expresses – all men coming to Christ... The P. Candle is good. I've put the gold on – it's a good design, good idea, not badly painted, and the Christ is better than I deserve or expected – He looks "risen" if not more than roughly.'

In May Eularia opened up her studio again as she had in 1966. This time it was Sidney Mullarkey himself who urged her to advertise more. Once again the exhibition began slowly, but this time she set up her painting studio in the attic so that she could continue to work while the exhibition was on downstairs.

The following day was Ascension and Eularia's birthday, also her first day back teaching after the half-term break (despite being out at work she was in the habit of leaving the exhibition open). She returned home for lunch and had just pulled up in the Mini van feeling very grubby:

> '…when a big car drove up, Cormac, Fr. Lawrence, and a third figure. I said, "golly" – it was the Bishop!! I felt so awed. They looked round and the Bishop read all the notices and looked carefully at everything, in his purple socks, and the other two chatted with me and I was so thrilled, that I was rather preaching, I couldn't help it!'

The 'preaching' was always a challenge for Eularia. The more nervous she was the more she tended to talk, although few seemed to realise that it masked a lack of confidence. Michael Gedge was her worst critic over this. He wrote to her, after a visit to Fareham with some pictures:

> 'Do let me urge you when you show your pictures anywhere to try very hard not to talk. When you came here the other day I think that literally you didn't stop talking from the moment you came into the house till the moment you left, except when I shouted you down once for about ten seconds. You could not know how exhausting this is: it simply leaves everyone exhausted and drained dry – and what is far more serious it makes it quite impossible to see the pictures, because one can't take in a picture when someone is talking all the time, particularly the artist – to whom one has got to pay *some* attention…Let the pictures talk for themselves.'

Despite Michael's warnings (and Eularia knew that she talked too much) she just couldn't help herself. After all the years of feeling that the clergy weren't interested, this was a major event for Eularia and the Bishop's visit was the first time that she expressed an intention of leaving the paintings to the Portsmouth diocese.

Even Sidney Mullarkey went to see the exhibition and told Eularia he had meditated on the paintings (she was out teaching). So what had begun as another rather low-key exhibition in the end was a great success from Eularia's point of view and she realised how important her captions for the paintings were. Everyone read them and some visitors told her that they were as good as the paintings.

The possibility of more exhibitions was increasing. Eversley Belfield began organising an exhibition at Southampton University for the autumn, David Mahy talked about arranging one at the school in Portsmouth, so with these and the one at Corpus Christi College also scheduled for the autumn she had every reason to be feeling optimistic. She concluded, however, that:

> 'I'm never going to be a really good painter, technically I'm rough and incompetent, but nobody else, just now, paints these things.'

One firm supporter of Eularia's was missing from the visitors of the exhibition. Pat Murphy-O'Connor, whose health Eularia had worried about on her last visit, was in hospital having surgery. She visited him in Leigh Park when he was supposed to be recuperating:

> 'I went to the priests' house and there was Pat doing the accounts (Parish priest!) – he said he'd been told to go carefully but he wasn't going to. I looked at him and he looked back, his eyes were full of light, he was all translucent, we both knew that he's going to have a short life, at his own wish. These people need his work, he's going to die for them, probably painfully… I felt fortuitous in being able to do the Stations for him.'

She credited Pat with a return of prayer that she experienced:

> 'Just as I left I knelt on the carpet and (*he*) blessed me and as I said "I never waste priests, do I?" I recalled the time in hospital when he taught me to bless myself. Since then I've felt the live presence of God and the longing to stop hating people, but in some cases it's *so* difficult.'

Eularia followed up the success of her home exhibition with a letter to Raymond Lawrence (now Episcopal Vicar for Administration in the diocese) about the possibility of the diocese housing her collection in Portsmouth, which he had mentioned to her during the visit to the exhibition. His reply was practical, cautious, and refrained from making promises that he couldn't follow up. Eularia's collection consisted of over forty canvasses by this time. It was no small thing to find somewhere that could house them permanently. Inevitably Eularia took it badly.

I believe that as people we arrive at the time and place we are meant to, that Eularia was meant to be painting when she did, but it has to be said that if she were painting today it would be in a far more receptive and settled climate and her success is unlikely to have been in doubt. Even today there are few English Catholic artists and the Church is much more willing to appreciate the art it has. But post Vatican II everything was in such flux that there really was very little space to focus on a phenomenon as unique as Eularia.

The Vatican II changes were turning everything on its head and a considerable number of Catholics felt that they were fighting for the very survival of what they considered to be the core of the Church, the Mass itself. The clergy (many of whom were leaving the Church altogether) were desperately trying to keep abreast of a constant stream of new directives, which often seemed experimental and contradictory, and by the late 1960s and early 1970s the Catholic Press was full of letters of complaint and articles about the state of the Church.

Amidst all this turmoil Eularia was emerging as that very rare thing, an English Catholic Religious Artist. Once again, she was ahead of her time. On one hand her paintings are a reminder of the old Catholic life that was passing. On the other they reminded everyone of what the real core of the Church was, the Gospel living in our daily world, beyond politics, a deeply individual and heartfelt relationship with Christ Himself. It speaks to the state of things at the time that the only two of Eularia's paintings that have remained on public view for over forty years are the two she sold to the Methodists.

It is a little ironic that the organisers of the Methodist Collection say that her two paintings remain amongst their most popular with the public, and yet nothing has remained of her within the Catholic Church itself, not her Stations, not her *Last Supper*, not her original painting of Candlemas, not the collage she made for St John's Cathedral in Portsmouth, not the paintings she gave to the St Dismas Society. The only religious paintings that have survived outside the collection preserved by her family, apart from those in the Methodist Collection, are the icon of *St Joseph* that she gave to David Mahy, an icon of *Our Lady of Wilton* that David Mahy bought, *Palm Sunday* in the presbytery at St Peter's, Winchester, the *One True Vine* which she gave to Tim Russ and the three canvasses bought by Veronica Stokes.

Cormac Murphy-O'Connor was now secretary to Bishop Worlock and Eularia decided it was time to honour his request for a painting. She did give some thought as to which painting he should have and in the end decided on the original version of *Candlemas* (she had copied it by then). Sadly this too has now disappeared.

The idea of a collection all hung in one place was really beginning to ferment in Eularia's mind. Backed up continually by the remarks and observations of others, it was to become her greatest hope and dream for her work.

'I paint with knowledge. Nobody will be able to look at ordinary life without thinking... "it's like the gospels"... Every single person I meet, whether pagan, Catholic, non-devout; every painter and non-painter, man woman or child, every degree of education, they all produce the same reaction fundamentally, are powerfully struck, even if unwillingly. This is my strength, I can manage on this, no need of the approbation of locals, even though my loneliness cries out for local acceptance. One must be true to oneself...'

It's a far cry from the Eularia who had struggled in 1962 over what to do about *The Last Supper*. This is a far more certain and confidant Eularia, not prepared to give in to individual sensibilities and tastes, but prepared to stand by her own message.

She was watching the people on Meon beach one day during the summer:

'...and at that point I saw the connection between that frightful cathedral (St John's in Portsmouth) and the rather dull animal seaside life... families without joy, very careful of their babies, very unenthusiastic. And I saw them standing in the water among the sea-weed, with Him talking to them from the boat... My job is to PAINT. Not worry about my reputation, not seek consolation or friendship but PAINT...'

This inspired her next painting, which, in its own way, is a statement of exactly where she felt herself to be. *Preaching from the Boat* (Matthew 13:2) depicts exactly what Eularia saw on Meon beach. In it we find the boat full of lobster pots at the top of the painting and the hand of Christ draped over the side (we only see his face as a reflection in the water). In the foreground people watch amazed on the shore and others move through the general seaside rubbish floating in the water towards the boat.

Eularia's own caption for this painting tells us:

'I meant the people to stay on the beach as they did in the Gospel story, but somehow they kept walking towards the boat with Christ preaching, and I couldn't stop them, though it was a cold day and the sea very chilly indeed.'

It is full of typical Eularia detail. The murky green water, the cold-looking bather standing on the breakwater, the plastic bottles floating in the water, the young family wading out with the man clutching a small baby over his shoulder, and the sense of them all being polarised towards Christ as he is preaching. The fact that she chose this subject at a point when she was so clear about her own role can be no coincidence.

Eularia sometimes painted on very odd things indeed. She wrote to Rachael about an Action Man doll she had sent for her grandson Cuthbert's birthday at the end of August:

'...but probably all the children are dead by now, because I forgot to mention that I'd disliked his (*the Action Man's*) nasty un-human "killer" face, and painted on a sort of cheerful face with OILPAINT – so if anyone sucked it they are probably in Heaven now – *so sorry...*'

It was the only Action Man in history to have a rather insane, cheery grin and I'm not sure that we really appreciated it. "Killer faces" were much more in line with what all the other children had. It was odd that she should choose to attempt to sanitise the face of a plastic toy when she was so adamant about her own paintings showing real emotion.

My first really clear memories of Middle Road begin in 1967, prior to this they are a vague collage of images, smells and sounds. Apart from her paintings, one of my enduring memories is of the numerous pot plants everywhere, especially in the greenhouse, but also in the very eccentric and rather dimly lit bathroom (there was always ivy growing over the window), which smelt of her favourite French Fern soap. She rescued a large Harts-tongue fern from a house that was about to be demolished and installed it in the bathroom where it added to the general cave feel:

'...it's really happy! Dangling its 2ft fronds between the bath and lav – it seems to think it's between two wells! Visitors gasp...'

35

No Old Age

Rachael's family came to visit her for two weeks in August after two years' absence. Eularia was looking forward to this visit a great deal but inevitably she fell into a 'Martha' role. With four children of seven and under Rachael had her hands full, but she was used to the routine. Eularia was not. Already tired and tending towards breathlessness, our stay exhausted her but she did manage to refrain from making an issue out of it with Robert and Rachael.

She enjoyed her grandchildren as much as her energy would allow but felt that Robert and Rachael were very scathing and sarcastic about her work. Rachael's interest in Catholicism was waning, and Robert was one of the many who was becoming increasingly disillusioned about the changes. Eularia was greatly warmed, however, by her grandchildren's interest in her paintings, especially Cuthbert who asked her about them endlessly with great excitement.

It is difficult to tell from Eularia's diary how much of her reaction was simply her feeling unwell, making her more sensitive to having two weeks of wall to wall people, mess and noise which she wasn't used to; and how much was genuinely a sense of disagreement between herself and Rachael. What is clear is that she did not let on this time how she was feeling, but at the end she was convinced she couldn't cope with so much family.

Once again Rachael was probably expecting her mother to be supportive in the way that most mothers were, but Eularia had changed.

She had left her mothering role behind and embraced her artistic self, which made her much less flexible in domestic situations and less inclined to be maternal or a 'Martha', so once again the visit did not end on an entirely happy note.

We children were oblivious to these undertones, we loved her far too much and we greatly enjoyed her. Compared to our other grandparents she was fun, and we loved Middle Road. Not long before we arrived she had finally cut off her long hair, something I regretted as I used to love watching her comb it out, falling forward over her face in a long dark wave.

Eularia with myself, Cuthbert and Austin at Middle Road with her paintings on the wall (1967)

On the other hand she was very pleased when James was given a director/scriptwriter job on the BBC documentary series 'Man Alive' and would be moving to London, so much closer for visits.

Once we left she began *Come Down Zacchaeus* (Luke 19:5). Her model for Zacchaeus was Michael Gedge (now moving to a new parish of his own at Holbury), and it shows a tree of autumn leaves with Zacchaeus clinging to a branch with his pocket full of notes as Jesus and a sea of faces look up at him, others hidden among the branches watching him. In her caption Eularia described this as a straight Gospel illustration, but she added:

'The rich nations are perhaps being asked to be a bit poorer so as to restore justice all round? The people in the trees are secretly asking what there is in Christ, if anything.'

Come Down Zacchaeus (1967)

It was while she was taking four paintings to an exhibition by the Catholic Artists at All Hallows Church in London towards the end of the summer that she realised just how poor her energy was, and it persisted along with a noticeable loss of weight. Then she fell ill with a bronchial infection that simply wouldn't go. The news wasn't good. The doctors discovered that Eularia had a collapsed lung, and once this was diagnosed she was moved to hospital where investigation showed a cancerous tumour in the pleural lining. Unfortunately she was given some sleeping pills not long after admittance, which she reacted badly to and she was very sick. It was in this state that Richard Davey, the new curate and current hospital chaplain at the time, saw her and realised how serious things were. Sidney Mullarkey then came in person and offered to bring her Communion himself on as many days as he could:

'Everyone has been marvellous; the pagans sit cracking jokes (to take their minds off the ugly thought); the Catholics come in endlessly and are *so* comforting and cheering! Four priests a day is common (I'm the only R.C. for miles) and you should see Canon (*Sidney Mullarkey*) sailing firmly through the bedpans and breakfasts with his Swan Vestas and his Pyx (I have to help him with the English prayers!) Francis and June came, (June was *so* human!) Chr. (*Christopher*) and Clare, rather sophisticated, James *superb*, and says Holy Faith is definitely his aim – which is the best result of all. Mrs Cornes does the Visiting the Sick Poor act, Fr. Sutherland brought four nuns in sea-green habits, Pat (*Murphy-O'Connor*) and Fr. M (*Mahy*) pop in and out the back entrance, and Alicia and Catherine wrote such *wonderful* letters in the expectation of my early death (*if* it could be called early!) that I only hope they won't be less kind when the anti-climax occurs as I "respond to treatment".'

Eularia's bedside must have seemed like Piccadilly Circus. She wasn't exaggerating in this letter to Rachael, she had visitor after visitor, neighbours, local Catholics, other friends, family. Once they had drained her lung and started treatment she began to feel better:

'The radium man says it's the same cancer as seven years ago, only its got onto the pleura. I'm to have drainage, and tablets and injections, and I might live six months or six years, it's quite unpredictable. In other words, borrowed time – but definitely no old age – I'm very glad of that.'

It was the visits from the priests that cheered her most, and Sidney Mullarkey, true to his word and in a clear demonstration of how much he cared about her, took over the duty of bringing her Communion almost every day despite the fact that the hospital was his curate's responsibility. He didn't confine his visits to just once a day for the practical purpose of Communion either, but often popped in at other times too. What Eularia never mentions in her diaries (it is quite likely that she didn't know) was that, before he died, John Henry King made Sidney a Vicar General for the diocese, which meant that he had much wider responsibilities than just his parish work. David Mahy said that Sidney always played this down (and even stuck to the title of Canon although he was now a Monsignor), so for him to fit in sick visiting on such a regular basis would not have been easy.

But it was David Mahy who was the most perceptive of all.

'Conversation flowed so easily, he'd come to see that I get oiled, to tell me how cancer does not always kill, but a shrewd question occurred, did I *always* feel so optimistic, or did I get frightened sometimes? This was what priests seldom ask... or doctors, or relations, or friends. He went off, blessing me with his hand on my head – this should upset the cancer badly.'

It was the end of her art-teaching days, which she was very happy about. She was eligible for £4 sickness benefit a week and the cancer seemed to have given her the life she had been longing for, time to paint without interruption.

A strong incentive for her to get better was that her painting was beginning to bear fruit. While she was in hospital her paintings were shown again on television. Eversley Belfield was putting into place the exhibition at Southampton University and the second Corpus Christi Exhibition was about to open in London. Her brother, Christopher, and his wife, Clare, delivered the paintings to this exhibition and David Mahy collected them. David, who was now Administrator (Dean) of St John's Cathedral, told her of plans to house the paintings in the Cathedral Baptistery, for an exhibition in Portsmouth the following April, and to have the *6-inch Stations* at the chaplaincy in Southampton. David even told her that he was willing to be Executor over the paintings if she still decided she wanted to leave them to the diocese:

'I'm cheerfuller than ever, because of life's rich promise – so absurd, with a disease in me which might be fatal; soon. But the utter peace of letting God do what he wants, and following the course with trustful interest and appreciation (as long as it's easy and pleasant). The comic opera continues.'

Treatment for cancer had come a long way since 1960, although her condition was serious and the doctors weren't joking when they said it would eventually be fatal. They were extremely pleased with how well she responded to treatment. Eularia saw her passage through this bout of cancer as entering into a new life:

'I am a very tough woman, and the only religious painter with an obsession.'

The visitors continued and predictably she began to become impatient with them. She knew how lucky she was and how much people cared about her, but the artist in her was calling again and to create her art she needed peace, quiet and uninterrupted time. Everyone was offering her places to recuperate, Catherine Dupré in Frant, even Michael Gedge at his new parish in Holbury.

Eularia was very funny about Michael. With a new parish he hadn't been able to visit her, but he had phoned and written. She wrote to Rachael:

'He's awfully fed up, and hoped I'd die and edifying death, even offering me a room in his new presbytery for the purpose!'

She started to paint again and very quickly ordered a new larger easel and a batch of new paints. The forthcoming exhibitions were a big incentive. She began to improve some of her earlier paintings with a view to exhibiting, although we do not know how many or which ones.

She also began *Search the Highways* (Luke 14:23). This painting is full of ordinary people being dragged by the apostles to a glowing altar, behind which is an even more glowing figure of Christ. This painting can be seen as the final dragging of Eularia to her destiny and reflects a period in her life when she was absolutely certain of her calling as a religious painter doing God's work. It illustrates the story Jesus tells of the man who had invited guests to a banquet who subsequently made excuses not to come, so instead he commands his servant to go out and pull in whoever he finds to share the banquet, blind, lame, poor, sick... For Eularia, as a choice of subject, it undoubtedly reflects her experience of St Peter's at the time. With the departure of Pat and David the dynamic of the parish had changed. No matter how much he felt it was his role and duty to implement the changes of Vatican II, Sidney appears to have been quite traditional at heart (hence Eularia having to help him with the English translation of prayers in hospital). Like many priests, he had far too many years in the old ways to facilitate change easily and he had to rely heavily on his curates to implement them.

Of his two new curates, Roy Bennett was expecting to be given his own parish at any time, and Richard Davey was newly ordained, young and had yet to find his feet and his confidence. By his own admission Sidney Mullarkey felt that he had been in the same parish too long. The net result was that implementing changes at St Peter's, especially the musical changes, which mattered most to Eularia, had hit the doldrums. Sidney was not musical enough to take the lead. Will Thomas was a traditionalist and Sr Mary of the Filippini Sisters did her best but, in Eularia's opinion, often managed to choose hymns that no one knew.

To someone who enjoyed using music as a form of worship as much as Eularia did it was a sad state of affairs and is reflected in this painting, the implication being that the original guests had turned away and it was time to pull in new ones.

Despite the fact that she had been unable to attend either, the Catholic Artists and the Corpus Christi College exhibitions in London were well received. The Catholic Artists' exhibition even produced a request to purchase *Maundy Thursday* from a clergyman in Esher, which Eularia refused. With these successes, another television slot and at least two new one-man exhibitions coming up, Eularia began to worry that she wouldn't have enough paintings:

'I've only *just* enough as it is, and not very good. So the answer is the same as Catherine Eularia (*her great grandmother*), never a day without a line.'

Part 5
A Painter of Religion
1967 – 1970

36

Never a Day Without a Line

Having been so glad of all the visitors, they now became a chore as they distracted Eularia from painting and left her feeling tired. Within only a couple of weeks of leaving hospital she wrote:

'Alone, alone I primed canvasses and enjoyed my quiet hearth. I don't want anyone. Up with Trappism!'

There was a change in Eularia after this bout of cancer. It was ironic that just as she came out of hospital she was plunged straight into preparing for the Southampton exhibition, an interview for ATV and then a talk for a late-night television show called *Epilogues*. Once again she was caught between that old rock and hard place. On the one hand she tired easily and the treatments often left her feeling low. On the other, all the activity involving her paintings was just what she had wanted. But the cancer had sapped her confidence in her ability to cope and she became panicky very quickly at the prospect of such things as entertaining, driving the car, travelling and even publicity.

She did not handle fear well, and whilst she was fairly good at self-analysis she wasn't always able to act on the results. The consequence was that many good-natured friends suddenly found they were being given the brush-off and being told not to come and visit her. She tried to do this as nicely as she could but if she was very frazzled, as she was when John Amos rang one day, she could be extremely rude and hurtful.

It was a self-protection. She knew that she couldn't cope with constant interruption and that people drained her, especially if they were not able

Eularia's poster design for the Southampton show (1967)

to talk about painting or religion and required her to make polite inconsequential conversation, or simply to listen to their woes. At first she persuaded herself that it was because she was getting somewhere and they were now beneath her, but deep down she knew this wasn't so. She was afraid. She had a disease eating at her and she reflected this outward into the feeling that people were eating at her. She could be very irrational in this state, seeing demons and slights in the smallest comment, or the most innocuous correspondence.

But she also saw the cancer as a gift:

'More and more I see the advantage of a genuine, classified impressive-named disease; it has ironically, given me so much radiant health! No more struggles to do more than I comfortably can, and the result is definitely a better life altogether. No other disease could do exactly this, free me for painting without any perceptible weakening of physique.'

The Belfield's collected the forty-two paintings for the Southampton exhibition (which ran from 4–16 December) and hung them. Eularia was very glad of this as she didn't feel up to the stress. It was the first time she had been required to do a poster and biographical details for an exhibition, but despite giving a copy of the poster to Sidney it was not displayed at St Peter's (Mary Fairburn's had been). Felicity Belfield said that she was very cross with Sidney Mullarkey for not putting it up, even though she had asked him to herself. We will never know if this was oversight or intentional, but Eularia was not to forget it.

The Southampton exhibition was a success and well reviewed in the local press. The University authorities told Eversley that it was the best exhibition they had had that year, which included Art Council exhibitions.

With so many exhibitions coming up she was aware of the need to produce more paintings and began *Mending Their Nets* (Mark 1:20). This was her second painting of the calling of St John the Fisherman by Jesus (*Weighing the Catch* was the first). Eularia said in her caption:

'John was getting on with the work, and it sounds as if he was called quite suddenly. So I suppose it was a shock for him. Priests have sometimes told me what a shock it is to be called. They thought, what ME? The younger Zebedees and the parents have got into the picture because I had been watching an ordination and there was the memory of the new priest's family receiving Holy Communion from him. The location is the shore at Hill Head near Titchfield.'

A review in the *Southern Evening Echo* (author unknown) described it very well:

'One of the most successful of Mrs Clarke's compositions at several different levels... The skilfully observed beach scene with its innumerable holidaymakers, digging, knitting, love-making, or listening to transistor radios is in itself composed with considerable skill. Against this background the face

Mending Their Nets (1967)

of the fisherman in the foreground on whose head the hand of Christ is resting, has a look of sudden realisation of what he will be expected to renounce if he becomes one of His disciples. It does not need any particular knowledge of doctrine to understand one at least of the points which the artist is putting over in this particular picture.'

Once again the painting reflects where Eularia considered herself to be at this point in her life, that God had removed any obstacles to her becoming a full-time painter. The other reason for choosing this subject was because David Mahy had taken over the organising and storing of her paintings at St John's Catholic Cathedral in Portsmouth. She was immensely grateful to him for this. It was a burden removed and she added a codicil to her will leaving the paintings to the diocese with David as executor. The subject of St John was, therefore, very prominent in her mind:

'It is a positive joy at realising my vocation at last, yet something even more than that – it is the overflowing life in my heart, the singleness of mind and direction – quite calm, for I am not doing this myself. And the dropping-away of all needs and obsessions and worries, for the doctors diagnosis stripped away these requirements, and the amount of health and activity needed for painting, and the freedom and solitary life.'

She did an interview for Southern Television and the Reverend Tom Devonshire-Jones, later founder of the Art and Christian Enquiry Trust (ACE), was instrumental in arranging an exhibition in the Guildhall in Portsmouth for January 1968. Devonshire-Jones, then the Church of England Chaplin to the Portsmouth College of Technology, had seen some of the paintings at the Bishop's house in Portsmouth after David Mahy had picked them up from the Corpus Christi College exhibition in London. He wrote to Eularia:

'My main impressionional theologically was how incarnational they were – your meditation on Our Lord and your portrayal of Him is gloriously earthy, and you seem to be passionate about His divinity too, so the Christology is very rich and full. Each of them provided no end of food for looking and for prayer...'

Eularia was overjoyed with this letter, as she felt that Devonshire-Jones was the first person since Fr Alberic who had actually showed her that he both completely understood and appreciated her paintings. It threw into sharp contrast how much more openly appreciative and knowledgeable he was than the Roman Catholics.

Despite stiffness in her right hand causing her to cramp whilst holding a paintbrush, she began *No More Wine* (John 2:7), which she once told me was her favourite, and was reviewed by the *Southern Evening Echo*:

"Water into Wine' her interpretation of the marriage at Cana at first appears a slightly bazaar marriage feast in a garden. Look more closely into it and you will find guests in the background impatiently waving their empty glasses, a bored over-dressed woman in an elaborate wedding hat is only just stifling a wide yawn, a small child helping himself to food while his elders' backs are turned. The detail is endless.'

Eularia's caption asks:

"Why did the servants obey such a peculiar command by a quite non-famous preacher? Did they have a hunch that here was the Vine himself, with power over things like water and grapes?'

By Christmas the doctors declared her lung clear of fluid. She seemed to have made a remarkable recovery and she was in remission, so perhaps the idea of miracles was not so far from her mind, but for someone recovering from and still undergoing treatment for such a serious condition her workload during the autumn was exhausting, even though she enjoyed it. Then she attempted to take a step too far by going to York for Christmas. She opted to go by train, the thought of which caused her anxiety attacks, but the noise, the movement, the crowds, the thought of having to travel across London, all proved too much so she gave up at Woking and returned home to a Christmas alone with a small chicken and a tin of strawberries.

Southern TV's *New Approach* programme had asked her to give a series of late-night talks called 'Epilogues' just after Christmas. Once again she found this daunting. Eularia's teaching had always been very practical, showing people how to do things, not talking about it.

There is a sense of her going from standing still to running at full tilt during this period. Consequently, to handle this sudden leap in success, she tended to fall back on the strength of character she had inherited from her Aunts Sylvia and Dorothy, which had the downside of making her feel very superior and above 'lesser beings'. It was the family snobbishness (so prevalent in its women folk) which had surrounded Eularia as a child and was now so desperately out of place and counterproductive. But under it lay that deep sense of inadequacy and a growing fear that she might be a fraud. For all her eccentric appearance and character, Eularia still worried a great deal about what others thought of her. Her snobbish pushing away of 'lesser mortals' (her diary is full of it at this time) was really a protection, a fear of being 'found out'.

She did recognise the tendency and wrote:

'Aunt Sylvia, Aunt Dorothy, that *cruelty*... The answer is, I suppose, to be kind as far as possible, and let people think it's illness and hard work at painting rather than contempt. Let the tentacles loosen very gently.'

Just after Christmas 1967 she began *Widow's Dead Son* (Luke 7:14). A painting about raising the dead is a fairly obvious subject given Eularia's recent experience, but it may also reflect the fact that after so many years of seeing hardly anything of James, now that he was in London (and settled with a wife and a baby on the way) he was visiting every other weekend and had become a very practical help and support for Eularia. It must have felt to her as if he had 'come back from the dead'. Her own caption for this painting reads:

> 'A widow could be left quite destitute, with no social security, if her only son died; which makes Christ's compassion stand out, and the miracle so beautiful and also very disconcerting.'

The painting is sombre and monochrome in colour with the exception of the bier, which is covered in yellow and golden chrysanthemums. We see the hand of Christ extending over it from the right of the painting, bringing the colour into it with him as if he is returning everything to life. Almost in the centre of the painting is the widow herself, with a face stricken with grief as she looks up with a faint glimmer of hope towards Christ.

Despite the fact that it was her own choice, Eularia worried about her lack of contact with St Peter's. She had been attending various other local Catholic churches for Mass – St Edmund's in Southampton where she knew the priest Fr Francis Isherwood (Fr Ish), the hospital, Chandler's Ford and even on occasion the Cathedral in Portsmouth – but St Peter's remained her parish church, although she felt more than ever that she didn't belong there. She found the music very disappointing and she resented the lack of support over her exhibition, which wasn't even mentioned in the parish newsletter:

> 'Yet how will I paint or broadcast properly without? Is there any other way? Won't I become a sort of Stanley Spencer painter, not genuine, laughing at faith, even deriding it? This could happen. And it would be the end – I'd have lost everything, the ordinary teaching, all friends, everyone's trusting and liking, all my raison d'être, and the devil would win completely.'

It is hard to know now why Sidney Mullarkey didn't support Eularia by advertising her exhibitions within the parish. He had the information, but for some reason he never felt able to get behind her in the way that other clergy did (Francis Isherwood had written to her specifically to say that he had her poster up in his church porch). Eularia was too sensitive not to feel this and, when I interviewed her, Felicity Belfield backed up Eularia's position, confirming that Sidney had not supported her despite requests from the Belfields. Eularia always did her best to be optimistic about this, and not to let it colour her whole experience of worship and Catholicism. Certainly her other clergy friends helped, but it reflected too strongly the old feeling of lack of support in her home environment and it undermined her.

Sidney did try with Eularia. She went into St Peter's just before Ash Wednesday and Sidney was there and asked after her health and whether she was painting:

'I realise that I'd missed him in the last 4-5 months of not seeing him, and I sensed that he missed me, and that his cruel lack of backing wasn't due to personal dislike. Then what was it? Why does he leave me out, when he butters up every other parishioner who "does something" of note?'

We will never know the answer to this. Eularia never discovered it and David Mahy, who knew them both well, does not know either.

Amidst all this Eularia had a powerful image in mind for her next painting:

'I felt the new painting coming, stand out into deep waters... Christ pushing out the boat and the young apostle hanging out in front shining a lantern down, and the churches sticking out of the shallows with seaweed on them, and scum, and the deep water full of people looking at the lantern...'

Into Deep Water (Luke 5:4) illustrates the story of the apostles having been out fishing all night and catching nothing. Jesus tells them to put out again and the subsequent catch is the largest they have ever had. In the event the only thing missing from Eularia's original image of this painting are the submerged churches. In every other respect it is as she first described it, complete with young apostle holding the lantern over the water and a sea of faces looking up at it. Eularia's caption reflects something of her state:

'They were exhausted with all night fishing, but they were ordered to go out again, into different waters. What does this involve for us? Does he want us to fish?'

Many times over this period in her diary she talked about feeling as if she was moving into deep water with the new direction that her life was taking. The sense of exhaustion and yet having to launch out again reflects her physical state very strongly, and we can see this in the faces of the apostles as Christ pushes the boat back into the water. But the sense of having to move into different waters is also reflective of her questions about whether she should find a different parish to belong to, where she would feel more at home.

Into Deep Water (1967)

37

Into Deep Water

Eularia's 'Epilogue' talks went well and she quickly found her rhythm with them. Needless to say the film crew all warmed to her and she got on very well with the interviewer, Ian Currie. The *Southern Evening Echo* reported on Eularia's appearance on 'Epilogues' with an accompanying photograph of her discussing *Glastonbury, Taking up the Crosses.* Another local paper also featured her (the clipping does not include the name of the paper) under the heading 'Change of Will has happy results' referring very publicly to the fact that Eularia had decided to leave the paintings to the Portsmouth diocese.

Hot on the heals of 'Epilogues' came the exhibition at the Portsmouth Guildhall during a week of prayer for Church Unity. Tom Devonshire-Jones had been true to his word, and now that the paintings were stored at the cathedral Eularia didn't have to think about transporting them:

'The Portsmouth Guildhall Exhibition was a hoot, hung very badly in a hurry by the poor overworked clergy, and lit by orange, dim lighting, so the paintings looked very grim and dark, and the Book of Comments kept saying "gloomy and gruesome" – also it said "SHIT" and "AGREED" and "A Load of Rubbish" and "The best religious paintings since Raphael" – all very interesting, as I don't believe many of the visitors have seen modern painting before! The nicest comment was, "Very bloodthirsty but true cause of what happened." (I suspect a child of about 8?)'

She had a good write-up (the clipping does not say from which paper. The author was probably Tom Devonshire-Jones):

'The 44 paintings represent the artist's understanding of the Creed, but have nothing of the stuffiness of conventional commercial Church art about them.

'Victorian stained glass window saints – fisherman daintily toying with nets – are out. Instead, hefty real-life figures are seen reacting to Christ in their setting of work, commerce, and home...

'The artist has a message for believers and non-believers alike; she leads them to reflect on the nature of religion and is content that her paintings should stimulate discussion.'

Eularia kept many of the comment books and sheets from her exhibitions, regardless of whether they were flattering or not. She was interested in all opinions and knew that there would be many who did not like her work. So long as she didn't know the people who had made the comments she didn't seem to mind much. But she received many good comments too:

'For all their modernity and freshness these paintings have an authentic 13th century atmosphere...The artist may not know it, but she was born with an invisible Franciscan cord – and it shows through the painting. Giotto didn't get as close as this.'

'Something quite unusual, probably fantastic. This throws an entirely different light on religious paintings to what I have been used to. Some of the figures in the procession somewhat elementary but, not as bad as what we are used to seeing. These paintings show the real life – and the real Christ – not a Christ standing in a nightgown with deep blue eyes and soft complexion.'

As a result of the 'Epilogues' the Quaker Meeting House in Alton asked to borrow some of the paintings for an exhibition in June. This amazed Eularia (her appeal to non-Catholics always amazed her) but she was very pleased. It spurred her on to produce as many new paintings as she could. She established that she liked the morning light best to paint in, especially between 10am and 12 noon, so began organising her day around this, leaving household chores until evening.

The Catholic Press was beginning to take an interest in Eularia. Winefride Wilson of *The Tablet* had written about her, and Kathleen Rowland at *The Universe* also contacted her to do an article. A local paper (probably the *Hampshire Chronicle*) did a big article of the Wessex Artists show using Eularia's *Search the Highways* painting for the photograph. This was quite a coup as there were 149 works at this exhibition, half of which were by professional artists. In total there had been 1500 submissions and they had accepted all three of Eularia's. With only a handful of the accepted artists being mentioned in the article, Eularia gets two paragraphs.

Ideas for new paintings were now coming thick and fast and she was working on as many as three at once as well as finishing off the last of the *Stations* for Pat Murphy-O'Connor. 1968 would prove to be her most productive year, producing fifteen new paintings. This was possible because she was no longer having to work, so could put her whole focus into it, but on another level there was a sense of urgency. The doctors were of the opinion that she was getting better, she was certainly in remission, but no one knew how long it would last. The next three years would see her almost equal her output of the whole of the past seven years put together.

Christ, the Vine-Dresser (Luke 13:6) came next. It shows the story of the man who wants to cut down a fig tree that bears no fruit but the vinedresser asks for one more year to mulch it and tend to it. The inference is that Christ always gives us one more chance and will always prepare the ground for us to fruit. Once again it is impossible to ignore the reference to her own life, which a year ago had seemed barren and unfruitful and just a few months before had seemed to be ending. Yet here she was flowering and fruiting, as she never had before. She always gave credit to the doctors for this but also to God and her sense of prayer.

Her caption for this painting reads:

'If God made us, and knows our exact potential and our performance, all we are capable of and all we need, I suppose we shall get the appropriate treatment; He will let us be cut down (like that other fig tree) or he will go on giving us more chances of producing fruit, like the Vine-Dresser.'

For nearly a year she had been working on Pat's *Stations* and she finally began the last one (*Station twelve, The Crucifixion*) in the spring of 1968. As far as we can determine this is the only version of Station twelve that she ever painted because she found this particular subject 'so difficult, so impossible'. Traditionally it is the one that shows the crucified Christ. It is the one Station missing from the two surviving sets, and as Pat's set is no longer in existence we do not know what it looked like.

The completion of this set of *Stations* represented the last regular contact that Eularia had with Pat. They saw each other from time to time but their busy lives prevented them from seeing each other on any kind of regular basis.

Most of Eularia's contact with her old clergy friends over the next eighteen months would be at Portsmouth Cathedral, which was now the epicentre of her collection. Eularia never liked the drive to Portsmouth. In those days there was no M3/M27 making it fast and easy and she always got hopelessly lost in large towns and cities, even when familiar with them. But she persevered, firmly convinced that this was the best place for her collection.

She began the sixth painting of 1968 during Lent, *The Sowers* (Matthew 13:24). Here we see the arms of Christ loading up seed sacks onto the backs of sowers amidst a field with brambles on the left, unripe and ripe wheat down the middle and an empty furrow with a few seeds in it and bare ploughed field on the right. Above them in the foreground black, menacing birds fly, their red eyes alight for any spare grain. It is a visual representation of the parable in which we are warned about letting seed fall onto unproductive ground, which matched Eularia's increasing reluctance to waste time or energy on anyone who couldn't converse about theology or her paintings. Her caption states:

'The well known parable of the sower. Sometimes I just leave the Telly on (*she now had one*) because it's easier to watch mindlessly than to think. Often I get fed up with religion, it can be such a nuisance and a bore. BUT...'

Perhaps bearing her growing superiority complex in mind, she began her version of the Prodigal Son called *The Son Came Home* (Luke 15:20). Eularia's caption reads:

'The Prodigal Son, not quite home yet, but getting near perhaps the kitchen garden? Not knowing how to represent God the Father, I used the Feast of the Sacred Heart, because it is about God calling people back and loving them. Also, the red votive lights give a vaguely cosy look to the church, and the prodigal's father was nothing if not welcoming, he really overplayed it....And this is Christ's own portrait of the Father!'

Eularia was feeling a little prodigal herself in having paid less attention to God, caught up as she had been in her whirl of publicity. The returning son is seen in the distance opening the gate to a kitchen garden, complete with cinder path and beehives. This merges, as it moves to the foreground, with the church itself and leads to the focal point which is the statue of the Sacred Heart seen from behind and which is denoted by its heart-shaped stand for votive candles. Once again we are behind and above the action, the church statues all seen from the rear and in silhouette, and the quiet and respectful church attendees lending an air of calm to what is an otherwise emotional scene of reunion. Eularia plays this aspect down, unusually for her who was so keen on drama. One is left with the feeling that the stage is set but the drama is yet to unfold.

She said of her paintings in her diary at this time:

'They are getting simple, non-intellectual, yet the ideas lie underneath the first appearance, they are my own ideas. Like the early Fathers, who put all sorts of meanings into the gospel narratives.'

The Son Came Home (1968)

Nevertheless she did feel a loss of inspiration. This she put down to finding St Peter's so dull and unattractive, but it could just as easily have been the sheer volume of output during 1968:

'The paintings depend on love of Church, the "Religious Act", but Church is either the horrors of St. Peter's, or gloomy doubts coming from ecumenists or protestants or agnostics. When I think of Christ, am I just thinking of some imaginary person I'd *like* to love, to worship? Have I invented this image because I don't fit in with people? Because it brings me a sort of fame?'

This doubt would remain with Eularia, but it was always countered by something deeper that she could never quite define. The original impetus behind the Vatican II reforms was increasingly becoming lost under the divisions between liberal reformers and conservative hard-liners. The Catholic press was full of letters of criticism and disagreements about what was happening. The status of the ordinary priest had been downgraded in favour of bishops and the laity, religious vocations had plummeted to an all-time low and many felt their faith was challenged.

The younger clergy, like Pat Murphy-O'Connor and David Mahy, who had been around when Vatican II was first convened, and who saw the original vision, remained keen to implement it, but older clergy like Sidney Mullarkey must have felt very tempted to remain with what they had known all their lives, and it is possible that Sidney had given in to pressure from very vocal conservatives in his congregation. Consequently, while things had not returned to how they used to be, they hadn't moved forward as much as was hoped either.

Eularia was also becoming concerned about how well-looked-after her paintings were in Portsmouth. David Mahy had been thrown into the deep end with his new post as 'Administrator' at the Cathedral (having been promoted over several other much more experienced and older clergy) and, at only 30, was in charge of the primary parish of the Portsmouth diocese in a large and busy seaport. That he was not more available to support Eularia is a lasting regret to him. But the late 1960s was a particularly challenging time for priests, even with experience. With the foundations of Church organisation and daily worship shifting beneath them the calls on their time were immense.

Perhaps it is not surprising, after such an intense period in which she had equalled in a few short months her previous annual output to date, that she went into a period when she really felt unable to paint at all. She felt she had lost all inspiration:

'I don't know what "darkness" is – how can I? Spiritual darkness, is there any, or only a sort of depression? Last night was thick with it, I saw that I've gone and committed myself to a huge faith which looks increasingly subjective and imaginary, a sort of tradition, now breaking up and held only by dim people against a huge wave of modern thought. I think of Christ, who was written about, has been followed, prayed to, worshipped. I've expressed something very powerful, but it may well be myself simply seeking comfort and love, blown up in typical Baines fashion into something exciting, pictorial, dramatic... To go forward means more painting, it means loyalty, love, participation, worship, sacrifice. And this has all gone, all that is left is the Baines tendency to be dramatic. However the sun comes out and brings a sort of trust.'

Given that she was working on more than one painting at a time, it is difficult to know exactly when one is finished and she begins another, but certainly at this time of 'dark night', rather ironically, she was working on *Finding the Ex-Blind Boy* (John 9:35). This is the story of the boy who was born blind that Jesus cured on the Sabbath day. The Pharisees threw the boy out because he refused to say that Jesus was not from God so Jesus went to find him. The painting illustrates the moment that he was found and is set at Osmington Mills, near Weymouth. We see him on the cliff tops confused with wide staring eyes, being chased by an angry crowd and Christ just behind him rising from behind a rock and touching him gently. Eularia's caption says:

'His very first experience of SEEING – and everything spoilt and made unhappy and frightening by the arguing and the bullying, and then being thrown out. Then Christ took the trouble to find where he was, and came and cheered him up.'

As a subject at a time when Eularia was feeling so spiritually blind, and rather cast out by her own parish, it could easily be expressing her deep confusion and despair. It is possible to discern some of her own 'dark night' in the expression of the boy, along with the hope that she was still being held by Christ, even if she couldn't see it.

It is easy to see why Eularia might subconsciously identify with the blind boy. Her painting reflected the changes that were happening in the Church itself. Bringing the Mass into the vernacular was a way of bringing it into the present day and people's ordinary worlds. Eularia's paintings were doing exactly the same thing but visually. The housekeeper at Pat's presbytery in Leigh Park brought this home to her:

'His housekeeper very sweetly criticised my Stations, very kindly and openly; I was glad, yet I see that I've launched a really difficult thing. And I see how people must truly *prefer* the traditional Stations, clean white nightgown,

18th century carving, exactly in a certain, beautiful manner. She wanted a beautiful girl for Veronica, too. And I see that – a lovely dream-world Veronica, the ideal nun, all dewy over Him.'

One of the key purposes of good art is to challenge and provoke, to lift us out of ourselves into something else. By ignoring the tradition of Catholic Art, Eularia's paintings were doing exactly this.

It has often seemed to me, and to Eularia too, that one of the biggest problems with religious faith is its inability to cope with being challenged, with people seeing it from different angles and in ways that are neither traditional nor safe. It has lost ground because of this, especially in the world of today. Whilst Eularia's work is deeply rooted in her Catholicism and the Christian faith, it represents a major step towards expanding and changing traditionally held and safe views. The idea that each of us can experience Christ and the Gospels in our everyday lives means that we cannot avoid His teachings in a very practical sense. The underlying message is that it is impossible to simply be a 'Sunday' Christian. In every moment we have the choice of how we express the living gospel.

Eularia was very aware of this, which is why she often gave herself such a hard time about what she perceived as her character flaws. But she couldn't escape the sense of 'ploughing that lonely furrow', the only English Catholic Religious Artist painting anything that wasn't traditional and easily digestible, the only Catholic Artist attempting to alter the perceptions about how people had seen their faith for centuries.

But she wasn't entirely without allies. The Catholic Artists Committee elected Eularia to send in two paintings to the Sonning Exhibition of Religious Art due to take place in the summer. This was quite an honour as she would be hanging alongside Spencer, Piper and other well-known artists.

With all this success and support it seems extraordinary that she embarked on what is her worst painting. Even Eularia thought it was bad and she never framed it or included it as part of her collection. *All This Waste* (Mark 14:4) shows Mary Magdalene drying Jesus' feet with her hair. Set against a backdrop of willow trees, the figure of Mary has her usual drama and fluidity, but the figures around her are curiously angular and stilted, even menacing. There is a powerful sense of Mary being overwhelmed by criticism and forces ranked against her. It is a shame that Eularia didn't pull it off.

38

Walling In

In the summer of 1968 Eularia bought herself a large bag of cement and became addicted to hard landscaping, creating ponds, a wall imbedded with old bottles and glass and pebbles that she picked up from the beach, along with many other small garden projects. It became the perfect antidote to artist's block, which, as usual, she suffered from dreadfully in the summer. She loved the feel of the cement and the act of creating with her hands. The only downside was that it increased the stiffness in her right hand, which made painting even harder.

This urge was partly driven by her increasing need for privacy: 'I want to wall myself in from all view.' Rather like the desert hermits. It was almost certainly a reaction to increasing public recognition. But she couldn't paint without absolute peace and quiet; noise and interruption prevented her from connecting with the inner experience of God that she so relied on.

Her 'war' against unwanted guests and interruption continued to the point where she finally realised that it was having a detrimental effect on her. She was visited late one evening in April by a young seminarian that she knew. He was just the sort of guest she would previously have encouraged and enjoyed, but instead she did everything she could to force him to leave (other than asking him directly) by leaving all the doors and windows open with no heating on. Unfortunately he had a warm jacket on and she only had a shirt. It brought her up short and helped her to realise how ridiculous she was becoming about it, but she found it very hard to say no to people and turn them away. Nor were they used to her doing it.

Having only Eularia's accounts to refer to it is sometimes difficult to find objectivity about all this, but she felt that people resented her vocation and her success. In an era when women still played a minor role in the life of the Church she was preaching through her Art (her term for it) and, with so many friends among the diocesan clergy, including being known to the Bishop, she was occupying a place that no woman had yet occupied in the memory of the local Catholics, without being a nun:

> 'But I behave badly, I despise people... the criticism and high standards I bring to painting are big drawbacks when judging *people*.'

She was finding it increasingly hard to balance the hermetical life needed for her art with the fame that she began to attract, and to include ordinary casual relationships alongside it.

She became a grandmother again, this time to James' first child, a daughter called Camilla Matilda. Camilla was the last grandchild that she would live to see, and despite the fact that she had to brave the combined forces of Cousin Alicia and Clare (Christopher's wife), she went to London to visit them.

As she was anxiously waiting for news as to whether the three paintings she had sent up for the Royal Academy summer show had been accepted, this rather distracted from the event. So far she had always had outright rejections but this year, the last year she would make the attempt, she got three D rejections which meant that they were only rejected at the last minute during the hanging. She did try not to mind this but inevitably it mattered to her. The Royal Academy still represented acceptance by the proper artistic community, but it spurred her on to find other exhibitions nearer home.

The Alton Quakers chose twelve paintings for their exhibition. It was Eularia who had to go to Portsmouth, pick up the paintings and deliver them, but as she was always concerned about damage during transit at least she could make sure they were well wrapped.

Much to her surprise Sonning also wanted more paintings as she told Rachael:

> 'I have just been to Sonning-on-Thames where they have a Festival of Art (!!!!!!) and after seeing the five paintings I first took, they demanded five more, hung in the vicarage, and I was the V.I.P for a few hours, as the visitors

all enjoyed them as much as Cuthbert (*her grandson*) did, and ganged up to interview me and shake hands... this being "Stanley Spencer Land". A nice, black, parson – (chaplain) – has asked for 40 in November at the Imperial College of Science – do you think the scientists will spray them with pest-destroyer?'

The vicar at Sonning even asked her to give Lenten addresses in the church the following Easter. It was all a stark contrast to the complete lack of interest that she always met at St Peter's and, for Eularia, cut all the deeper because all the interest was coming from Protestants and not Catholics.

Despite the fact that she was finding it very difficult to get back into painting she had ideas for three new works:

'...the Baptism, with the usual canoes, vertical shaft of light, pollarded willows. Visitation with hen-coop, enamel pie-dish, tethered lamb, blackthorn, Elizabeth in cameo brooch leaning over gate, Mary coming up from the bottom R, basket, espadrilles, striped frock, jersey over basket, shining abdomen between stripes, against dark hedge. These will be two very easy, "sweet" paintings. Then Barabbas.'

Mary Practising the Magnificat (Luke 1:40) is just as she envisaged it, with a few minor changes, but despite the fact that it is painted on canvas on board she returned to her beloved gouache:

'... (*I*) painted quite a lot of the Visitation, doing it in the remaining poster-paints, partly for speed in drying, partly to use them up, partly so as to smell the tobacco-plants and carnations. Also, there is something in the medium. Flat it may be, but it's very fine and accurate.'

She didn't use the actual Magnificat as the Gospel quote which, given the caption and the eventual painting title, is intriguing:

'Mary sang it (*the Magnificat*) to St. Elizabeth, so I assume that she had been composing it all the way to the Hill Country as she walked. My Hill Country is Monmouth-Brecon up above the Wye. The cade-lambs came into the picture naturally because Elizabeth was pregnant with John the Baptist whose sign is the Paschal Lamb.'

She was never entirely happy with this painting though, considering it to be too M. W. Tarrant in nature, and it is rather sweet by Eularia's standards with bright, jolly colours, a very bucolic scene.

But both the paintings Eularia did in the summer of 1968 have a

Mary Practices the Magnificat (1968)

lightness and colour about them, the other (also in gouache) being *Baptising in the Jordan* (Mark 1:10 and John 1:29). She felt that this painting became a rather '...muddly affair, too much willows etc.? But rivers are like that – no clear view from the bank.'

The willows, the canoes and the vertical shaft of light are all included and these two paintings make an interesting pair to have chosen to do together, the first being the meeting of the two expectant mothers and the second being the meeting of their sons so many years later. Because they were done in gouache both paintings were wax varnished.

Eularia enjoyed the summer of 1968, despite the fact that she didn't feel her painting was going very well. She was exhibiting, meeting new people and most of all she was alive and, against all expectations, apparently cancer-free. Because she was no longer teaching she could take off in the van whenever she wanted and frequently went to the South coast to swim in the sea, which remained an abiding joy even on dull and chilly days. She was enjoying her garden, her cementing and all the wildlife that was making its home there. Sleeping in the greenhouse with doors open meant that the birds often flew in while she was still in bed and became quite tame. She stocked her new ponds with snails and fish acquired from the pools where she collected her pondweed and she bought a large old tin bath in order to make an internal pond in the greenhouse.

She made an observation in her diary during the summer which described her sense of there always having been something more than the merely human:

'A really warm night – like those nights in Spain; further back, the nights at Mitcham (*where Cyril's parents lived*) ... nights which never quite satisfied me, but only increased my hunger for something beyond, and my knowledge that no human could satisfy my human needs. Tonight, as every night, I am internally fed.'

It was her success that renewed her enthusiasm for her work after the end of the Middle Road Curia:

'I woke up with a new sense of direction. My vocation is to show all these technical artists that there *are* other subjects than the crucifixion and nativity.'

Despite the hot weather she began two new paintings *Corpus Christi* and *White and Dazzling*. *Corpus Christi* (John 6:48) is her version of the traditional Catholic procession on the feast of Corpus Christi, which falls in the first half of June. In her caption she said:

'Since Christ said "This is my Body" the awareness mounted and mounted until in the Middle Ages it began to be expressed in processions and adoration of the consecrated bread which is the special sign of Christ's presence. The processions are still kept up in honour of this mystery, rose-petals are still scattered by the First Communion children, and honour is given to Christ as a king of his subjects giving him public honour as far as we are able.'

In the painting we follow the procession of priests and white-veiled girls in a cloud of rose petals from behind as it turns a corner, as if we are part of the congregation. David Mahy helped her with the ecclesiastical detail. As this was the painting she was working on when the professional photographs of her as an artist were taken we can see her painting it.

Eularia painting Corpus Christi (1968)

Although *White and Dazzling* (Matthew 17:1–3) was begun in the summer it took her a long time to complete. This was her second 'Transfiguration' painting, the first being *Transfiguration in the Valley* in which the three apostles and a bright light can be seen in the background of the painting on a slagheap. Rather than attempt to show the transfigured Christ along with Moses and Elijah, she chose to show the very human reactions of the three apostles, with Peter's face being the only one the viewer sees. Her caption says:

> 'The only mountains I've been up have been cut by deep narrow gullies with splashing streams. This is the first moment of shock and awe, before the disciples had taken in any details.'

We stand just behind and above the three disciples, which encourages us to look at what they are seeing. It is a clever device as the figures of the apostles are far more substantial than Christ and one naturally looks at them first. We then follow the gaze of an awed St Peter to the transfigured Christ. Eularia finished two other paintings before completing this one as she was very aware of not wanting to portray an ethereal M. W. Tarrant-style Christ, so for that reason, we are only given his foot. The rest is left to the imagination.

39

Where Will The Paintings Live?

Now that the Middle Road Curia had disbanded and she no longer
attended a regular parish church because of her disaffection with St Peter's,
she was beginning to feel less a part of the intimate priest circle. This came
home to her with some force when she attended the annual ordination
service in Portsmouth, a spectacle she always enjoyed, and went to return
some of her work to the storage cupboard by the sacristy afterwards only
to find the area full of priests:

'I had some paintings to put back, but I drove them home, I felt I might be
de trop in the happy gathering of males, the Church, this love-affair of man
with God, this alliance, it hasn't much room yet for women.'

There is a wistfulness here which during the next two years would
become much more focussed and define her relationship with the clergy
for the rest of her life. It went hand in hand with a concern regarding the
paintings, which she noticed were being bashed about in the cupboard at
the Cathedral, along with a slight tendency towards damp. Now that she
was having more to do with other denominations over the paintings she
began to notice how much less care the Catholics seemed to be taking
of them.

The brutal fact was that, despite any misgivings she might have had, no
one else was offering to house them as a collection, despite the growing
interest. The only other option open to her was to take them all home.

She began what she referred to as the "Tent" painting. Once again the
subject ties in neatly with where she was at and her sense of not having a

home for her work, but she wrote in her diary of it that 'it's got the right mixture of real and imaginative, material and sacramental.'

Ultimately entitled *Master, where do you live?* (John 1:38), it illustrates the moment when the two disciples, who overheard John the Baptist referring to Jesus as the one, followed him and caught up with him. Jesus is shown on the edge of a campsite in the early morning, just as everyone is waking up. In the background a mother cooks breakfast on a primus stove, just like Eularia's own, a woman is seen brushing her long hair in much the way that Eularia used to before she cut it short and in the foreground a man is drying his face after washing. The tents are rather shabby and there is washing hanging in between. Eularia's caption says:

'Unfortunately I didn't notice that it says "the tenth hour" so I painted the visit of Andrew and the other disciple to Christ's home in early morning; it ought to be 4pm. But I expect there were a lot of these visits. I was remembering, too, the sight of the empty open Tabernacle on the altar on Good Friday. And "The tent of God among men".'

In August she began the only painting she made using an Old Testament reference, *The Valley of the Shadow* which was based on Psalm 23 (The Lord is My Shepherd). She said of it, 'It may be comic or bizarre, I don't know.'

Eularia referenced much of her own experience for this painting as it is set in a hospital ward, but with a grassy stream from which sheep drink running down the centre. The feet of Christ walk beside it with a shepherd's crook gently herding them. Eularia's own caption says:

"A memory of a Medical Treatment Ward combined with the psalm "The Lord is my shepherd". The sheep were on Swainby Moor, up in North Yorkshire.'

Eularia was uncertain about both *Master, where do you live?* (The Tent) and *The Valley of the Shadow* (The Hospital) while she was painting them:

'The Tent is a puzzle – it ought to be quite good, but something is vaguely wrong – or is it my fancy? As for the Hospital ... I don't know at all.'

In the early autumn she began a painting, which she did not list as finished until 1969, *A Manchild is Born* (John 16:21). Eularia's is an unusual interpretation of this gospel passage in which Jesus uses the metaphor of a woman giving birth to help the disciples understand that suffering is nothing once the joy of the new birth is felt: to be born is to leave one state and move into another. Jesus is referring to his risen state after his death.

Eularia appears to take the metaphor literally in her interpretation, but, given her understanding of theological texts, she would have understood the true meaning of this passage and its context. Eularia, being a mother herself, knew about birth in a way that no man could and she chose to speculate what experiences in Jesus' ordinary life had led him to choose this metaphor with such accuracy. In her caption she says:

'Christ knew how a mother felt, after all the tussle of birth, and I wondered if he remembered the look of joy and relief when he described the Second Coming. Did he come in with the other children after the births in Nazareth, while Mary and Joseph helped their neighbours? He chose this illustration, so we may expect joy and peace and well-it-was-worth-it from his words.'

The painting shows the moments after a new child has been born. The setting is a simple kitchen and the new mother, lying in bed, is being helped by Mary while the midwife holds the squalling new baby in newspaper to clean it. Joseph, carrying a bunch of sticks for the fire, and many other children, look on joyfully. Among them in the foreground is the child Jesus by a table loaded with dirty cups, jam pots, butter, milk bottles and sliced bread. It is a picture of cosy domesticity and the joy of new life.

Just as she began this painting on 20 August, the Russians invaded Czechoslovakia. In one of her very few diary entries that refer to world events (other than religious ones) with anything more than a passing mention she wrote:

'War? James! Comes the instant dart of worry. And the sudden, well-remembered feeling that all else will be of no importance if there is a major war; only survival. These promising beginnings, the lovely babies, Robert's and my and James' work – nothing. All our beginnings, our professions, hobbies, interest, enthusiasms. Possessions – nothing.'

This was a very real fear for someone who had lived through the last war as a young adult, and seen the fall-out of the first war as a child. It might go some way to explaining why the cosy domesticity and new beginnings of *A Manchild is Born* were put to one side and only completed with the start of the new year some months later.

Once again inspired by Evelyn Underhill (this time her biography), an author she had returned to several times over the years since she first discovered her as a teenager, she made a statement about her own journey in her diary:

A Man Child is Born (1969)

'My own call is much more adventurous though I've none of her qualifications or qualities. I must stand into the deep water after a tiring and unsuccessful life, and be battered by storms and criticisms and uncomprehension. I must preach, via paintings, to the thousands who'd never open a spiritual book, never hear a sermon, and take the consequences, living with no help, no support or sympathy, no holidays even – yet free and alone.'

It would always be Eularia's default position, even if people or events came along that alleviated things for a while. Once again she referred back to her mother's diary of them all as children:

'I never had the interest in listening to music which the boys did – I thought about other things, they thought about music... I also note my lack of demonstrative affection, my contentment on my own, amounting often to sheer selfishness; this is part of the training of an artist I fear. I see that I lived largely in a dream world, was this a sort of perception of the supernatural in embryo?'

The autumn of 1968 was an odd period artistically for Eularia, as if her fear of war deterred her from doing any serious painting. Instead she diversified and experimented, first with collage icons and then with another portrait, this time of *St Thomas More*. She painted this directly onto board in oil and coated it with what was probably a polymer varnish, as its original destination was an external one. She was inspired to paint it when passing the St Thomas More chapel at Four Marks and on the back of the panel she wrote "for the *outside* (facing London Road) Four Marks Chapel". This was not a commission and needless to say it never ended up there.

Eularia was feeling increasingly beleaguered in her faith and as a Catholic, as many were:

'I heard Baroness Stokes (on the radio) talking to Mervyn Stockwood (*Anglican Bishop of Southwark*) and was appalled. No Transubstantiation there, no "eat of my Flesh"... to him, it's just a sharing out of bread; a remembering of the Crucifixion, a witness. The Baroness described a Jewish Passover feast, and said it was just the same as Communion, he didn't *quite* agree. She raved furiously about Doctrine and Apostolic Succession, and they were both very, very anti-roman. I must go on painting R.C. pictures.'

The autumn of 1968 was also a hard period health-wise. It was a year since her cancer and she suffered a severe drop in energy along with backache, which the doctor first diagnosed as lumbago, but they then ran tests to see if the steroids had weakened her spine. Her health affected her ability to paint and she found she just couldn't get down to it after she had completed the *St Thomas More*.

She slipped into a depression partly triggered by a row with James over money, but she was also increasingly concerned by the eventual fate of the paintings. Nothing much seemed to be happening in Portsmouth. The nuns at Park Place were keen to have them there, however, and were even going as far as planning a 'sort of gallery' by their chapel. But Eularia felt that burying them in a Convent School would mean less public access and wasn't keen on this. Once again she doubted David Mahy's enthusiasm for her work. But David came up trumps:

'Fr. Mahy was exploring what was thought to be cellars under the 1940 Parish Hall, and he found a *huge underground room* – under a foot of water, but splendid for paintings – he at once decided to hang them all in it, (when drained.) I'm very pleased, as it's a splendid location, between the station, Guildhall and Victory, handy for everything, and will eventually be skylit which is the best of all. Christian painting began in Catacombs, and so it's nice that in England it should begin in an underground cellar!'

It was everything that Eularia wanted, and despite her own slight misgivings and Rachael's concern about the damp, she felt that it was a good option:

'Christian art began in a catacomb, and will be reborn in one. Darkness, artificial light, prayer, silence... splendid, splendid...'

The room was not as ideal as all that. It was narrow and high ceilinged with no natural light – all things that Eularia knew did not work terribly well for her paintings, but she remained optimistic nevertheless. At the very least it meant somewhere the paintings could be better stored and hung so that anyone wanting exhibitions could easily see them without constantly having to shift them around and damage them.

To have them all in one gallery was always her dream, right from the time when Adrian Stokes had first stimulated it back in the early 1960s. That they would always be available for loan to exhibitions or for clergy to build sermons around or discuss at retreats was a part of that dream. This was why she was so keen to leave them to the Portsmouth diocese and not to her family. She never saw them as personal possessions. They had a job to do and they could not do that on private walls.

Privately, though, Eularia's inner struggles continued:

'...Last night I saw more clearly than ever that Alicia might be right, that I'm just one of the flock of unattached women who gather in this fold of man-run religion, gathering a circle of spiritual husbands, fathers, sons. Even Christ *may* be the make-believe husband – but this I doubt, because I sensed Him even as a child, and especially just before marriage, that time when I used to cycle over to Westcote to the church, and told Cyril in such joy that I'd "found God." And he kissed me. I doubt if God is a substitute husband, but the priests may well be a sort of substitute family.'

Meanwhile the exhibition at the Imperial College in London went ahead, despite her worry over student riots. Her paintings were hung in the foyer of the Department of Mechanical Engineering and the Bishop of

Kensington celebrated the Eucharist amongst them. Eularia was worried about attending as she was not feeling strong, but her London-based family were all very keen, as James had organised a party for her, so she felt she couldn't let them down:

> 'I seem to be up against destructive forces. Each little symptom, even the detail of sore tongue, seems to threaten defeat. But I suppose I prefer this to what life might have been – unicus et pauper, this is what I keep saying. It is dark and cold and hostile everywhere. But nothing to be done. ... Pauper et unicus...absurd, I've lots of money and the family's full of every kindness. Also the hand of God, completely invisible and impalpable but *there,* felt by the inmost soul, God who is possibly using me for something.'

40

Unicus et Pauper[1]

As 1968 drew to a close Eularia was still feeling low. She hadn't picked up a paintbrush since she'd put aside *A Manchild is Born* at the end of the summer. But with the opening of the new gallery set for spring 1969 she had an incentive, so she began work again. She began *It Was Winter* (John 10:23).

Some of Eularia's bleakness can be seen in this painting. In the foreground are a huddled mass of people, all looking cold, none taking any notice of Jesus who is under a Grecian-style portico (she set it in London). In the background are an angry mob throwing bricks at him. Her caption says:

'Winter in Solomon's porch; they threw stones because Christ wouldn't explain himself clearly. Winter for all of us when the Christian Thing looks so unreal and obscure. When some groups are attacking Christ and the vast mass seem indifferent – symbolised by these Central London crowds going to work in frost and fog.'

There is a sense of the world closing in, of the 'unicus et pauper', the forlorn and friendless quality that Eularia had been feeling, despite renewed contact with the family and an easing with the parish priests. It was in her low moments that her illness and awareness of approaching death came through and this scene is one in the prelude to Jesus' death on the cross.

Light was shed on the growing stiffness in her right arm when the

---

1   From Psalm 25 verse 16. Respice in me et miserere mei quia unicus et pauper sum ego. Pity me, Lord, as thou seest me friendless and forlorn.

doctors discovered a lump in her right shoulder muscle, which they decided should be removed. She was very worried about this because of the importance of her finger muscles in her right hand, and was concerned about any chance of loss of feeling or movement. She lectured a gathering of doctors, stripped to the waist, on the importance of muscles and nerves in the hand if you are an artist:

> 'My fingers moved perfectly (on the stretcher I'd kept saying, Lord into thy hands... Lord Jesus receive my soul).'

Her confusion about the Church and her place in it weighed on her for the rest of her life. As an intelligent and educated woman she simply couldn't find a way of fitting in and having her talents accepted. Yes, there were individuals, like Pat Murphy-O'Connor, David Mahy and Michael Gedge, who were exceptions, but the hierarchy and organisation of the 1960s Church really had no place for a women like Eularia. Eularia was doubly tied by her gender because the art world in general was slow to support its female artists. It is a poignant reminder of just how hard it was for the pre-feminist generation of intelligent and talented women to be accepted as anything but subservient mothers. Once again Eularia would prove to be ahead of her time. As the feminist movement was just beginning she was approaching the end of her life.

She referred to this period as the 'dark night of the nervous system' and it worried her because of the family patterns of depression. In it she felt that she had lost her faith and any sense of religion and found it almost impossible to care about the paintings. In fact she was finding it very difficult to adjust to the reduced physical health brought on by the radium treatments and adrenal suppressants. She had much less energy to do anything, people and crowds especially were stressful and tired her out and she began to hate attending Mass, not least because she found it very uncomfortable to physically sit through a long service.

Eularia was realising that it wasn't the framework of Catholicism that sustained her but the opportunity for friendships with like-minded intelligently spiritual people, who also had a calling to follow Christ and were dedicating their lives to it. But she felt that this was wrong; that it shouldn't be about the priests and that because it was she had somehow failed. Despite all her experience of prayer providing evidence to the contrary, she began to feel that she never really had a connection with God at all and her sense of ploughing that lonely furrow became very strong.

Every artist is inspired by something, and many by the people around them; that her priest friends helped to inspire her art is not unusual. But inspiration leads us on to other things. Through these inspirations she found a voice for her early experiences of God and that was what she expressed in her Art. Occasionally Eularia saw this:

'As for the falseness of my painting, it could be a necessary factor. Grace builds on nature, and we must paint spiritual things from natural models. If God is real, and it looks like it, then he could only use what I have – my loves and my longings, which at least are genuine. My emptiness and inability to form relationships may even have been divinely planned.'

If Eularia had lived in a more artistic and bohemian community in London she would probably have felt much more at home. Her parents had always been on the fringes of the bohemian. Her father had tried to fit into normal life by having a respectable job and it had never suited him, leading to depression. Her mother had been trained as a professional botanist at a time when respectable women rarely worked. The Distributist ideals of self-sufficiency and her father's Heath-Robinson inventiveness would clearly have set them apart from gentry in a small Cotswold village. Eularia's brothers, especially Francis, had unconventional careers for the period they were in and Francis in particular was a noted eccentric. It was Eularia's uniqueness and eccentricity that made her so attractive to others, but her enduring judgement of it was that it isolated her, and it fed her low self-esteem. The recent publicity she had received, and was about to receive with the opening of the Cellar Gallery, only served to emphasise it. For all that she wanted to be famous, she wanted to be accepted more, and most of all by her local community:

'I contemplate my successes fascinatedly, I am an elderly narcissus, I watch my success grow and am full of self-admiration.'

Deep down she had very little self-admiration. The successful Eularia was a very shallow, rootless aspect of her personality and was not, in any way, connected with the part of her that had a deep sense of self and God. It was too concerned with externals and she had insufficient belief in it. Consequently when she was swept up into it she lost touch with the part if herself that really mattered to her, just as she had when she married and had children.

Anyone who has suffered bouts of depression and illness will know how it can take over every horizon and seems to cut us off from everything that we value. Eularia was no different, and every time she began to focus on her success and image she inevitably ended up depressed and feeling cut off.

How appropriate then that in early 1969 she should choose as her next subject *Stones Into Bread* (Matthew 4:3) which is a depiction of the forty days Jesus spent in the wilderness resisting temptation. In my opinion it ranks among her strongest works. The image of Christ struggling to hold back the dark cloud of red-eyed devils whilst the rocks round him merge into white sliced loaves is a powerful one and very representative of her own sense of battling with inner devils, especially her success.

Stones Into Bread (1969)

Her caption for this tells us:

'If a person was desperately hungry, I gather that everything would become hallucinations of food. Did the desert rocks look unbearably like bread? So here are the sliced white loaves appearing in the wilderness with Christ fighting blackness away. Temptation seems more like a "dark thing" than a man.'

Despite surgery on her shoulder, the lack of energy and the pain in her arm were making it increasingly hard to paint. But Eularia was still convinced that she was beating the cancer and discounted the radium as a cause. Instead she put her low mood down to a loss of faith and another bout of hatred of the Church.

Two things contributed to this. The first was the stress of the regular drive to Portsmouth (given her poor health) coupled with the belief that she was always something of a nuisance to the clergy there. David Mahy denies this as they always enjoyed seeing her, but Eularia was too reliant on their good will in relation to her paintings to feel good about it. The second was the apparently odd behaviour of Sidney Mullarkey. When Eularia returned from York after Christmas she made a concerted effort to return to St Peter's (even singing with the choir again) and she enjoyed it for a while. The choir were welcoming, but for some reason Sidney was not. Whether he was fed up with his rather uncooperative flock, simply feeling overworked, or whether he couldn't cope with Eularia beginning to pressure him once again is unclear, but one day, according to Eularia he blew up at her over announcing hymns.

According to her diary there were other instances. He snapped at her over the Bible Study group, roared at her over attempting to get the altar boys to join in the "People's Mass" and still refused to publicise her in the Parish newsletter. Eularia may have been a nuisance at times at St Peter's. She had certainly championed the musical changes, and she could be forthright and persistent, but her accounts in her diary during 1969 give the impression that Sidney seemed to have very little time for her. It is odd after his support and dedication in visiting her when she was in hospital, and something does not quite add up. What is certain is that Eularia chose to interpret Sidney's behaviour as dislike of her and she ceased to feel welcome at St Peter's because of it.

But the clergy as a whole were not immune from this miasma:

'I heard (*on the radio*) a whole hour of opinions about the Clergy of

Tomorrow. Everyone spoke *except* a single R.C. diocesan priest. And God wasn't mentioned, nor Christ, nor the Holy Ghost – only secular relationships, relating Theology to Sociology. Nothing supernatural at all. We shall see a dwindling there, a calamity. The C of E run by retired brigadiers! I must bear witness to the supernatural. How?'

Once again Eularia shows herself to be ahead of her time. There is a natural curiosity in humans about the supernatural. The more that religion has become secularised and watered down, the more the younger generations have voted with their feet and sought the supernatural elsewhere. In attempting to make God more accessible it could be argued that the Christian Church ended up with something too prosaic to capture the imagination and the sense of awe and wonder that, over the centuries, has inspired humans to create some of our most amazing art and architecture, and kept them coming back for more.

It would be a mistake to confuse the fact that Eularia set her paintings in the modern day with a need to make everything very ordinary and sociological. She was attempting to show how the supernatural is still important to our daily lives, that the gospels that Jesus preached are as relevant now as they were then, not because they had been updated but because they were eternal and applied to every moment.

Despite her protestations about needing her solitariness and being glad not to be involved at St Peter's, she always missed it. The support she had found there, especially from the priests, had been very important to her. She justified her own sense of rejection by rejecting the St Peter's flock and, increasingly, Catholics in general, with the usual refrain that they were not her type of people and they were beneath her. Once again her snobbishness became her protection.

The spring of 1969 was to see the last flowering of her friendship with David Mahy, who had arranged for the cellar to be pumped out and re-plastered.

'It's a bit more difficult to be my worst self when a saintly man is there.'

Perhaps reflecting her own doubts about her faith, she began a painting of the scene when St Thomas doubts that he is seeing the risen Christ. *Give Me Your Hand* (John 20:27) shows Jesus, with a gaping wound in his chest in which can be glimpsed a radiant heart (not dissimilar to the traditional Sacred Heart paintings) grasping the hand of a very surprised St Thomas. Behind him we see the locked door and in the foreground is an old-fashioned oil lamp. If Eularia ever wrote a caption for this painting it no longer survives, but it is unlikely that she bothered as she only ever lists it being shown at the Southampton Painters Progress exhibition in 1969. Captions tended to be written for her one-man shows. As a painting it is powerful and typically uncompromising. The only comment she made about it is in her diary: 'I love the fierce, "give me your hand" – and the slightly macabre gesture.'

There were five exhibitions in the offing: King Alfred's College, Christchurch, Lymington, Alresford and Saxmundham in Norfolk. In the event the Norfolk one was postponed until 1970, but despite that she had to have a large number of paintings available to cover them all, so she began to rework some of the Lourdes paintings to bring them up to scratch. *Water from the Spring* and *Touching the Walls* were two of these.

She noted that she had three types of public:

'The pure art ones, who enjoy line, colour, composition, and simply don't take in the subject. Then the "people" public who enjoy the human scene, the details, the story. Thirdly the religionists, who can take in the doctrine and theology behind the story and human scene.... I must leave it to God to act on them when and where He will – and not make enemies – not resent one group, or another. Not even try to "preach to the poor". He may have other plans...'

The first of these exhibitions was at Lymington in April and was well reviewed. Only ten of her paintings were on show in, of all places, the bar of the Community Centre, which Eularia found amusing and appropriate. It was to be her first showing at Lymington and it received good reviews in the local press. Many of her paintings returned there in December for the Lymington Arts Festival.

41

The Cellar Gallery

Right from the start of the Cellar Gallery period Eularia found the regular drive to Portsmouth very tiring. Nowadays twenty-eight miles does not seem any great distance, especially with a fast motorway, but one has to take into account the fact that she took whatever route she could to avoid the main roads, which scared her, and the Mini van was not in good condition by this time. She also put in a great deal of work moving the paintings and hanging them once she got there. In typical Eularia style she always did this alone because she never asked for any help.

Ironically, after wanting success and limelight for so long, Eularia also found this unexpectedly stressful and exhausting. It was a marked change from her first emergence from cancer in 1967 when she seemed to be carried along on a wave of support and enthusiasm. At that time she really believed that she would beat the cancer, but it was beginning to look as if she hadn't. Lack of energy, feeling unwell and increased physical pain all served to drag her down and left her feeling less able to cope.

It was easy for her to lose her sense of self in the fear and she did, frequently. At such times she would question everything, her faith, her art, her friendships and relationships, and it was now that she saw how much of herself she had put into her paintings:

'The paintings are all about myself, my life and psychological states, my experiences, needs and emotions – not about the gospels... or are they?'

Inevitably they are about both, the personal and the transpersonal, just as Jesus was. If one sets out to illustrate the life of someone who was both human and divine then it is not surprising that both those elements will come into play in the finished work, and in ways that the artist was not even aware of at the time of painting.

The Cellar Gallery opened in April 1969 and attracted attention, at least to begin with, so for the first time we have much longer published articles about Eularia and her work. These provide an insight into the public face that she presented to the world. There are two that survive, kept by Eularia herself, both written by Joan Grigsby (Bryer) and published in April 1969, around the time that the gallery was opened. Grigsby says of the gallery itself:

'Entering it down a rough wooden staircase is rather like coming upon an underground chapel whose walls are decorated with rich mosaics.'

She went on to describe Eularia as:

'...a cheerful, voluble and extremely articulate grandmother in her middle fifties whose apparently happy-go-lucky, humorous attitude towards life initially masks a profound belief in what she is determined she has been called upon to do. She feels that through her paintings even though they may disapprove of them, she can arouse people to a consciousness of what religion is about – or even that it exists at all.'

'But what of the pictures themselves? Comparison with Stanley Spencer is inevitable, but Eularia Clarke has her own beliefs and views and these bear little relation to the intensely personal mysticism of Spencer.

'"I think," she says, "it is typical of us English to make jokes when we are deeply moved by a thing: you know how an adoring mother mocks her new baby or a loving husband caricatures his wife. If English people painted religion (which they don't) I think it would be full of those same Punch-like, loving jokes. I don't think we idealise things or people easily... Also there's the medieval view. My grandfather and uncle were both medieval historians, and as children we saw a lot of medieval religious art... cheery little people doing religion very naturally in their own setting. Nothing a bit grim or sentimental... and it all seemed very real."

'That is one aspect of Eularia Clarke's painting, and together with the fact that to many people it will evoke things remembered from childhood and perhaps since forgotten it may be the one that is most immediately apparent. To this one must add the purely visual appeal of skilfully thought out pattern and design and the really singing colours of many of the pictures which are lost in black and white reproduction.

'But to Eularia Clarke herself the paintings are, one feels, far more than this since, each picture to her is an intellectual and spiritual exercise, each of the main figures a basis for prayer and meditation. It is perhaps this side of her painting which makes a particular appeal to priests and clergy of all denominations and enables them to find in them the ground for sermons and discussion.

'How far this last aspect of her art will get through to the general public it is difficult to say, but (that) it is pre-eminently important to the artist herself is obvious after a very short time spent in her company. Art "with a message" is bound to be open to suspicion and misunderstanding, but if it is good in itself it must survive. Eularia Clarke's work seems to me to be worthy of attention on its artistic merits alone, but it has a flame of sincerity which makes it impossible to ignore.'

The other article was printed in *The Times*, also in April 1969, and they sent a photographer down to Middle Road, which Eularia thought very comic, as she wrote to Rachael:

'I've trained the cobwebs carefully over everything and made things extra typical.'

Cheerful and voluble is how most people remember Eularia. They never got to see the fearful, depressed and sick Eularia. She was very careful about hiding that aspect of herself as far as she could. But whatever her private fears, it is very clear that Eularia did not want her paintings to end up on private walls where access to them would be challenging if not impossible. She was painting them to be seen by as many as possible with the easiest possible access. Eularia didn't mind if people loved them, were shocked by them, or even hated them, because she understood that by prompting a reaction they had done their job and made the viewer respond and even think, too, about what she was portraying – religion.

Two more nodules were discovered and the pain in her arm was worse. It was a difficult period and it showed in her next painting, *Christ, the Good Samaritan* (Luke 10:33). Her choice of subject was probably influenced by her own feelings of being incapacitated and needing help, but it is possible to discern the restriction she was experiencing in her hand and arm in the execution of the work. Compared to her other paintings it lacks her usual flow. There is a rather half-hearted feel in the illustration and the detail seems over-fussy and rather stilted. She was never really happy with this painting as a result. She felt that it never quite worked. Her own caption stated:

'This was to have been an ordinary straight illustration to the parable, but I began to notice who was telling the story. It seemed to hold the firm promise that, if we were in a really bad way, God wouldn't treat us less kindly than his Samaritan-figure; so in the painting the Good Samaritan turned into Christ.'

The viewer takes the victim's point of view as he watches Christ tending his wounds. The usual details are there, his checked duffle bag lying on the ground with his possessions scattered around, a pub in the distance, but it lacks the impact of her other paintings as if she wasn't quite present while painting it. In her dairy she said:

'...it may be a flop as it feels funny, like illustrating a fairy-story.'

Without St Peter's and the priests the television became her main resource for information and it was this that made her realise that she might still have something to offer:

'I see that the public is calling out for the "Carpenter" and have abolished the "stained-glass window". But I have produced an image of Christ which is a splendid carpenter, divine as well, haloed and work-worn, carrying the sacraments to people, carrying them himself. But nobody will see this, especially not the Catholics.'

Eularia had always sought to portray both the very human world of the Gospels and the divinity of Christ. One of her objections to Catholic Art and the Catholic mentality as she saw it at the time was that it still hung on to a very idealised 'stained-glass' image of Christ, one which was for Sundays and which most Catholics were happy to leave in the charge of the priests. Eularia's experience of God was far too personal for this and it made no sense to her to preserve this 'fictional' image of someone who was clearly human as well as divine. It was another perceived gulf between her and the Church, but it also reflected her own struggle to bridge the gap between her very human experience, especially in illness, and her experience of God:

'I shall always be eccentric arty, shabby, unimpressive, and that is right for a Christian painter.'

Eularia's need for seclusion was becoming all-consuming:

'If I attempt to assimilate into the group, I become estranged from the thing at the centre. People, relationships antagonise, and I get cut off from the source of the inspiration, my own vocation and metier; I lose my peace and ability.'

Largely for this reason she decided that it would be a mistake for her to continue with clerical friendships, although she greatly appreciated the ones she had had. Her fear was that they would lead her into parish politics and the inevitable upheavals, which she now realised caused her too much nervous stress, a worsening in her symptoms and subsequent energy drops. She had good reason to be concerned about this, as she was facing the prospect of more radium for a new lump on her shoulder and she had been experiencing increasing tightness across the chest. Then in her bath she felt a new lump on her ribs. She still hoped for a cure but realised that it might not come, and inevitably her thoughts turned to death. After watching some sticklebacks she had just released into a stream she wrote:

'Will death be like that, the big clear-running stream after the thick cloudy green tank? I think about it constantly, suspecting secondaries, wondering what the outlook is? Yet I know it's unimportant. People die so often, some so much too late. And I've actually achieved something, which should make it miles easier....'

Eularia was beginning to accept that she wasn't going to get better, that death was inevitable, she simply didn't know how long she would have. With this she gained more peace, and the endless round of discovering secondaries and subsequent treatments began to become a debilitating routine that she learnt to manage.

Having been away in the North, and with her preoccupation about secondaries and general ill-health, Eularia had not been to the Cellar Gallery for a couple of months. Despite being drained and decorated, the Cellar Gallery was never a good site. The steep ladder staircase made it challenging to visit, and the skylights had not materialised. She also discovered from David Mahy that people were scared of the cellar because three people had drowned in it during the blitz.

People had visited it over those two months, although the number had dwindled by June, but Eularia's problem was that she wasn't on the spot to see this. She rarely made it to Portsmouth more than once a week. The likelihood is that no one had really made a sufficient thing of it being a gallery. There was no entry fee, no curator and to many it was seen as little more than another storeroom. David didn't have the time to curate it and Eularia didn't dare, feeling that she was already adding to David's burden as it was.

Having forgotten her original romantic notion of Christian Art in the catacombs, she also began to worry about the paintings being 'buried' in the cellar:

'Last night I had dreadful horrors about the paintings, and couldn't sleep. I saw how they'll always be ill-treated and knocked about, people don't respect either a woman without solid reputation, nor paintings with no sales.'

As an experiment it was successful in that it allowed those interested in her work to go and see what was there and make selections for exhibitions of their own. One such group were people from The Red House Museum in Christchurch who made a selection for a summer exhibition. This they had done in the spring not long after the gallery had opened, but when they came to pick the paintings up they found that they had grown a blue and green mould due to the damp conditions. When Eularia arrived there the day after the paintings had been picked up, she found '...two walls bulging and cracking with damp, several paintings covered with mould, and clear realisation that nobody had, or will ever, descend those stairs.'

No one had noticed. David Mahy had not had time to check and Eularia took this to mean that she wasn't wanted there, which wasn't actually true. Her dream of a gallery and a permanent home for the paintings was a flop. She was tempted to think of David as incompetent, but no one at the Cathedral knew anything about looking after paintings or the kind of conditions they needed. Eularia knew that the cellar was damp and Rachael had warned her about it, but her joy at having a permanent gallery, and her gratitude to David, had overruled this very practical detail. She was the one person who could have pointed out that the cellar wasn't suitable to house paintings.

She was, however, very happy with the exhibition at The Red House. They had cleaned up the paintings they borrowed and had hung them very well. The Belfields stepped in to see if some solution could be reached and they discussed the possibility of a Trust, but in the end Rachael said she would take charge of them, so Eularia changed her will in favour of her children, Rachael and James. She felt very bad about cutting David Mahy out but she didn't see much choice. She collected the remaining paintings from Portsmouth, including one that was on display in the Cathedral porch and on which someone had carved some graffiti, not an impressive end to her dream and rather fermenting her growing conviction that Catholics didn't know how to look after paintings.

Middle Road once again became the storage space. She moved her studio back up to the attic from the greenhouse, which she found ideal for working on several canvases at once as well as framing and storing. Now she had no reason to go to Portsmouth (she probably wouldn't have been physically able to keep up the visits anyway) it meant that she lost regular contact with the last of her priestly allies and close friends, David Mahy. David's parish duties only allowed him very intermittent visits to Winchester so he did not know how ill Eularia was until after her death. She did not tell him and because she was no longer in regular touch with St Peter's he didn't hear through the grapevine either.

Increasingly during 1969 and 1970 it was James who became her main support over her paintings, although they didn't entirely see eye to eye about them. James had always been of the opinion that they wouldn't become known if she didn't sell and they wouldn't be published unless pushed by rich and powerful patrons. Eularia concluded that he saw them as works of art and did not understand the mystical side of them or their message. While she was extremely glad of James' interest and support, Eularia clung fast to her belief that the paintings were her ministry and not merely objects of art to be bought and sold. This was very important to her and became increasingly so. She knew that it was impractical and uncommercial but that wasn't why she had painted them.

Her garden became her refuge. The cellar incident knocked all her resolve to paint and she achieved very little during the summer of 1969, but Eularia was increasingly aware how much the grandchildren, especially Cuthbert, loved and appreciated the paintings. This became her new motivation for a while, especially Cuthbert.

With this growing self-acceptance a much more contemplative Eularia was beginning to emerge:

'Sitting here over my cup in the soft rain, watching the green dimpling pond and the wrought-iron lilies, I am very content. I can be last and waste time. I try and try to pray but my mind wanders away – yet it does help so much. It produces a calm and well-being, even the muzzy attempts at prayer. I look ahead and see that all is unpredictable, except that I'm free – free from the struggle to be what people want, free to be myself, kept from doing damage or bossing or criticising or putting my oar in, free from intruders and tiresome visitors, free to say no, free to smell the wet greenery...'

She began what she at first called the 'Sleepy Servants', eventually entitled

Trying to Keep Awake (Luke 12:37). Given the fact that, at the time of painting this, Eularia was either having trouble sleeping or finding that she slept too much, one can see the relevance of the subject matter. But it also speaks to her determination to keep on praying and staying spiritually awake, not allowing the discomfort from the cancer to send her to sleep. Her own caption states:

'A mysterious promise, that the "Master" will be so glad to find anybody waiting up for him, that he will actually be grateful...with the images of bringing the supper and even serving it! This is the worst time of the night, just before dawn, and in ordinary life the servants most likely to be up are mothers of small babies, so I put one in.'

This period, just before the dawn, was the most common time for her to wake with terrors and fears, so especially relevant. In the background the luminous arms of Christ can be seen carrying loaves of bread and bottles. Next to him, looking out of the window and holding a baby, is the mother. In the foreground is a table over which the servants are slouched, some doing their best to stay awake, others clearly asleep. Gone is the rather stilted style of *Christ, the Good Samaritan* and back is her characteristic flow and expression.

Eularia says that as she contemplated this painting:

'I wept over it, longing for it all to be true. The promises, which all the best people have rejected, and all the most ghastly people cling to. The promise of Christ. What is to be done about the promise of Christ?'

This painting went very slowly to begin with. As summer took hold and the heat began she could do very little. Even sitting through Mass was hard due to physical discomfort. But she was determined not to give in to depression and set herself the job of achieving small creative tasks every day, which helped:

'It seems odd, as there is no real reason or incentive; just the intuition that I'm alive for this purpose, and the sense of fulfilment when I've actually finished a bout of work. My capacity is less and I tire easily, but the ideas come; not divine inspiration nor enthusiasm for the R.C. thing, only a powerful longing which demands expression, a longing for something once glimpsed, some ideal and perfect and transcending joy-giving thing which would transcend all my life's miseries and failures. The psychologist would call this a "Compensating Factor", but I think it's too powerful to be merely that. It is never far away, but it exists at a deep level, so that my mind is never convinced about dogmatic truths, in fact I grow less and less concerned with all these things, feasts, liturgy, ceremonies and clergy; probably even sacraments may become unimportant as I get less able to "frequent" them.'

It was a challenging time to be a Catholic and Eularia certainly felt this. Pope Paul VI was proving very unpopular with many since the publication in July 1968 of his encyclical letter entitled 'Humanae Vitae', which is most famous for its prohibition of all artificial forms of contraception.

As the daughter and granddaughter of two vocally pro-contraception women (Constance and Peggy), Eularia was almost dismissive of this encyclical but 'Humanae Vitae' was, and remains, very controversial and many left the Church because of it. The ensuing turbulence, which swelled right into the summer of 1969, caused Eularia to believe that the old structure was 'toppling fast' and she expected to see celibacy go after the Pope's death. But she was not in touch enough with other Catholics to realise that her own doubts and struggles with faith were being felt by many, and therefore did not seek or receive support in working through it. Instead she decided she had to do it alone.

Consequently she began to read more authors who had found spirituality outside the Church such as C.S. Lewis, who she greatly admired, and 'the Paradise woman' (this is Eularia's name for this author and because she never gives her real one I have been unable to find out who it is).

In her diaries Eularia indicates quite clearly that her growing disenchantment with Catholicism was fed by disillusionment regarding the direction the Church seemed to be taking post 'Humanae Vitae'. This was combined with her belief that Sidney Mullarkey really didn't like her, her belief that the curates at St Peter's treated her as a troublemaker, and her general ill health. She did persevere with Mass attendance but the success of it depended greatly on which priest was saying it and how involved in the service she was. At Alresford, and later Chandler's Ford, she found Mass easier because the services were more modern and brisk, and she had no history with the parishes there, so she took a more active part and even sang. This took her mind off her physical discomfort so she enjoyed it more.

She began work on what is, I think, one of her loveliest paintings, which she originally referred to as 'The Cockles' but became *The Mixed Sheaf* (Matthew 13:30). This is the parable of the wheat and the tares. Cockle is the word for tare or weed that is used in the Rheims-Douai translation of the Latin Vulgate Bible and is the clearest evidence we have that it was this version that Eularia used as her reference for her paintings. In her caption for this painting she refers to 'Tares' which is given in the Knox and the St James translations, but this is almost certainly because the caption is written for the exhibition at Winchester Cathedral where she knew it would be largely read by Anglicans who would not know the Rheims-Douai reference. In English one tends to think of shellfish when cockles are mentioned, not weeds:

"What will be done with us who produce practically no wheat, and a whole lot of tares and weeds? This is a painting of hope; that Christ will somehow sift out the odd ear of wheat among the thistles.'

The Mixed Sheaf (1969)

The Mixed Sheaf shows the moment of gathering in the weeds and the wheat. Christ is directing the man carrying the weeds (a beautiful bunch of cornflowers, poppies and wild grasses) to take them away whilst the other harvesters bring the wheat into the barn. The fact that the bunch of weeds is so attractive whilst the bundles of wheat all seem very uniform and rather limp has to be a reflection, even if unconscious, of her feelings about the Catholic 'flock' and how different she felt from them, along with her feelings of being alienated. It could also be a reference to how attractive the weeds can be, as it is the bunch of weeds that provide the colour in the painting, that and the sunset sky. But this painting really is Eularia back on form.

During the painting of *The Mixed Sheaf* she had a return to her state of prayer, which had been illusive for a long time. Her inner experience of God had been very eclipsed by feeling ill. Instead she had begun to hear a voice in her imagination, which would sometimes reassure her if she became too desperate.

The 1969 diaries really have two themes. The first is her increasingly ill health and the second is her struggle with her faith and the Catholic Church. She could be very inconsistent. One day she was being kind to Catholics, the next she was criticising them fiercely and wanting to cut off from them. The only thing that remained consistent was her assertion that without the Catholic Church her paintings would not exist.

At the root of her battle was always the same issue:

'Did God choose me out for all my misfortunes, failures, blows of fate, let-downs etc., so that I might have nothing to turn to except religion – or do I turn to religion because I've somehow failed to succeed in the fundamentals of life?'

It was a question that she never really found a satisfactory answer to.

42

Not Looking Back

She started *Not Looking Back* (Luke 9:62) in the autumn of 1969 and it is the closest to a self-portrait that Eularia ever painted. Throughout her 1960s diaries she talked of ploughing a lonely furrow in life, especially as an artist, and she always referred to this painting as 'The Lonely Furrow'. It is very evocative and Eularia at her very best. Amidst the small farm cottages a lonely ploughman is seen, from above, pushing his hand plough uphill in a field full of stubble, creating a furrow in the red earth. Life is going on in the cottages around him as normal, but very apart from him. In her caption she says:

'Ploughing in midwinter in the early morning setting out when the kitchen is nice and warm, this must be peoples' experience of following Christ in these days...'

It is easy to gain a sense of how she felt about her own journey and this was always her theme. Eularia was the lonely ploughman, solidly pushing her plough uphill, breaking up the soil so that a new crop can be sown. No one is helping, no one is even displaying an interest and yet she toils on.

She was spurred on to do more painting by news that the Congregationalist Centre in Basingstoke wanted forty paintings for an exhibition in January 1970 and Canon Maundrell at Winchester Cathedral wanted forty for an exhibition there in the autumn of 1969. She was very pleased about the Cathedral exhibition, as it was to be in the North Transept. It was exactly the kind of local support she had been hoping for.

Not Looking Back (1969)

But painting *The Mixed Sheaf* had brought awareness of a new pain under her ribs which made it very hard to do more than half an hour's work at a time. She found a new growth on her right side. The doctor prescribed painkillers and sleeping pills but she was determined to stay off them as long as possible.

Ill health inevitably brought more bouts of depression with it and the thought of death scared her, but in the end she concluded that as she wasn't going to get better, and because she didn't seem to make herself worse with activity, she might as well just get on with life and do what she was capable of without worrying about over straining herself. This was a good choice as activity invariably helped her to feel better. She was determined that the 'paintings will *go on*.':

> 'Where is God's love? Yet I know it is there, and it brings tears when I think of it, the Islands and the singing, like last night's V.W. (*Vaughan Williams*) Theme of Tallis – it's in that, the land of heart's desire.'

As with most terminally ill people she still hoped for a cure, that a new treatment would emerge, but inevitably she was left with a lack of motivation. When one is approaching death the question of whether or not to start new projects is always present, but she refused to give in:

> '...as for "what's the point?" the point is that while there's life there's creative possibilities.'

As autumn approached and she began to put away her summer clothes she found herself wondering:

> 'I feel so strongly the sense of its being the last this, the last that. Will I ever wear summer clothes again?'

One of the gifts of Eularia's diaries in these last years, despite their often harrowing nature, is the clarity with which she describes the journey of someone with a terminal illness. Whilst she may have disguised how ill she was to her friends, she openly expressed her vulnerability and her feelings in her diaries. She was no saint, she did not approach death well, she was often afraid, angry, bitter and hateful of the world, pushing people away, refusing to allow herself to be helped although she desperately wanted it. Her deep distrust of the good nature of others and their desire to be kind and friendly eclipsed any overtures of help or concern and sent her running in the other direction towards isolation.

There were increasingly few exceptions to this. Close family was one, James and Rachael, but few others. She had not told her brothers about her current state of health, nor did she want to, and she had temporarily fallen out with the only other family member she had any time for, Catherine Dupré.

More than anything Eularia dreaded having to give up her haven at Middle Road if she became too ill to manage on her own. But she was practical enough to realise that it was a possibility:

'I must be ready to leave it all, soon or late, and the less I grow attached to it the easier it will be to uproot for good.'

Detaching is the theme of the second half of 1969. She had withdrawn from the Church, from most of her friendships, from Winchester, from Portsmouth and one wonders if there wasn't a subconscious drive to do this so that when the time came to 'leave for good' there would be nothing to remain for. Eularia's great fear of things having a claim on her comes through very strongly here. The only local friends that she still kept up with were the Belfields and it was Felicity who took Eularia's entries to the Southampton Painter's Progress exhibition in September for her.

Saddest of all was how her illness changed her attitude to her paintings. She completely discounted any previous inspiration or meaning in them:

'I shuddered when I had to read the gospels to get references, and I saw how little the paintings related to the truths in them – how many twists and eccentricities and individual interpretations, how much mockery and caricature and cartoon and how little reverence. I don't understand my old self, the self who painted them, it's a closed chapter.'

Closing down her more emotional, feeling self as she was (it was just too physically uncomfortable), she was left with only her intellectual capacity and fell prey to an increasing cynicism. It is sad that she felt the need to sweep away the old Eularia and completely discount her contribution. By doing so she was losing contact with the very qualities that had made her so unique in her family, and instead she fell into their trap of cynical non-attachment and disbelief. It was not a good place to be, it was, after all, what had contributed towards her own father's suicide and was one of the things she had so consistently disliked about her cousin Alicia.

Eularia was mourning her old self and, although she was never a natural Catholic, for someone who had consistently stated that she had felt the presence of God for most of her life (except when she was raising her children) it would suggest that her increasing ill-health had pushed her away from her true self. The Eularia who was writing at the end of the summer of 1969 was being shaped by her illness.

Her mood did pick up in the run-up to the exhibition at Winchester Cathedral. Forty paintings were exhibited in the North Transept for a month, from 21 October to 22 November. This was coupled with a renewed interest in religion inspired by the author Eularia called 'The Paradise Woman' (lack of any proper name or book titles prevent me from identifying her):

'If I seek prayer in order to find relief for depression, serenity, peace, joy – then my search is not only hopeless but wrong. I must seek it because I want it for itself, and know it will come and is waiting – even though I shall gain nothing, owing to my sick nerves. Secondly my quarrel with the R.C. thing – the book tempts me to chuck the whole of this, to be a "goat" – and I believe this is a very common reaction, Ida Gowes, Simone Weil, there must be so many thoughtful women of all religions or none who are repelled by the whole Catholic Thing. Some have been novices, even nuns; others have carefully avoided the Church which they feel would interfere with their spiritual freedom or (Paradise woman) scoff at their experiences because they are given "outside the R.C. shop". Well, I must accept honestly that I got prayer and painting of religion – as a Catholic receiving Sacraments, not as a free-lance outside any church. I must not deny this because I feel e.g. that the official Church doesn't appreciate my gifts, or that it's more "me" to be a goat. I must learn to live with complete discomfort, spiritually among Catholics, physically with increasing cancer; there is to be no security and no comfortableness; no "belonging". And still Mass pulls very oddly.'

The Paradise woman did more than anything else to pull Eularia out of her summer blues, despite the fact that Eularia did not entirely agree with her. What she had done was stimulate Eularia to consider her questions regarding spirituality once again. Perhaps more than anywhere else, it is here that the loss of Pat Murphy-O'Connor, David Mahy and Michael Gedge as friends is observable. She missed engaging in conversation about this kind of thing. It was what stimulated her inspiration. In many ways her painting was her own search for truth and answers through the Gospels.

So why did she not make friends with the new curates at St Peter's? She had certainly made a connection with Gabriel Cave (the newest curate) but had actively decided not to pursue it and instead dismissed him along with the rest of the Catholics. It may be that there was something in Eularia's assertion that it was to do with her recognition as an artist and their lack of apparent acceptance about this. It is possible that Eularia was correct in asserting that they did not know how to treat her. She wasn't an average Catholic. As a Theologian and someone who had been on her own spiritual journey for the past ten years, she had grown. It must have felt that going back to St Peter's was like a senior school student being sent back to the kindergarten again. She had grown up with Pat, Michael and David, spiritually speaking. But most priests, especially those with large busy parishes like Winchester, would automatically assume that she had the same level of understanding and education that the rest of their flock did and treat her accordingly.

With a new stirring of inspiration, and feeling a little better, she continued to work on *The Mixed Sheaf* and *Not Looking Back* as well as beginning *Following with Faint Hearts* (Mark 10:32). The title alone is enough to show how closely this choice of subject reflected Eularia's current frame of mind.

Her caption says:

'When the road goes into a beech wood, in dark weather, it suggests tragedy, the fallen leaves can look almost like blood, there is this dark tunnel ahead. Who could possibly want to go with Christ on the road to Jerusalem?'

The painting focuses on the reluctant followers, those who are losing heart or struggling. We find them at a crossroads with a broken signpost against which some of them lean, exhausted or fed up. In the distance Christ can be seen disappearing into an autumnal beech wood, the red leaves lying around. Some of the followers are going in the wrong direction and once again we see the mother holding her baby calling those following Christ back, perhaps a reference, conscious or not, of those blank years when she was looking after small children and had to bury her own calling.

What is also significant about these later paintings is how much briefer the captions were. In her diaries she spoke of finding them increasingly hard to write and how she missed having her cheerful priests popping in to discuss them with.

Following With Faint Hearts (1969)

43

A Big Thing

Just as Eularia was beginning to emerge from the worst of her anti-Catholic mood, she went to Mass at St Peter's only to find that it was the feast of St Thérèse of Lisieux, often referred to as 'The Little Flower'. Eularia hated 'the Little Flower' with a passion. She represented everything that Eularia feared and disliked in women: weak submissiveness and sanctity.

One of the priests at St Peter's misguidedly gave her this advice:

"I must just follow the Little Flower, doing Little Things perfectly, the way she attained the heights of sanctity". But God has asked me to do a large thing, not a little one – and to do it against illness and weakness, on my own. NOT a small thing, out of date anyway by now (*Little Flower*) but a large thing, too large. To do it far from perfectly, rather badly, but for the present day, not warmed-up Victoriana. Naturally the priests prefer *little* people and little things – they suit women and make them nice and inferior and easy to manage and look down on. I mustn't be encouraged to do large things, things which no priests has ever done... preaching to thousands outside any church.'

Perhaps with this in mind she began *Under My Roof* (Matthew 8:8). It was David Mahy who had suggested the subject of the Centurion's servant and Eularia had very clear ideas about how it should be portrayed:

'The Centurion painting won't be a fine officer being praised. I keep thinking: "I will come and heal him." That's what I like. "Lord I am not worthy." The servant lying sick in a very low tent, and the altar-bell ringing while the priest – what does he do then?'

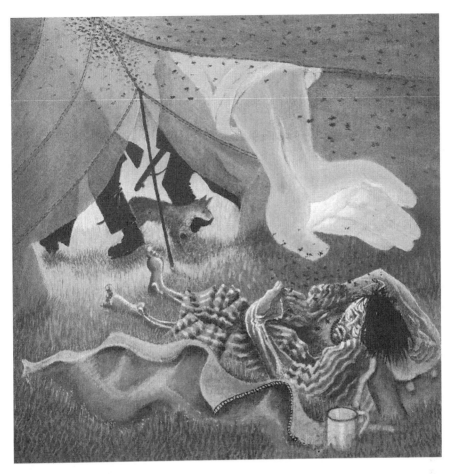

Under My Roof (1969)

And this is exactly what she painted, with the omission of any priestly activity. Instead we see the servant lying on the grass under a low tent surrounded by buzzing flies and the hand of Christ coming through the canvas roof above him to heal him. Without the caption it isn't immediately obvious that this is the healing of the Centurion's servant, as there is no visual reference to the meeting between Jesus and the Centurion himself, but it does illustrate the heart of the story. Eularia felt that too much emphasis was placed upon the faith of the Centurion in traditional renderings of this work and not on the miracle of the healing itself. She very clearly puts this right. In her caption she says:

'The Centurion's servant, at the moment when Christ did the famous remote-control healing miracle. Catholics used to say "Lord, I am not worthy to receive you under my roof" before receiving communion; the idea being that none of us feels suitable to receive Christ; hence the flies buzzing and the absence of status conditions.'

Eularia does a powerful job of depicting lack of self worth in this painting. It was something she readily identified with and which is why it was so hard for her to relate to a saint like St Theresa who, she felt, was being vaunted as an example of perfection that all (women particularly) should aspire to. Quite rightly she felt excluded by it. She did not relate to St Theresa's spiritual journey and she did not feel worthy of that kind of holiness, she knew it was a state of perfection she could never attain. All it did was alienate her even more. The fact that the Centurion (rather like a priest) is taken out of this story in her version and we see Christ directly interacting with the servant reflects her strong desire that she could have a personal relationship with Christ without a mediator. It was not that Eularia hated the Church, she had, in fact, outgrown it, but she had no idea what came next.

It was around now that she finally brought to a close her friendship with Michael Gedge. She recognised that she simply didn't have the stamina for him anymore, he was too rough and forceful and she couldn't cope with it. Gone were the days when she felt she could meet it like for like.

After the Little Flower incident Eularia began to see her painting differently:

'...not to convert to R. C'ism, but to inspire other goats, preaching the love of God, no longer love of the Church.'

She made a very profound observation, having read William Law:

'(I) find it very, very English. Rational, sober, pious... this is what God wants everyone to be, and when considered, it's right and good. But it's very male. The female side of every human cries out for something a bit personal and dramatic, surely?'

But even so, despite her determination to rid herself of all things Catholic, she wrote:

'I must stick to the fact that Catholics are very religious; leading a Catholic life is a good religious formation, if you want to go all out, no religion could be better – and this is the truth. I couldn't have done all that painting on St Paul's Winchester, or even on the Cathedral; only on this small detestable group of immigrants, lonely, stupid and of no account... this provided the catalyst.'

For Eularia the exhibition at Winchester Cathedral was her first major exhibition on home territory and in the largest and most prestigious building in the city. Despite the rather poor lighting in the North Transept it attracted many people and stirred a lot of interest. It said something for the Cathedral that it hosted this. The late 1960s were still a period when ecumenism was in its infancy and Winchester Cathedral had not yet had any exhibitions by modern artists, let alone Catholic ones. The fact that Eularia was both said much for their willingness to embrace the new.

This was noted in a review in the *Hampshire Chronicle* (author not given in the clipping):

'Provocative, ancient and modern. These are the characteristics of the forty paintings by Eularia Clarke to be shown in the Cathedral's North Transept.

'Provocative because they are the result of an individual's meditation on God's creation, the living, redemptive work of Christ and the power of the Holy Spirit active in the world of everyday and in the Church. A book for comments placed alongside a group of Mrs Clarke's paintings recently exhibited in Portsmouth Guildhall, was eloquent of the mixed sense of shock and gratitude produced in the minds of hundreds of viewers of all ages, and of all religious denominations. Some of the most startled and puzzled reactions came from school children – that most conservatively-minded section of the community where religion is concerned.

'Ancient, because the artist has recovered the aim of religious painters of long ago. She points with simplicity and directness at the Biblical scene she is representing, and lets it speak for itself. Preachers note! A Theology graduate of Oxford she knows her subject, but does not parade it, or dress it up.'

'Modern, because with a refreshing naturalness and unselfconsciousness her Christ moves in today's life and takes his place in scenes of home and work. Hefty men at work and harassed housewives see him among them finding it unnecessary to change into Sunday best before having him in their company.

'In being at home to these paintings by a Roman Catholic the Cathedral is making more than an ecumenical gesture. It is offering the people of Hampshire (a County poor in post-war paintings for churches compared with neighbouring Sussex) the chance to view at leisure a collection of paintings which raises in a fascinating way questions about the role of the visual in the evangelistic, apostolic and teaching work of the Churches today. Already seen on television and industrial, educational and civic surroundings, works like these need integrating into the life of the Churches. The worlds of education, industry and advertising know that it is not only children who respond to visual images; the Churches need this visual element as an accompaniment to their often all too verbal and conceptual means of communication.'

As soon as the paintings were hung they attracted interest and Eularia made a set of much more ecumenical-style captions for this exhibition. Inevitably Eularia noted the difference in the level of support between the Anglicans and the Catholics. The Cathedral was only too willing to help. It was a sad irony that it was the Protestant religions that were most supportive over Eularia's work in the end. Of the twenty-five one-woman exhibitions that she had during her lifetime, only five were organised or hosted by Catholics, the rest were all thanks to other Christian denominations and in the end it is the Methodists that have kept her in the public eye.

Eularia enjoyed this exhibition, especially when she saw her poster on the West Door of the Cathedral, which inevitably cast Sidney Mullarkey in an even worse light. No poster for it at all had been put up at St Peter's and there was nothing in their newsletter, despite the fact that she was a Catholic of their parish. She did however discover third hand that Sidney had been to see the exhibition and had been enthusiastic about it.

The Cathedral exhibition gave Eularia the opportunity to reconnect with old school friends from St Paul's. News had reached the Old Paulina's (the old girls' school network) and several of them came to see the show. They were impressed enough to offer her an exhibition at St Paul's Girls School itself the following year. The Catholics weren't a complete washout either. Fr Roy Bennett, who was now parish priest at Fareham, came to see the exhibition and it was to inspire an exhibition at Fareham the following summer.

Although Eularia was hard on Catholics at this time she recognised that by becoming less involved with them she was making herself available as a painter for other denominations. In fact she was going through a transition and in typical Eularia fashion was doing it kicking and screaming. Her sense that the Catholic Church didn't seem to want her paintings, and was incapable of looking after them properly, came from a deeper recognition that, whilst they inspired them, the clergy were neither worldly enough nor practical enough to do anything sensible with them.

Finally she accepted that she was too individual to feel comfortable belonging to a group or a flock. It wasn't the fault of either the groups or the flocks, it was simply that she was designed by providence to do something unique. Like many artists she was happier in her own space, doing her own thing and not feeling that she had to conform to a set of standards. After years of attempting to find a space in society, having felt so outcast because of her position, she finally realised that society didn't suit her.

She began *The Rich Young Man* (Mark 10:22), which is not one of her most successful works. It shows a private swimming pool by a very stormy sea with Christ and the apostles (eating fish and chips) calling the rich young man to follow them. We see only the man's hands (complete with gold watch) raised, palms towards them and covering Christ's face. Her caption for it is brief:

'The private swimming pool is nice and safe and cosy, but Christ calls people to stormy sailing and shipwreck.'

The symbolism is all there, and from that point of view it has a strong message, but, in the author's opinion, there is something in the execution of it that doesn't quite work visually. It feels confused, which would reflect Eularia's own confusion at the time about her own call to Christ versus the trappings of fame and success. Eularia agreed. She felt that it was '... dubious owing to the bad shape.'

Don't Bury It (Matthew 25:18) was begun in late 1969 and not finished until 1970. It is a powerful image, more so than *The Rich Young Man,* and would become increasingly so for Eularia in the first part of 1970. It shows the servant about to bury his talent, wrapped in a red spotted handkerchief, in the earth as the hand of the Lord grasps his jumper at the shoulder. Significantly, the hand of God, the handkerchief and by default the talent, are the only source of warm colour in an otherwise blue painting set at night with only the cold moon as light source.

It is as if you can feel the servant reluctantly impelled to hold the talent out to the outstretched hand instead of burying it. In her caption Eularia tells us:

'We mustn't bury our gifts – but perhaps he was an older man who wanted peace and quiet and security, not business transactions. But he was told off. The red handkerchief is to enable him to find the talent in the earth later.'

Eularia felt ruefully that her Winchester Cathedral show was the peak of her career. There were other exhibitions already in the offing but they were on a smaller scale. Forty-two of the paintings had been hung in the Cathedral for a month, and she was right. She would not live to see such a big exhibition in such a prominent and famous place again.

Don't Bury It (1970)

After the Cathedral, ten of the paintings returned to the bar in Lymington Community Centre for the Lymington Arts Festival and she received a very good review:

> 'It is, in fact, very difficult to look at any of these pictures and remain completely indifferent to them. They make you think about the story they are telling; and that is what the artist intends.'

The doctors were quite pleased with Eularia at the end of 1969 and told her that she was in remission again, but her faith in them began to decline and she was right, she wasn't in remission. She knew she wasn't well and she never would be, it was just a question of coping with the periods when she felt worse and making the most of those in which she had more energy. Her last diary is that of a woman subconsciously preparing for death:

'The relief was strangely dim, no uprush of joy, somehow I feel I've been so far, on such a dark journey, that I've come back quite different. Lazarus wasn't one of the apostles, he just sat at the feast. He had journeyed too far, and so have I. There is no more earthly joy.'

But she remained optimistic throughout December because, despite her inner misgivings, she really wanted the news of remission to be true. Her energy was fairly good and the uncomfortable symptoms had receded for the time being:

'I'd asked for a bit more time, a bit more health, so as to learn more, to learn how to cope with eventual death.... And this is exactly what I got. What I asked for.... The cloud has lifted from my life for the time being. It may come again quite soon, or it may keep off for many years. It has taught me a lot; how to face horrors alone, without making trouble and scenes; how to accept weakness and helplessness; how to be thankful for small blessings.'

44

Don't Bury It!

Another bout of flu over Christmas 1969 brought Eularia low once again. What emerged from the fall-out was a necessary releasing and clearing of the decks. It was through this period that she finally let go of her past relationship with the Catholic Church and, although she always remained a Catholic, she was never a fully engaged Catholic after this. Her paintings were separating themselves from the purely Catholic vision and the need to convert people to it. They were not meant solely for Catholics, conversion was not their purpose. They were meant to be seen by everyone and to make them think and question their relationship with the divine, and in order for that to happen Eularia herself, as their 'mother', needed to gain a measure of distance from Catholicism:

'I really only need what I had at 18, a Bible and concentration… I have once more become myself, for better or worse.'

This may seem like an odd thing to say, especially if you are a Catholic, but how many people today remember that Jesus was a Jew? It was Catholicism that gave birth to the paintings, Eularia was always adamant about this, but the paintings themselves were not Catholic. They were beyond that. Even those of Catholic worship can be seen in this way, as Eularia noted herself once she became more stable in her new position. They are images of activities that humans have performed in one form or another as far back as the beginning of recorded history: the need to engage the sacred and the supernatural through symbolism and ritual. What Eularia never lost sight of was that underlying yearning in us to find a voice for this relationship, to express it in some way that gives it meaning. Ultimately it is not whether we are Catholic, Anglican, Methodist, Muslim, Jew, Hindu, Buddhist or even Pagan that is at the core, it is our relationship with the divine and how we experience and express that. What Eularia always struggled with was the fact that it was not just an intellectual concept (the Theology of it) but a much deeper, much more 'felt' thing, which was almost impossible to define and yet which had given birth to so much religion and art:

'I am now a Seeker, having failed to become a Catholic because I am not a joiner-in of groups. How does a Seeker express religion in art? '

It could be argued that Eularia had always been a Seeker. Her urge to join the Catholic Church was driven by an urge to have questions answered, to belong to a community, and she certainly did find something under their influence. There were 'the years of prayer', a return of her experiences of God and something supernatural from her childhood, and the inspiration to produce what remains an extraordinary body of work – but she was never a natural Catholic, nor a content Theologian. Her persistent flu at the beginning of 1970 was the culmination of the doubts and struggles with faith over the last year and one can see glimmers of a new direction emerging. Had her health sustained her it might have heralded a whole new direction for her painting. But health became the over-riding concern. Eularia was not one of those people who could shine through illness. The family depression patterns were too strong for that.

We can be fairly certain that Eularia would have moved beyond the confines of Catholicism even if she had not been so ill. She wasn't wrong when she felt that her paintings had an ecumenical appeal and destiny, they still do today. As a painter of religion she was necessarily an observer of it, not a participator, inspired by her own inner sense of spirituality from a direct relationship with God. But culturally this didn't fit and she didn't have the confidence to be a complete and assured eccentric walking her own path as her brother Francis did.

For so much of her life Eularia had wanted to fit in, to belong. It was, perhaps, her greatest paradox – being called to a unique and unorthodox path and wanting the safety and acceptance of society – the two never sat happily together. Had she been male, like Francis, it might not have been so hard. There were plenty of examples of eccentric male artists following their own paths, there was a degree of acceptability about it, but being female and a mother added a whole extra twist to the dynamic. Even in the late 1960s women of Eularia's generation were still, for the most part, either respectable mothers and grandmothers who stayed at home, looked after the house and their families and didn't ask or expect too much of life, or they were bluestocking spinsters, like her cousin Alicia, teachers, matrons, or some other respectable profession.

The necessity of giving a talk at Alresford Community Centre was the incentive to become clear about where she now stood as a painter of religion:

'The real problem is how to speak of religion now that I have "no denomination". The answer is that I did this painting up to marriage, and the shock of the new religion revived the urge. The fact of loss of faith in the Church isn't fatal. A vocation is a vocation, and I'm lucky to be a laywoman, not committed to any specific religious jobs... But the summons is welcome however alarming. I did *want* to be a speaker, to be asked respectfully to speak, and I wasn't suitable while militantly Catholic, now I'm much more suitable perhaps, owing to my semi-lapse...'

It was inevitable that Eularia would make a good speaker. She had kept small audiences of friends entertained for years, and the talk at Alresford proved it. It is as if this acceptance of expansion, of freeing up from the purely Catholic milieu, reawakened Eularia's experience of faith:

'Last night the distant intimation of prayer... and there was God, without any reason – no church, no priest, no sacraments, nothing. I was shocked. But there it was...For God wants apostles; the priests don't, they want sheep, and the sheep want other sheep, not apostles. Yet what else am I?'

In Eularia's mind the paintings were never really divorced from the Catholic 'thing', just as she never truly felt divorced from Cyril, and she did not give up Catholicism altogether. The church at Chandler's Ford was now her favoured place to attend Sunday Mass and she enjoyed singing with the choir, but she was very aware of staying in the background and not causing trouble. She didn't want to run the risk of being 'thrown out'. Music was still her most important way of worshipping and she described how, listening to a group singing 'Jesu Dulcis Memoriae':

'...something hardened and twisted in my mind, resisting it fiercely. The same thing lies behind Mass, very far behind, very deeply buried treasure. This "thing" is behind the paintings.'

The very things that most bothered Eularia about the Church by now were exactly those things that it was attempting to address, but through the post Vatican II confusion and conflicts she couldn't see it. It was a desire to return to these more simplistic roots that the council, and indeed priests like Pat Murphy O'Connor and David Mahy, wanted to recapture, the essence of worship and responsibilities being shared by a group of like-minded believers. The problem was that Eularia wanted that simplicity but couldn't cope with the reality. She always ended up judging it as unintelligent and beneath her. She just wasn't prepared to play the game. Whilst recognising that she had her own resistance to the 'buried treasure' that fed the paintings, she began to see that the resistance also existed within the mechanics and ritual of Mass. The place she had been told that she ought to be experiencing God was exposed as the one place that she did not.

The fact that she was a woman also had increasing influence. Undoubtedly her attitude to the clergy was tangled up with her attitude to her own brothers and the resented sense of superiority she felt in them, especially Anthony, the older brother who failed her by not being interested in her. She wrote in her diary about Michael Gedge wanting to stay on top and still be King. Her view of the Church and the clergy had shifted in line with her view of men. She no longer saw them as sources from which she required praise and attention, but as falsely superior beings who had too much power in her world. Essentially, as her life had panned out, this was true. She herself had allowed them all to play this role and the only way she could stop it was to effectively evict them all from her life. She did this as pleasantly as she was able, declining offers of sick visiting from Michael, David and Richard Davey (another St Peter's curate). As for her brothers, she saw and heard little enough of them anyway so it did not matter. The only male that she continued to have close contact with was James.

Having finished *Not Looking Back*, *The Rich Young Man* and *Don't Bury It*, Eularia was once again wondering what her next subject should be. The fact that she had three overlapping summer exhibitions on the cards meant that she would need every painting she had and this spurred her on.

She finally chose *The Angel of the Lord* (Luke 2: 9). This is the moment when the angel tells the shepherds of the birth of Jesus. Perhaps there is an irony in the fact that she chose a subject in which a being much greater than the male shepherds is telling them what to do. She set the scene around a shepherd's hut on wheels, very much as she would have seen them in the Cotswolds, populated by a group of very surprised shepherds with their sheep. Each shepherd is being held by a luminous hand emanating from a swirl of light and energy above him. Eularia tells us:

"This is a sort of Christmas card. Shepherds used to live, day and night, during the lambing, in little wheeled huts. As for the angel – how did he attract their attention and convey the message? Was it just light, or was there a sort of action?'

But her next subject would not come. She could only do so much work on *The Angel of the Lord* before she had to leave it to dry:

'...of all the possible subjects not one will start me off. Plenty of simple illustrations could be done, but I need something a bit deeper... also the eroding thought keeps occurring, that it's all nonsense, why paint it? Yet this didn't stop much great painting in the past, mythological subjects, battles, fantasies, dreams. My song is love unknown – *very* unknown indeed. I want to paint.... My search for love and fulfilment continues, but there is a chance that, like Aunt Rose, I shall retire into a land of unreality, having got tired of all real things.'

In the end her subject was *The Eleventh Hour* (Matthew 20: 6-7) the parable of the workers in the vineyard and their hiring. Eularia sets it in a market that is in the process of closing up at the end of the day. Amongst all the stalls and jumble is an elderly couple sitting on a bench, just watching and minding their own business. But Jesus stands behind them with a hand on their shoulders, calling them at the eleventh hour of their lives and of the marketing day.

In her diary she cites as part of her inspiration for choosing this subject a programme she saw about a woman who credited her great age of 107 to belonging to Christ. Eularia says:

'The opportunity to broadcast this, at the "eleventh hour"... sunset, market place, closing down.'

She found the detail in *The Eleventh Hour,* which at this point she called 'The Market Place', hard work, which is probably why she took the unusual step of sawing two inches off the right hand margin giving it a rather unsatisfactory balance. But Eularia, too, was in her eleventh hour. These last few paintings and the exhibitions of the summer were her swan song before Christ finally admitted her to his vineyard, so to speak. Eularia tells us:

''The market packing up at the end of the day, and the couple resting at the end of their working lives. But Christ turns up and hires them...'

By this time Eularia's captions were much shorter and more cryptic. Instead of the confident and lengthier explanations of the early and mid 1960s, we are now posed riddles and more questions. She is no longer preaching, she is prompting us to think.

The Eleventh Hour (1970)

45

Back To Nature

It was now Lent of 1970 and one evening, as Eularia drove back to Winchester from Romsey with the setting sun in her eyes, she found the inspiration for her next painting:

> 'Just as I drove into Winchester I realised why Mary M. (*Magdalene*) didn't recognise Christ... was the rising sun behind him, and a lot of gardening tools around, as in every spring? The new painting.'

Thinking he was the Gardener (John 20:15) is the moment when Mary Magdalene encounters the risen Christ and mistakes him for a gardener. Eularia gives us the luminous bright yellow sky of the rising sun and silhouetted against it is the figure of Christ, amidst a sea of daffodils. He is holding out his hand, complete with nail hole through which the sun shines, imploring Mary not to cry. In front of him is a stack of gardening implements and Mary is seen clinging to a branch looking up at him tearfully, directly into the rising sun. It is a powerful image, even as a direct illustration of the Gospel scene, but it also reflects something of Eularia's own struggle, that to see Christ is to be blinded by the brightness of it all. It is a play on light and what that means for us. By using the ancient images of the sun returning and the son returning combined together, Eularia blends the ancient and the less ancient in a modern setting. This gives it timelessness and yet places it firmly in the here and now with the modernity of the gardening tools and a Mary who wears a hooded duffle coat. Once again her caption, by posing a question, forces us to think:

Thinking He Was the Gardener (1970)

'Why did Mary think he was the gardener? Was it because the sun rose, and she was crying and couldn't see clearly and only took in the gardening implements? Anyway the image of Christ as a gardener stuck in ancient tradition, which is nice in these days. Few of us are shepherds or fishermen, but most of us are gardeners by forty, if not sooner, so the connections between Christ and the spade and hoe brings him closer.'

Eularia was entering a period of relative calm with regard to her faith and her painting and wrote a retrospective of the last two years in her diary:

'I've been over-enthusiastic and consequently made a fool of myself, in public, TV and papers. Yet fundamentally I have been true to myself, and accepted the Catholic challenge, undertaken what I thought was a deeper journey into the Christian religion. It caused tensions with my heredity and education, and has resulted in what may yet prove a purer type of Catholicism, clear of all the "toys and games", the superstitions, and the smug piety which puts its trust in outward forms and observances. Yet these *do* help simple people.'

This is a spiritually much more mature Eularia despite her willingness to discount her publicity. Even the understanding that some people need outward forms and observances can be seen as wise as opposed to arrogant. Eularia perceived that the outward forms and observances of religion and ceremony give our minds space to adjust to what already is, they allow us space to integrate it. The blinding image of the sun behind Christ in *Thinking he was the Gardener* momentarily eclipses our ability to see something we can relate to, a physical presence, a reality, and so the mind attempts to place it by using the physical tools that give it context – the gardening implements.

The last six works that Eularia painted reflected her more assured and unique spirituality. Only four of them have Bible references and only one of those is a direct Gospel illustration, the other three are visual interpretations of teachings of Jesus. Of the remaining two, one deals with death and the other is an unfinished interpretation of one of the Gnostic Gospels.

The fact that she ordered sixty-two yards of new linen for canvas just before Easter showed that she had no intention of giving up just yet. But, with the spring approaching, she was increasingly turning once again to her garden.

Much of her correspondence with Rachael by now was about her garden and the swapping of seeds and notes (Rachael was also a keen gardener), and it is increasingly common to find plant and gardening to-do lists on the backs of envelopes and inserted into her diary as loose sheets or scribbled on the end pages. The garden was more than merely a hobby by now for Eularia and this shows in her choice of *Thinking He was the Gardener* as a subject, despite the fact that she didn't think the composition for the painting worked:

'The garden. She found Him in the garden, just like "The Secret Garden" where the voice said to Mr Craven "in the Garden". The garden of the soul. "One is nearer God's heart in a garden" in the poker-work texts. This is the present direction, peaceful manual labour combined with painting, seclusion from people, the despised "communing with nature" which seems to have inspired not only poets and painters but also St. Francis and the desert hermits. Also it fits in with the present state of glandular imbalance, avoids all trouble and strife, and may tide me over the present crisis of religious practice, the giving up of the Catholic habits and customs. The idea of the door, opening on to pasture, might be possible though very difficult. Also the Crux Fidelis one...'

Here she clearly gives the next two subjects for her painting inspired by her love of and connection with the garden. Her reference to pokerwork texts relates to pyrography (writing with fire) – the art of decorating wood with burn marks. It is an interesting subtext to what would be the choice for her final painting, *Fire on the Earth*.

Eularia did indeed find a close relationship with Christ through her garden in those last months. Some might say that it is a much more feminine path to spirituality, the classic organised path of religion being more male perhaps. There is evidence that Eularia agreed with this but it is only now, at the eleventh hour, that she began to really find the courage to identify with it and stand by it:

'Yesterday more gardening, and well-being - I sleep well, and today I woke up full of the strong love of Christ yet it's the new (?) sort. The constant inner cries may not have been mere expletives. They go with this constant preoccupation, not with Christ in the Tabernacle, not even in Communion especially – nor in the Passion or resurrection, nor in my neighbour (alas). It is Christ close to me day by day, within me, that holds my attraction. Not anybody else's experience, but my own unique one, as the Bournemouth man said. It may be an illusion, but I cannot any longer think of priests as his representatives.'

She began painting *I Am the Door* (John 10:9) which was the subject she had felt rather daunted by. The painting is as she described it in her diary. The upper body of Christ seems to emerge from the rock of a cave, as if organically part of it, and is shown drawing many to him. Where his chest would be is a doorway opening on to beautiful green pastures and distant hills and from which a stream bubbles. In contrast, the world this side of the door is far rockier and more tunnel-like. There is the usual human drama present in the figures, some are climbing up to the open door, and one is repeatedly beating upon it with bloody fists, apparently oblivious to the fact that it is already open. One is sitting on a rocky cleft to one side ignoring it completely. Eularia's caption states:

'One of the promises of Christ, what does it mean? We can go in and out of Christ and have a bit of Paradise; Conservation Years so that we can have beautiful places for car-trips, and the Garden Centres booming because we try to make Paradise in our gardens. Is this all part of our instinct to get back into the Garden of Eden? And how difficult is it? The man knocking hopelessly on the door which is wide open, the river of Paradise runs out and brims over, and the people press on towards the pasture which Christ promises...'

The fact that Christ himself appears as a part of the Earth that holds us is a very feminine idea, far removed from the more distant and either human or more God-like images common to the Christian religion.

She attended Easter services at Chandler's Ford and was dismayed to find that, although the last supper was enacted in a way that was much more accessible, and that laymen read the Passion, she missed the pomp and ceremony of the old Latin Mass. She found the new English service dull, as did many, and mourned the loss of the old.

She did wonder if her desire for it all was purely artistic, the new Mass having nothing visual in it that inspired her artistic eye. She also observed that when it came to kissing the cross on Good Friday, a subject she had painted in 1961, only the altar boys did it:

'I was amazed at how disturbed I was, but in fact the congregation all "crept to the cross" at the end of the service, and although there was no blood between the toes, yet it was very beautiful; I saw the point of "tradition"; for these folk, especially men and boys, would not have done this if newly introduced; they'd done it as toddlers and seen parents and grandparents do it, so they performed the strange action quite naturally.'

By contrast she watched *The Word of the Cross* on television (which focused on an Anglican Easter service) and wrote:

'...but (*I*) was happily disappointed, a group of white-robed "U" Anglicans performing a bloodless ceremony like Trooping of the Colours in perfect precision. A hundred miles from Padre P (*Pio*). They did *not* kiss the cross. And I saw how I truly belong to both; I love my country, but I belong to the intense and traditional thing, Catholic worship, low-class ritual done by uneducated priests and dim Irish peasants. And in my paintings this comes out.'

Perhaps, rather unsurprisingly, her next painting was the Crux Fidelis (Holy Cross), a revisiting of *Kissing the Cross, Good Friday* (1961), and was entitled *The Holy Tree*. In her diary just after Easter in 1970 she wrote:

'The painting of the Wood of the Cross came to me, an enlargement of the Good Friday one with the leaves and branches.'

It is interesting to compare these two. Essentially the two subjects are the same although the 1970 version is significantly larger and the crucifix, which is the focus of attention, merges with a soaring tree newly in leaf, giving again a much more earthy organic feel to ceremony. The 1961 version is set in St Peter's and is a straight representation of the Good Friday ceremony of kissing the feet of the cross, as it was pre Vatican II. In the 1970 version the body of the church itself has receded to the point where, although an altar can be seen in the distance and the chair on which the cross rests is clearly on a parquet floor, we could just as easily be out in nature as in a church. It is as if she has left us to decide which way we see the ceremony, as external and part of nature, or as internal and part of an organised ritual.

Firstly, the execution of the two shows Eularia's growth in technique and stature as an artist. In both paintings the central focus is the same, a crucifix on a wooden chair over which a woman in a checked coat leans with an altar boy standing behind. There are similarities in other details, but in the first many of the congregation sit and in the second all are standing. *The Holy Tree* is a much more accomplished version of the earlier work.

Secondly, the two show Eularia's own spiritual growth and the change in her relationship with the Church and organised religion generally. *Kissing the Cross, Good Friday* is a faithful rendition of a ceremony that had been performed for hundreds of years by Catholics all over the world. As Eularia herself said, it was a tradition that had been handed down through generation after generation. She does not attempt in any way to expand it. In her very early Catholic period of 1961, *Kissing the Cross, Good Friday* was only the seventh canvas she painted, all but one of the others having been Lourdes paintings. She was still a relatively new Catholic and enamoured and awed by the ritual and ceremony of the Church.

The Holy Tree is a Eularia emerging from a dark night of the soul, which she was never fully to escape. Having been brought up in a very male-centric household and society and then become part of a very male-centric religion, she had never really engaged with the more feminine

Eularia Clarke   *Painter of Religion*

Kissing the Cross, Good Friday (1961)

The Holy Tree (1970)

aspects of her character or spirituality. Finally in 1970, as disillusionment set in regarding the Church, it began to emerge in her painting and her relationship with her garden. Gone are the more rigid stances and lines of *Kissing the Cross, Good Friday,* along with the sense of tradition as a duty. The rather bored and strained faces and postures of the 1961 version are replaced by softer poses and more meditative and thoughtful expressions in her characters. There is even a sense of devotion that seems quite free of any set ritual. This is achieved by the introduction of the tree springing into new life, emerging as it does from the crucifix and chair. Any semblance of Mass-type ritual, with the exception of the one altar boy standing by the crucifix, is pushed into the indistinct background where it is possible to discern activity from clergy around the altar, as if they have nothing to do with this quiet moment of devotion.

Eularia never showed *The Holy Tree* at an exhibition so she never wrote a caption for it but in her diary she wrote:

'The idea came alive splendidly. Painting the mysteries is really my best thing – the gospel illustrations are like pot-boilers, too simple. People will hate the Holy Tree, it won't be chosen, but it's my true self speaking.'

Whereas in the past Eularia had always considered herself equal with men and resented being treated as 'merely a woman', now she began to champion her gender, as if, for the first time in her life, she was proud to be female and not male.

On this vein there was a particular reading during the Easter Vigil service which she attended at Chandler's Ford which really annoyed her:

'I heard the lector reading the prophet, "God hates your sins like a woman's menstruation;" and I noticed that this passage is chosen to be read in public, not any other. The prophet's simile from primitive life, utterly out of tune with the new understanding and wonder and admiration of God's making of a baby in a human woman. One can see what the prophet meant, for female hygiene in the O.T was hardly possible – and the stench was still around in the years before the war. Yet it needn't have been retained in the new version in English – except that the all-male committee may well have wished to humiliate the new, uprising female sex, the new threat, the stealers of priests, the good professionals. I looked around and saw the sanctuary full of men and boys, the male lectors, the male offering collectors and ushers, the male choir man who shouts down everyone in unison, the good female organist patted on the head... I thought of Worlock "Hands up boys who serve at Mass. Hands up girls who help their mothers to clean the church." Yet it is natural. This old-fashioned and mentally inflexible group can't catch up yet. Equality of the sexes would wreck this male stronghold and expose a terrifying equality of gifts and education and ability. A female "strike" would almost empty the churches, on weekdays and non-Sunday services. Yet nothing can be done, we must bide our time and watch the advance take place, and note the strange savage prophecy of Mary in the Magnificat.'

Eularia's reference to the Magnificat here is a different interpretation to the one most commonly held by the Church. She is reading Mary's statement as a praise of God for exalting woman from her lowly humble state and casting down proud men. For the first time Eularia was standing by her gender as a whole, and she was perceptively realistic and down to earth about it. She was certainly reflecting a growing wave of feminist thinking (1970 saw the publication of Germaine Greer's *Female Eunuch*). Eularia would probably never have considered herself to be a feminist in the way that Greer espoused but she did support the idea that women were as capable and as intelligent as men, and just as able to represent Christ on earth, after all that was what she was doing.

This led her to choose what would be her last illustration of a miracle from the Gospels. *The Bent Woman Straightened* (Luke 13:13) is the story of a woman, who had been bent for eighteen years, simply going about her business when Jesus saw her and straightened her. This might not have been a problem if he hadn't done it on the Sabbath, which caused him to fall foul of the authorities. Eularia's painting shows the moment Jesus performs the miracle and the woman stands straight. She has set the miracle in a church during a service. The altar, clergy and servers can be seen once again in the distant background with their congregation, all with their backs to us. Jesus is in the foreground, as if at the back of the church, with the woman, a handful of men, who appear to be ushers, and two children, only one of which is a girl. It is as if they are not part of the service at all.

Again this painting was never shown at an exhibition so Eularia never wrote a caption for it, but in her diary she wrote:

'Yesterday I got on with the Bent Woman. It's a good story. How the Church has always neglected it, preferring the Issue of Blood woman, who was what they like women to be, ashamed, frightened, unclean from the female state, furtively, almost "stealing" Christ's healing and creeping away. But the Bent Woman! Bent by an affliction common to both sexes, not furtive, not even asking for a cure. But Christ saw her and went to her of his own accord, and healed her rather spectacularly, and she *at once* began praising God. A joyful and inspiring scene – but not one which would suit Church Authorities. Not a word about men, or priests, only the usual about healing on the Sabbath – Christ *against* the Church, in fact.'

The Bent Woman Straightened (1970)

Of all her works this is undoubtedly her most feminist, and was intended to be. Eularia had never identified with the image of the weak and humble woman, not even as a mother. She saw it increasingly as an entirely male construct, which women bought into. She had never been happy as the 'Martha' figure, the cook and bottle washer who took care of everyone else and missed out on her mission in life, which was a dangerously 'male' one – spreading the word through her Art (either the job of priests or male artists). Even today the bulk of our celebrated artists are male.

46

Beyond the Church

What is significant about Eualria's 1970 paintings is their strength. A stronger, more original voice was leading Eularia to choose challenging subjects, not just for her but for her audience too.

'I can't give my whole allegiance to an organisation which discourages criticism, yet is so openly anti-women. A trial of strength is on; I don't want to destroy but to reform.'

She makes a very insightful observation about how the conflict between a devout religion and the modern world can lead to problems which are still as true today as they were in 1970. In 1970 it was the IRA and the Irish troubles, which were increasingly in the media, and the IRA (certainly to Eularia's mind) represented Catholic Ireland:

'Perhaps humans shouldn't say Father to another man all their lives – is this why Protestants become more adult and civilised? Yet the R.C. thing is a mixture, very entangled, of this ridiculous subservience and something else which is not ridiculous. The close-knit flock enables a very intimate religion to be practised. No explanations to strangers are needed, no allowances made to the stranger and observer, the priest leads his flock and talks to them in a special language, and the atmosphere seems to be very supernatural. End-results are not good, certainly by everyday standards, probably the tensions produced by these two worlds are frightful, living in one, worshipping in another. So the Catholic doesn't grow and develop as a social being in the modern society; he remains a savage child.'

This modern secular world does not allow for the practice of religious faith, increasingly so (Islam is the faith that now most strongly illustrates this). What Eularia understood is that a relationship with God permeates through your whole life. It is not possible to shut it off in order to go to school or to work. We like structure, and thus religions emerge to organise our relationship with God and to attempt to legislate it. Whenever there is tension between the structures created by religion and those created by secular society extremists will always emerge – it is the point where the pressure cooker explodes, inevitably in violence.

The treatments were not working anymore, and it was she that was diagnosing new growths and then pointing them out to the doctors rather than the other way around. She knew that this was the pre-death period and this was probably why she chose death as the subject of her next painting.

He Shall not Perish is not her most successful work, but it is one of the most challenging, all the more so when you realise that, although the subject of the painting is male, Eularia must have been seeing herself in his place as she painted it. There is no Bible reference for this painting as it deals directly with Eularia's own feelings about death and what might lie beyond.

The painting shows a man on his deathbed in a hospital, surrounded by family and a nurse. But the focal point of the painting is not the dead man but the swirling light that is leaving him helped by golden disembodied hands. Again there is no caption for this painting as it was never shown and possibly never even completely finished to her satisfaction, but in her diary she wrote:

'I have two books out, about death, but neither really touches the realities. There are the fancy bits, the fairy-tale with only a spark of likelihood. There is the painful detailed theology of Boros, who works out each aspect of after-life according to propositions thought up about 1100–1300 A.D. There are beautiful deaths, and these are always sudden, ecstatic and full of faith, deaths of people in good health recently, able to do the job well. There is the recurrent theme of "joining one's dear ones," which means little to me, for I had little love for any of my dead, nor they for me; I wasn't exactly cherished owing to my character and circumstances, so I'd rather have my children than my "dear departed". There is only the C.S Lewis comfort, that all our secret ideals and longings will be somehow realised in God. My appallingly vertical relationship may somehow be changed into a genuine joining up, I shall love to be loved without barriers of fastidiousness or criticism...the High Country.'

Eularia believed in an after-life, hence the strident nature of the title, *He Shall Not Perish*. She was intelligent enough to know that she did not really know what it would be like. I can remember Marita (James' wife) telling me, some eight years after Eularia's death, that she lost even her faith in the end. Lost sight of it perhaps, it's not always easy to focus on God when you feel really ill as she undoubtedly did in her last days, but it would be entirely out of character for Eularia to lose the sense completely. What most of her family never understood, and fail to understand today, is that she always had that sense of God. Everything else was simply an attempt to express or explain it, to understand it, but it was only really in her diaries that she stated it clearly. She knew it became dormant from time to time, but it never left her completely.

Eularia had exhibitions booked right through to September. The first was a small showing at Henley Congregational Church, followed by a big one at Yoxford, Saxmundham (postponed from 1969), then St Paul's Girls School, Hammersmith, Eularia's old school, arranged by the Old Paulinas. In July a large proportion of the collection went to the Sacred Heart Church Hall in Fareham (organised by Roy Bennett), then many went on to St Swithun's School, followed by West Downs School. Her last exhibition was at St Peter's Church, Basingstoke.

Getting paintings ready for exhibitions, even if she wasn't transporting them herself, was hard work for Eularia, given her state of health. Those organising the exhibition would visit her in advance and go through the paintings deciding which ones they wanted. Eularia then had to bring them all downstairs and make sure they were protected for their journey. She then had to take them back upstairs afterwards and repair any damage to paintings and frames that had occurred in transit. Having recently done this myself for only twenty of her paintings I know just how physically demanding this is. That she did it so many times over this summer when she had so little stamina and was often feeling sick and in pain is an extraordinary testament to just how much she believed that the paintings should be seen. She, of course, did not let on to anyone about how ill she really was and so offers of help, that might otherwise have been forthcoming, did not materialise.

In May she bought something that was to bring her much joy for the rest of her life, her bus shelter. This was the nickname the family gave to the small, three-sided, cedarwood shelter (six foot by four foot) that she installed by the apple tree, because it looked just like a bus shelter. The first thing she did, once it was up, was create a raised platform from bricks and wood and put a mattress on it. It was exactly the right size for a bed and it meant she could sleep outside even when it was raining.

Eularia borrowed a book of the Gnostic Gospels from the library and the Acts of John 90 inspired her only attempt to paint a much more mystical subject, *His Head Touching the Stars*. Eularia copied out the relevant paragraph in the back of her diary (any misquotes are Eularia's own):

'Again in a like manner he bringeth up us three into the mountain, saying, Come ye with me. And we went again, and we saw him at a distance praying. I, therefore, because he loved me, drew nigh unto him softly, as though he could not see me, and stood looking upon his hinder parts. And I saw that he was not in any wise clad with garments, but was seen of us naked, and not in any wise as a man, and that his feet were whiter than any snow, so that the earth there was lit up by his feet, and that his head touched the heaven so that I was afraid and cried out, and then turning about, appeared as a man of small stature and caught hold on my beard and pulled it and said to me, John, be not faithless but believing and not curious...'

Eularia wrote in her diary:

'The Apocryphal Acts of St John speak of a tradition (written about 160) that John sometimes saw Christ as an Ugly Little Man, but when he prayed, his head reached up to the heavens. Sometimes his flesh was hard, sometimes insubstantial. This is heretical, Doetic, Manichaeism, but it describes my feelings about the Church, the ugly little man who, when praying, touches the heavens'.

It proved to be a tricky subject to express and she changed the painting more than once, eventually running out of time as the cancer caught up with her. Had it been completed it may well have proved to be one of her most powerful works. What we have is the sketching out and rough filling in on canvas of the painting. It is set on a ledge up a mountainside, possibly a cave entrance, overlooking what might be sea. The foreground is the most finished with two blanketed figures asleep by a campfire, their feet glowing red with the warmth of the flames. On the left in the background is a jutting cliff face and to the right an immense being of light, of which we only see the feet and legs reaching up to the stars and surrounded by flying birds. A ghostly, unfinished outline of John appears behind this figure, only there are two of him. Eularia disliked the first version and painted it out but a faint hand and head can still be seen. The clearer outline was to have become her newer version of John.

His Head Touching the Stars (unfinished 1970)

As Eularia tells us, the idea of being a small and ugly 'little man' who is suddenly elevated by prayer was one she not only identified with, but had also experienced. She had written about it but this was her only attempt to paint that inner experience.

Eularia was still coming up with ideas for new paintings. She mentions Barabbas as a possible subject, and one of the disciples dancing at the

Ascension, neither of which would ever materialise. In fact, besides the unfinished *His Head Touching the Stars* she would only ever paint two others after *He Shall Not Perish*.

The subject for the first of these came from the parable of the sorting of the fish. *The Judgment* (Matthew 13:48) is a depiction of Jesus' teaching where he likens the Day of Judgment to a fisherman's catch and the sorting of the good fish from the bad. Once again there is no official caption as the painting was never shown, but Eularia gives us this in her diary:

'I meditated on the parable of the fish being sorted on the shore. I had been thinking, much nicer to be thrown back than to be killed and fried. But the story is about the state of the fish. Either we go straight to Christ – perhaps for a brief cooking before he eats us – or we are thrown back into life to learn a bit more.'

The painting is vintage Eularia. Her Byzantine Christ sits calmly on the seashore with a large net of assorted fish, which he is sorting through in order to put the good ones in his basket and throw the rest back into the sea. Next to Christ we see a figure bent over and pouring a pail of fish back into the ocean.

The Judgment is a much more finished painting than *He Shall Not Perish* and her last one, *Fire on the Earth*. This is probably down to her practise of working on more than one at a time and it is likely that while she did finish *The Judgement*, *He Shall Not Perish* and *Fire on the Earth*, although more finished than *His Head Touching the Stars*, were never entirely completed.

To Eularia's great joy she heard that her son-in-law, Robert, had got a fellowship at Worcester College in Oxford, which meant that Rachael's family would be moving to Oxford and be within easy reach for visits. She began to look forward to being able to spend more time with her grandchildren:

'I'd resigned myself to never knowing the grandchildren, never chatting with R, never watching their growing-up, and hearing them talk... How do I feel so normal? Does God want more paintings? Has God a soft spot for Art?'

She resolved to hide how ill she was for as long as she could, even from most of her family:

'The feeling of defeat, and yet there is anxiety to conceal this, to cover-up, not to invite pity, concern or even people's awareness; it is to be a secret suffering as long as I can.'

She wanted to stay healthy enough to cope on her own until Rachael (just about to move) or James (in the process of buying his house) were settled enough to look after her, but the cancer had now metastasised which meant more radium treatment. Eularia was resigned to this as being a part of her routine, but what was becoming increasingly clear, to her disappointment, was that neither the drugs nor the radium was stopping the cancer from spreading and there was a possibility that it had spread around her stomach and diaphragm.

Then out of the blue:

'At 3.15, the doorbell rang...I didn't go to the door. A Mini started up and drove off. And the Canon's (*Sidney Mullarkey*) card on the mat. 'I never see you nowadays, it makes me sad.'

Sidney Mullarkey may not have conformed to Eularia's requirements and may indeed have been dismissive of her art, but he had, over the years, shown her that she did matter, most notably when she was in hospital in 1967. He may not have liked her *Stations* (to be honest not many people do even now) but he looked after the painting she gave him (*Palm Sunday*) despite the fact that since 1960 St Peter's has moved presbyteries twice. Sidney ended his working life as a priest on the Isle of Wight and did not take the painting with him, perhaps because he felt that it belonged at St Peter's, the parish that had inspired the painting in the first place. To me, a descendant of Eularia, it is a lovely thought that her old parish still have a part of her.

She did have a kind of reconciliation with Sidney during the summer of 1970 when he visited her once again. The attempts to heal the breach were all on Sidney's side and they succeeded in having a 'pleasant' conversation, although it was not enough to tempt her back to St Peter's or the Flock.

By the summer of 1970 Eularia was leaning more towards the teachings of Teilhard de Chardin and finding God via science and nature rather than through 'the Vatican Thing'. She knew that people liked the Gospel paintings but doubted that she would do another one, leaning more and more towards the mysteries.

By this time most of her creative pleasure was coming from the garden and working outdoors in three dimensions. Concrete and cement were still what she enjoyed most. Eularia's garden is long gone and very few photographs of it survive. I remember it as being a wild place of shells, flints, coloured glass, tiered pools full of goldfish, shell-covered pots and old sinks crammed with flowers. The fact that we had a grandmother who did all her own cementing was in no way odd to us.

That she had the energy to cement is surprising because she described even the smallest amount of food causing her stomach to distend and swell very painfully, so she was eating less and less:

'The chill rain pours, the nights get darker, I feel the cold so much more. I keep crying out for mercy, yet what's the good? God must do this thing with me, and this is mercy. He can't change his plans because of pity, if he did, I wouldn't realise my potential. My cry for mercy is simply the expression of my sorrow.'

Eularia was in the habit of stopping off in woods on her way home from Mass at Chandler's Ford on Sundays to gather leaf-mould for the garden and wood for her fire:

'... and there in the summer woods I found the spiritual joy I had missed in Mass. I find, coming from Communion, that I look so eagerly through the open door to the landscape, Hilliers shrub gardens, and my back is to the altar and the sanctuary. I could easily be a "blue-domer"[2], and when I read Father's parish notices, rubical and so fantastically concerned with life lived round church-worship, I see why people turn against churches.'

She went on to say:

'There are ways of dealing with Christ. One can dispose of him by thinking of him as a baby, dominated by the Blessed Virgin who is the big figure. Or as a corpse, destroyed by men, also tortured and bleeding and completely controlled. Or as a consecrated wafer, which has to be locked up on the altar for security but somehow seems very much controlled by the priest who has the key. Or, one can dispose of him by dressing him as a first-century Jew, localised in time and geography, dead. But the Lord is not like that. The Lord is risen. He comes to live in us at baptism, he is so alive, so active, so interfering and so constructive....'

Eularia was increasingly adamant that God lives in us, not in some remote object of veneration such as the Blessed Sacrament. She could no longer agree with the clergy who insisted that in order to commune with God one had to attend Church and Mass. For Eularia God was as present in her praying at home, in her painting and in her garden as in church, in fact more so.

---

2   Someone who prefers to worship outdoors under the blue dome of the sky (heaven).

47

Fire on the Earth

New exhibitions were appearing on the horizon: at Southampton University in 1971, at Lymington in December 1970, at St Peter's Anglican Church in Basingstoke and at West Downs. Of these only St Paul's and West Downs would take place.

Fire on the Earth (Luke 12:49) is an ironically intriguing subject for what would be Eularia's final painting. The quote for it: 'I am come to cast fire on the earth. And what will I, but that it be kindled.' could be Eularia speaking. Her difficult relationships, the conflict she found herself in with the 'R.C. Thing', the inability to find an alternative in any other organised religion that suited her, the conviction that she had a message from God to express, could all lead to this statement. Once again there is no official caption, the painting was never shown, may never even have been fully completed as it does lack the finer detail of her more finished works, but there is a brief mention about it in her diary:

'Next, Fire on the Earth, and the pollarded willows, and dead reeds and barbed wire and tarred planks – the path by the river, the red sun... the people with dead reeds held up. Ice.'

The painting shows a blazing, Byzantine Christ in the sky casting fire upon a group of ordinary people amongst pollarded, winter willows and dead reeds. Some hold reeds up in joy to the fire and Christ, another is cutting a reed and has not yet turned to the fire, and two others appear to be hiding from the fire, one crouched right down and another facing us, uncertain.

Fire on the Earth (1970)

There is a simplicity to this painting, quite different from *The Judgment* which she had recently completed. It is a fine example of Eularia as a painter of religion. She shows all 'men': those who embrace the fire and God, those who are unsure or not quite ready, and those who are actively afraid and turn away. It also reflected her inner state, she who was so familiar with catching the fire of God in prayer wrote in her diary in August 1970:

'I know that if a spark of enthusiasm built up, I'd catch fire myself, and this at present I don't want – I need the flat, uneventful days of routine and non-involvement.'

It is possible to identify from this statement the woman peacefully cutting her reed with her back to the fire, the man who looks out at us uncertainly and the one who hides his face, crouched upon the earth. Her own journey had led her to understand that faith is never straightforward. We are often not ready, afraid or resistant, we even cut ourselves off from it, but the fire falls to earth nonetheless. As a final message it is powerful.

Weakness was setting in, she couldn't paint for long and she was in a great deal of discomfort around her diaphragm. A locum doctor, who knew something about cancer, saw her and insisted she had a barium X-ray. Once again as the illness, and her worry about it, reasserted itself, religion and faith faded into the background. She didn't have the energy to struggle with it anymore. There is a sense at this point of Eularia finally giving up.

Despite her downturn she didn't lose touch with God completely:

'When I woke from my rest.... a glory came down, a total glory and peace. It didn't change physical ills in any way, but I found myself saying, that if he could give me this joy, then I must grumble at none of his treatment. And once more I saw the truth of the thing. For physical euphoria may produce spiritual peace and joy *perhaps* – I don't know. But spiritual joy and peace is the middle of utter physical lowness – this must be supernatural.'

She wrote a rather sad letter to Rachael at this time bemoaning the fact that just as we had all moved to Oxford she was too unwell to help or visit, with hopes that she would soon be able to be a better grandmother. Eularia was never to make the trip to Oxford to see us. We did visit her for the day in Winchester but it was a strange visit and she was in bed for most of it. I recall the atmosphere at Middle Road being very different, hushed and disturbing. We children did not know how ill she was and I barely remember her on this visit, just a figure in a bed in the greenhouse. It was the last time I ever saw her.

Eularia wrote of this visit:

'I've not put off R (*Rachael*) and the family – after all, it's on the cards that I mightn't ever receive them here again. After this month of weakness and deterioration I realise that death may come soon, as was expected three years ago. It will be no surprise to learn this, and loose all ties quietly and finally. On the other hand it may not be the end at all – I've struggled out of some fairly deep dark pits lately. Whatever way, I've done over eighty paintings by hook or by crook, and this is what matters....Yesterday was oddly bitter-sweet, the flock of angels, all six of them, the four little white-golden heads and rosy faces and beautiful red lips and white smiling teeth. Everyone so, so lovely, so kind and good, and my heart so full of love for them, and my stomach full of hateful nausea and my body protesting at the visit; my love and my will fighting weakness and sickness.'

Eularia did not want to be seen as ill, she didn't want to be a sick mother or grandmother with all that that entailed. Rachael and James were aware but hardly anyone else knew just how ill she had become. She was admitted to Southampton hospital at the beginning of November and would never leave alive. What she hoped would be a short stay for treatment turned out to be her last decline into death.

The last thing she did for her paintings was to bring downstairs, at great personal effort, the twenty-four that were due to be shown at Basingstoke. Her hardback diary ends as she goes into hospital. She did not take it with her, but she did take an old school exercise book of Rachael's in which she continued to make entries until she was too ill to do so. The cancer had metastasised too much for further treatment.

Rachael and James spent as much time with her as possible, even Sidney came to visit her which touched her. She died in the small hours of 30 November. James had been by her bed for much of the time, but, characteristically, she chose a moment when she was alone to slip away.

Her funeral was held at St Peter's and she was cremated. Her ashes are buried in her mother's grave at Great Rissington, which she always thought was the loveliest graveyard in England.

Eversley Belfield said of her in her obituary in the *Hampshire Chronicle*:

'As a personality Eularia Clarke was unforgettable. She was most outspoken and voluble, but those who knew her found her conversation stimulating and her advice, though often unorthodox, was kindly and penetrating. For the last three years she had been suffering from cancer, but she was determined to persevere with her work, and the courage and cheerfulness she showed in her increasingly serious illness will remain an inspiration to those who knew her.'

48

Afterword

Eularia did not achieve the success she wanted, she felt that she had failed to get her message across or to ensure the kind of future that she wanted for her paintings. But ultimately it is not we who judge our own lives, but those who come after us. When I began this biography it was to provide a background to the woman who created an extraordinary collection of paintings regardless of whether you are Christian or not. What I have come to understand through writing it is that Eularia's legacy lies not just in the paintings she has left us but also in her extraordinarily revealing and frank diaries that accompany their journey into life. She has given us a deep insight into one woman's journey with God and faith, a very human journey. It is not glorious, there is no triumphant or happy ending, there never was a Damascene experience when all became clear, and eventually it was coupled with her struggle with cancer and approaching death. Many of us are not aware that our days are numbered, Eularia was: she lived with the full knowledge of her mortality and the experience of God and managed to be touchingly human about both.

Only five days after her death *The Universe* published an article by Eularia that she had given them some time before. As there is no mention of her death one assumes that they had not realised it at the time of going to press. It is entitled 'They May Not Hear Sermons or Read Books on Religion – But They Will Look at a Painting.' I have quoted bits of it elsewhere in this biography but I give it in full here as it sums up, in Eularia's own words, her feelings about painting religion.

'Painting seems a bit fancy, when I think of the things I keep reading about in The Universe. It's not in the same class as, say, relieving peoples' distress, or organising God's worship, nothing holy or heroic, just messy. Why write about it?

'Fr. Michael Gedge had an answer: "People who would never hear a sermon or read anything about religion, or talk with a priest, will often look at a religious painting in a public exhibition."

'This is true. Oil-painting is right in fashion, paintings arouse interest, the visual medium is "in".

'Paintings about Christ seem to produce extra interest and reaction from all sorts of people, believers, unbelievers and anti-believers.

'The various people who exhibit my "Paintings of Religion" always provide an exercise-book and pencil for visitors, and I get a wonderful collection of comments in these.

'Four-letter expletives from sixth-formers, and cries of dismay from housewives, and deep thoughtful criticisms from teachers, painters and clergy.

'Here are three comments, in their own spelling by young school children whose implications are specially interesting:

"The artest seems to think Jesus and his disiples are reel."

"Don't like mixture of religion with real things. The contrast is too obvius."

"Modern settins make it more like our own life."

'These children had thought, and it's worth a bit of painting to make a child think about religion for five minutes these days.

'Then there's television. Those superb technicians, the cameramen on both channels, told me how much they like to have paintings shown on the screen; they can focus their lenses on them, moving from detail to detail, and they find this a change from the "talking face".

Paintings, I'm told, hold the viewers' attention comparatively well, so are useful in religious broadcasting.

'I've even, surprisingly, had paintings shown on three teatime local news item programmes, which means "Jesus and his disciples" at family tea-tables over a wide TV area – to switch off would mean risk of missing something good after!

'Why painting? They demand so little.

'Think of books, sermons, plays, films, music. They need publishers, printers, customers, audiences, congregations, performers, cameras, projectors, tape-recorders, record-players.

'Paintings need none of these. A little free daylight, hooks and string, and they'll talk away quietly and continuously all by themselves.

'They cost little to paint, and last indefinitely. Yet, year after year, the books about religion pour from presses, music-publishers' lists burst with "sacred music", films, magazines, records abound but where are the painters?

'I've been asking this question for so long! When I was small, my elderly relations took me round art-galleries, and I wondered why Italians kept painting Jesus, while English painters stuck to views, and ordinary faces, and dogs?

'They showed me English religious paintings; I dismissed Joshua Reynolds' "Heads of Angels" and "Infant Samuel" as just little girls, nor did Blake seem interested in Jesus, nor did Stanley Spencer.

'Only Holman Hunt's "Light of the World" seemed to be of Jesus, not just a man but "Light" like in the Creed.

'Also I explored a lot of old churches, when my brothers had crazes for organ-stop lists, or medieval architecture.

I looked for mosaics, frescoes, paintings, but I found only reproductions of Italian Old Masters, or of Margaret W. Tarrant's dreamy, misty water-colours in the Children's Corners.

'Stained–glass windows didn't fill my gap, I was looking for Fra Angelico, but I found stone, wood, plaster.

'I still ask the same question; why has England never produced a specialist – or even near-specialist – religious painter of any stature?'

The answer, of course, is that it has – and her name is Eularia Clarke.

49

And Beyond

Eularia always referred to her work as paintings of religion, not religious paintings. It is an apt title for a woman who never truly felt a part of what she was depicting in the standard organised religious sense. In the end she wasn't interested in rules and hierarchy, but in the immediate and ever-present experience of God in her daily life. She used the Christian Gospels and Catholic worship to express this because that was what inspired her and that was the framework she knew; and it could be argued that she is one of the foremost religious artists that England has ever produced.

That she is not better known today is due to her early death. Her paintings were divided between her children, James and Rachael, neither of whom understood (or were comfortable with) their mother's vocation as a religious artist. James admits that Catholicism and the extreme religiosity of his mother's work is something he still does not understand.

By 1970 Rachael was a very luke-warm Catholic, maintaining it because Robert was still committed and for our sake. She had never shared her mother's fervour for religion, and with four young children simply didn't have time to think about it. She is herself an artist but freely admits that she is not comfortable with her mother's work. Consequently the paintings were largely stored away in attics and barns, a chosen few making it onto walls in our family living rooms. Nothing was done to promote Eularia, and without the two paintings in The Methodist Collection of Modern Art she would have faded completely from view. Ironically those in charge of the Methodist Collection today say that Eularia's two paintings remain amongst the most popular in their collection and are frequently used on their publicity material.

But Eularia always intended that her work should be seen, and seen as a collection. In the early 2000s my brother Chris (Cuthbert), who had always been so fascinated by Eularia's paintings as a boy, began an inventory, searching out where they all were. Fortunately my mother had preserved Eularia's own cataloguing and lists. What became obvious quite quickly was that not all the paintings were in good condition and many of the frames were damaged or substandard. This was brought home to both of us when we went to photograph the forty or so that were at James' house. A few had been reframed very well and looked very good on his walls but the rest had been stored in a stable with no glass in the windows and the elements and the birds were leaving their mark. We stepped in just in time.

It is no mean feat to store over ninety canvases for over forty years and, despite the fact that the paintings had suffered to a degree, Rachael and James have kept the collection intact. None were given away and none had been sold. Talks of setting up a Trust to take over ownership of the collection began, spearheaded by the next generation, Eularia's grandchildren, who are keen to make the paintings available once again to public view and who do not have issues about having a grandmother who was a religious artist, thus the website gallery was born. This was something that Eularia herself would have loved because anyone can see the whole collection on-line all over the world.

It felt important to me that her story should be available to accompany them and so I embarked on her biography, only to discover that not only did all her diaries still exist (despite the fact that no one had read them), my mother had kept all her correspondence as well along with a rich supply of newspaper articles, poetry and details about exhibitions. It is a remarkably rich and extensive archive.

There is a great deal that can be said about Eularia and her spiritual journey. In this biography I have concentrated as much as possible in presenting her life as she saw it and experienced it, with the help of her diaries. Inevitably much has had to be pruned and although I do paint I would never consider myself to be an expert on Art. She died when I was ten years old but through the writing of this biography she went from being a distant memory of a loved grandmother (who I remembered as being great fun, forceful and sometimes a bit scary) to being a very human woman I now know far more intimately than I had ever expected to. Despite this my feelings for her have not changed. She is still and will always remain the grandmother I loved.

Eularia Clarke   *Painter of Religion*

Sources

All unassigned quotes are from Eularia's own diaries. They are numerous and it would be far too boring to keep assigning them to this section. ECA = Eularia Clarke Archive

Chapter 1: Cheppers
From recollections supplied by Christopher Baines in the early 2000s: Sherlaw-Johnson family archives.
Peggy Baines: *Diary*, 1914. ECA.
Fr Michael Gedge letter to Eularia Clarke, 1962. ECA.
Peggy Baines: *Diary*, 1917. ECA.

Chapter 2: School
Eularia Clarke: *They May Not Hear Sermons or Read Books on Religion – But They Will Look at a Painting,* article published in *The Universe* 4.12.70. Clipping in ECA.

Chapter 3: 'Like Fra Angelico'
Eularia Clarke letter to Sylvia Percival, 1931 – ECA.
Eularia Clarke: *Biographical Notes for Exhibitions,* 1960s, ECA.
Cuthbert Baines letter to David Percival, 1932 – Sherlaw-Johnson family archives.

Chapter 6: War
Cyril Clarke letter to Eularia Clarke, undated – probably 1941. ECA.
Anthony Baines letter to Eularia Clarke, 1942 from a photocopy of the original in the ECA. Location of the original unknown.

Chapter 7: Survival
Eularia Clarke letter to Alicia Percival, circa 1947. ECA.

Chapter 8: Someone to Love
Cyril Clarke letter to Eularia Clarke, 1952. ECA.
From Rachael Sherlaw-Johnson: *Eularia Clarke, a Memoir,* an unpublished essay.

Chapter 9: Chief Cook & Bottle Washer
From Rachael Sherlaw-Johnson: *Eularia Clarke, a Memoir,* an unpublished essay.

Chapter 11: A Question of Faith
Eularia Clarke letter to Rachael Clarke, February 1958. ECA.
Eularia Clarke letter to Rachael Clarke, 1958. ECA.

Chapter 12: Priests
Eularia Clarke letter to Rachael Clarke, 1958. ECA.
Eularia Clarke letter to Alicia Percival, early 1958. ECA.

Chapter 13: A Year of Change
Eularia Clarke letter to Catherine Dupré, June 1959. ECA.
Eularia Clarke letter to Alicia Percival, June 1959. ECA.

Eularia Clarke letter to Rachael Clarke, spring 1959. ECA.

Chapter 14: A Wedding and a Funeral

Eularia Clarke letter to Alicia Percival, spring 1959. ECA.

Eularia Clarke letter to Alicia Percival, autumn 1959. ECA

Fr Angus Mason (*Pseudonym*) letter to Eularia Clarke, winter 1959. ECA.

Fr Michael Gedge letter to Eularia Clarke, 1962. ECA.

Fr Michael Gedge letter to Eularia Clarke, January 1960. ECA.

Chapter 15: Lourdes

Eularia Clarke letter to Alicia Percival, March 1960. ECA

Chapter 16: The Work Begins

Eularia Clarke letter to Rachael Sherlaw-Johnson, autumn 1960. ECA.

Chapter 17: Expanding Horizons

Eularia Clarke letter to Alicia Percival, March 1961. ECA

Eularia Clarke letter to Rachael Sherlaw-Johnson, July 1961. ECA.

Author's conversation with Canon David Mahy, 2014.

Chapter 18: Going Public

Iris Conlay: Article, *Catholic Herald*, 1961. ECA.

Fr Robin Noel letter to Eularia Clarke, autumn 1961. ECA.

Eularia Clarke letter to Rachael Sherlaw-Johnson, spring 1962. ECA.

Eularia Clarke letter to Rachael Sherlaw-Johnson, February 1962. ECA.

Chapter 19: Singing a Different Tune

Official exhibition caption, ECA.

Eularia Clarke letter to Rachael Sherlaw-Johnson, May 1962. ECA.

Chapter 20: Pat

Eularia Clarke letter to Rachael Sherlaw-Johnson, May 1962. ECA.

Eularia Clarke letter to Alicia Percival, November 1961. ECA

Chapter 21: Painting the Gospel

Eularia Clarke letter to Rachael Sherlaw-Johnson, August 1962. ECA.

Eularia Clarke letter to Rachael Sherlaw-Johnson, October 1962. ECA.

Fr Robin Noel letter to Eularia Clarke, October 1962. ECA.

Eularia Clarke letter to Rachael Sherlaw-Johnson, October1962. ECA.

Fr Michael Gedge letter to Eularia Clarke, autumn 1962. ECA.

Eularia Clarke letter to Rachael Sherlaw-Johnson, autumn 1962. ECA.

Fr Michael Gedge letter to Eularia Clarke, early 1963. ECA.

Chapter 22: Vision of Failure

Fr Michael Gedge letter to Eularia Clarke, spring 1963. ECA.

Fr Michael Gedge letter to Eularia Clarke, spring 1963. ECA.

Official exhibition caption, ECA.

Chapter 23: Blessing the Paintings

Eularia Clarke letter to Alicia Percival, spring 1963. ECA.

Fr Michael Gedge letter to Eularia Clarke, spring 1963. ECA.

Chapter 24: Oils

Fr Michael Gedge letter to Eularia Clarke, July 1963. ECA.

Eularia Clarke letter to Rachael Sherlaw-Johnson, September 1963. ECA.

Official exhibition caption, ECA.

Fr Pat Murphy-O'Connor letter to Eularia Clarke, November 1963. ECA.

Fr Hugh Farmer letter to Eularia Clarke, November 1963. ECA.

Eularia Clarke letter to Rachael Sherlaw-Johnson, January 1964. ECA.

Official exhibition caption, ECA.

Chapter 25: A Sense of Vocation
Eularia Clarke letter to Rachael Sherlaw-
Johnson, January 1964. ECA.
Official exhibition caption, ECA.
Fr Michael Gedge letter to Eularia Clarke,
February 1964. ECA.
Official exhibition caption, ECA.
Fr Michael Gedge letter to Eularia Clarke,
April 1964. ECA.
Eularia Clarke letter to Rachael Sherlaw-
Johnson, summer 1964. ECA.

Chapter 26: Half a Century
Fr Michael Gedge letter to Eularia Clarke,
May 1964. ECA.
Fr Michael Gedge letter to Eularia Clarke,
summer 1964. ECA.
Eularia Clarke letter to Rachael Sherlaw-
Johnson, September 1964. ECA.
Official exhibition caption, ECA.
Official exhibition caption, ECA.
Official exhibition caption, ECA.
Eularia Clarke letter to Rachael Sherlaw-
Johnson, September 1964. ECA.
Eularia Clarke letter to Rachael Sherlaw-
Johnson, autumn 1964. ECA.

Chapter 27: The Pops
Fr Cormac Murphy-O'Connor, letter to
Eularia Clarke, January 1965. ECA.

Chapter 28: Going Solo
Fr Hugh Farmer letter to Eularia Clarke,
spring 1965. ECA.
Official exhibition caption, ECA.

Chapter 29: Flames on their Heads
Official exhibition caption, ECA.
Official exhibition caption, ECA.
Official exhibition caption, ECA.

Chapter 30: The Passing of the Curia
Official exhibition caption, ECA.
Official exhibition caption, ECA.
Official exhibition caption, ECA.
Official exhibition caption, ECA.

Chapter 31: Er-Prayer
Eularia Clarke: *Er-Prayer, a case for encouraging,
understanding and helping passive prayer in
the laity"*, July 1966.

Chapter 32: Stations of the Cross
Second Vatican Council: *The Constitution
on the Liturgy*, Chapter 7, Paragraph 123.
1963.
Eularia Clarke letter to Rachael Sherlaw-
Johnson, September 1966. ECA.
Eularia Clarke letter to the *Catholic Herald*,
October 1966 edition. ECA.

Chapter 33: Sacred Heart
Eularia Clarke letter to Rachael Sherlaw-
Johnson, December 1966. ECA.
Official exhibition caption, ECA.

Chapter 34: Preaching
Official exhibition caption, ECA.
Official exhibition caption, ECA.
Fr Michael Gedge letter to Eularia Clarke,
October 1966. ECA.
Official exhibition caption, ECA.
Eularia Clarke letter to Rachael Sherlaw-
Johnson, summer 1967. ECA.
Eularia Clarke letter to Rachael Sherlaw-
Johnson, September 1967. ECA.

Chapter 35: No Old Age
Official exhibition caption, ECA.
Eularia Clarke letter to Rachael Sherlaw-
Johnson, October1967. ECA.

**Chapter 36: Never a Day Without a
Line**
Official exhibition caption, ECA.
Clip from the *Southern Evening Echo* (author
unknown), April 7, 1969. ECA.
The Reverend Tom Devonshire-Jones letter
to Eularia Clarke, October 1967. ECA.
Clip from the *Southern Evening Echo* (author
unknown), April 7, 1969. ECA.
Official exhibition caption, ECA.
Official exhibition caption, ECA.
Official exhibition caption, ECA.

Chapter 37: Into Deep Water
Newspaper clipping January 1966, author
and publication unknown.
Comments from Eularia Clarke's exhibition
books, no names given. ECA.
Official exhibition caption, ECA.
Official exhibition caption, ECA.
Official exhibition caption, ECA.
Official exhibition caption, ECA.

Chapter 38: Walling In
Eularia Clarke letter to Rachael Sherlaw-
Johnson, June 1968. ECA.
Official exhibition caption, ECA.
Official exhibition caption, ECA.
Official exhibition caption, ECA.
Chapter 39: Where Will The Paintings Live?
Official exhibition caption, ECA.
Official exhibition caption, ECA.
Official exhibition caption, ECA.

Chapter 40: Unicus et Pauper
Official exhibition caption, ECA.
Official exhibition caption, ECA.

Chapter 41: The Cellar Gallery
Joan Grigsby article in *Hampshire: the County
Magazine*, April 1969. ECA.
Joan Grigsby article in *Hampshire: the County
Magazine*, April 1969. ECA.
Eularia Clarke letter to Rachael Sherlaw-
Johnson, March 1969. ECA.
Official exhibition caption, ECA.
Official exhibition caption, ECA.
Official exhibition caption, ECA.

Chapter 42: Not Looking Back
Official exhibition caption, ECA.
Official exhibition caption, ECA.

Chapter 43: A Big Thing
Official exhibition caption, ECA.
Review from the *Hampshire Chronicle*,
autumn 1969 (author unknown). ECA.
Official exhibition caption, ECA.
Official exhibition caption, ECA.
Clipping of a local Press review (publication
unknown) by J.G (probably Joan Grigsby).

Chapter 44: Don't Bury It
Official exhibition caption, ECA.
Official exhibition caption, ECA.

Chapter 45: Back to Nature
Official exhibition caption, ECA.
Official exhibition caption, ECA.

Chapter 46: Beyond the Church
Typed out quote from the Gnostic Gospels:
Acts of John 90 (publication unknown).

Chapter 47: Fire on the Earth
Eversley Belfield: *Obituary of Eularia Clarke*.
Hampshire Chronicle, December 1970.
Clipping in ECA.

Chapter 48: Afterword
Eularia Clarke: *They May Not Hear Sermons
or Read Books on Religion – But They Will
Look at a Painting. The Universe*, December
4, 1970. Clipping in ECA.

Bible Quotations

Where it was appropriate Eularia gave a Gospel quotation for her paintings, sometimes more than one. Unless they have been quoted in the text of this biography they are listed here chronologically under the heading of the relevant chapter.

I cannot be absolutely certain which translation of the Bible Eularia used as a reference, but there is evidence to suggest that it was the Rheims-Douai translation of the Latin Vulgate, which was the translation in most common use by Catholics at the time of her conversion. For this reason, despite the rather antiquated English, I have used it as the source for the following quotes.

Chapter 21: Painting the Gospel
The Five Thousand. Matthew 14:20: 'And they did all eat and were filled. And they took up what remained, twelve full baskets of fragments.'
Buying the Wood. Luke 2:51: 'And he went down with them and came to Nazareth and was subject to them. And his mother kept all these words in her heart.'
Christmas Gospel. Luke 2:7: 'And she brought fourth her firstborn son and wrapped him up in swaddling clothes and laid him in a manger: because there was no room for them in the inn.'
Across the Desert. Matthew 2:14: 'Who arose and took the child and his mother by night and retired into Egypt. And he was there until the death of Herod.' &

Matthew 2:21: 'Who arose and took the child and his mother and came into the land of Israel.'

Chapter 22: Vision of Failure
Gethsemane, Vision of Failure. Matthew 26:39: 'And going a little further he fell upon his face praying and saying: My father, if it be possible, let this chalice pass from me. Nevertheless, not as I will but as you wilt.'

Chapter 23: Blessing the Paintings
Supper at Emmaus. Luke 24:30: 'And it came to pass, whilst he was at table with them, he took bread and blessed and brake and gave to them.'
Glastonbury, Taking up the Crosses. Matthew 16:25-6: 'For he that will save

his life will lose it: and he that shall lose his life for my sake will find it. For what doth it profit a man, if he gain the whole world and suffer the loss of his own soul? Or what exchange shall a man give for his soul?'

Chapter 24: Oils

Storm Over the Lake. Matthew 8:26: 'And Jesus saith to them: Why are you fearful, O ye of little faith. Then rising up he commanded the winds and the sea: and there came a great calm.'

Blessing the Babies. Mark 10:13: 'And they brought to him young children, that he might touch them. And the disciples rebuked them that brought them.'

Chapter 25: A Sense of Vocation

The Vinegar Bottle. Mark 15:36: 'And one running and filling a sponge with vinegar and putting it upon a reed, gave him to drink saying: Stay, let us see if Elias come to take him down.'
John 19:29: 'Now there was a vessel set there, full of vinegar. And they, putting a sponge full of vinegar about hyssop, put it to his mouth.'

Rescuing Sheep. Matthew 12:11: 'But he said to them: What man shall there be among you that hath one sheep: and if the same fall into a pit on the Sabbath day, will he not take hold on it and lift it up?'
John 10:28: 'And I give them life everlasting: and they shall not perish for ever. And no man shall pluck them out of my hand.'

Chapter 26: Half a Century

The Penitent Thief. Luke 23:43: 'And Jesus said to him: Amen I say to thee: This day thou shalt be with me in paradise.'

Chairs to Mend. Matthew 13:55: "Is not this the carpenter's son? Is not his mother called Mary, and his brethren James and Joseph and Simon and Jude?'

Weighing the Catch. Matthew 4:21: "And going on from thence, he saw other two bretheren, James the son of Zebedee and John his brother, in a ship with Zebedee their father, mending their nets: and he called them.'

Chapter 27: The Pops

The Lepers. Luke 17:12: 'And as he entered into a certain town, there met him ten men that were lepers, who stood afar off.'

Cave, Shroud and Angels. Luke 24:4: 'And it came to pass, as they were astonished in their mind at this, behold, two men stood by them, in shining apparel.'
John 20:12: 'And she saw two angels in white, sitting one at the head, and one at the feet, where the body of Jesus had been laid.'

Picnic on the Shore. John 21:9: 'As soon as they came to land, they saw hot coals lying, and a fish laid thereon, and bread.'

Maundy Thursday. John 13:4-5: He riseth from supper and layeth aside his garments and, having taken a towel, girded himself. After that he putteth water into a basin and began to wash the feet of the disciples and to wipe them with the towel wherewith he was girded.'

Chapter 29: Flames on their Heads

Flames on their Heads. Acts 2:3: And suddenly there came a sound from heaven, as of a mighty wind coming: and it filled the whole house where they were sitting.'

Hole in the Roof. Mark 2:4-5: 'And when they could not offer him unto him for the multitude, they uncovered the roof where he was: and opening it they let down the bed wherein the man sick of the palsy lay. And when Jesus had seen their faith, he saith to the sick of the palsy: son thy sins are forgiven thee.'

Coming up from the Water. Colossians 2:12: 'Buried with him in baptism: in whom also you are risen again by the faith of the operation of God who hath raised him up from the dead.'

Chapter 30: The Passing of the Curia

Miracle at Gadara. Mark 5:15: 'And they came to Jesus. And they see him that was troubled with the devil sitting clothed, and well in his wits: and they were afraid.' Luke 8:27: 'And when he was come forth to the land, there met him a certain man who had a devil now a very long time. And he wore no clothes: neither did he abide in a house, but in the sepulchres.'

Walking on the Water. Matthew 14:25: 'And in the fourth watch of the night he came to them, walking upon the sea.'

Village at Sunset. Mark 1:32: 'And when it was evening after sunset, they brought to him all that were ill and that were possessed with devils.'

Water from the Rock. John 4:15: 'The woman saith to him: Sir, give me this water, that I may not thirst, nor come hither to draw.'

Chapter 32: Stations of the Cross

A Boy Here. John 6:9: 'There is a boy here that hath five barley loaves and two fishes. But what are these among so many?'

Chapter 33: Sacred Heart

Martha and Mary. Luke 10:38: 'Now it came to pass, as they went, that he entered into a certain town: and a certain woman named Martha received him into her house.'

Chapter 34: Preaching

Preaching from the Boat. Matthew 13:2: 'And great multitudes were gathered together unto him, so that he went up into a boat and sat: and all the multitude stood on the shore.'

Chapter 35: No Old Age

Come Down Zacchaeus. Luke 19:5: 'And then Jesus was come to the place, looking up, he saw him and said to him: Zacchaeus, make haste and come down: for this day I must abide in thy house.'

Search the Highways. Luke 14:23: 'And the Lord said to the servant: Go out into the highways and the hedges, and compel them to come in, that my house may be filled.'

Chapter 36: Never a Day Without a Line

Mending their Nets. Mark 1:20: 'And forthwith he called them. And leaving their father Zebedee in the ship with his hired men, they followed him.'

No More Wine. John 2:7: 'Jesus saith to them: Fill the water-pots with water. And they filled them up to the brim.'

The Widow's Dead Son. Luke 7:14: 'And he came near and touched the bier. And they that carried it stood still. And he said: Young man, I say to thee, arise.'

Into Deep Water. Luke 5:4: 'Now when he had ceased to speak, he said to Simon: Launch out into the deep and let down your nets for a draught.'

Chapter 37: Into Deep Water

Christ, the Vine-Dresser. Luke 13:6: 'He spoke also this parable: A certain man had a fig tree planted in his vineyard: and he came seeking fruit on it and found none.'

The Sowers. Matthew 13:4: 'And whilst he soweth, some fell by the way side: And the birds of the air came and ate them up.'

The Son Came Home. Luke 15:20: 'And rising up, he came to his father. And when he was yet a great way off, his father saw him and was moved with compassion and running to him fell upon his neck and kissed him.'

Finding the Ex-Blind Boy. John 9:35: 'Jesus heard that they had cast him out. And when he had found him, he said to him: Dost thou believe in the Son of God?'

All This Waste. Mark 14:4: 'Now there were some that had indignation within themselves and said: Why was this waste of the ointment made?'

Chapter 38: Walling In

Mary Practising the Magnficat. Luke 1:40: 'And she entered into the house of Zachary and saluted Elizabeth.'

Baptising in the Jordan. Mark 1:10: 'And forthwith coming up out of the water, he saw the heavens opened and the spirit as a dove, descending and remaining on him.' John 1:29: 'The next day, John saw Jesus coming to him; and he saith: Behold the Lamb of God. Behold him who taketh away the sin of the world.'

Corpus Christi. John 6:48: 'I am the bread of life.'

White and Dazzling. Matthew 17:1-3: 'And after six days, Jesus taketh unto him Peter and James, and John his brother, and bringeth them up into a high mountain apart. And he was transfigured before them. And his face did shine as the sun: and his garments became white as snow. And behold there appeared to them Moses and Elias talking with him.'

Chapter 39: Where Will the Paintings Live?

Master, Where do you Live? John 1:38: 'And Jesus turning and seeing them following, saith to them: What seek you? Who said to him: Rabbi (which is to say, being interpreted Master), where dwellest thou?'

A Manchild is Born. John 16:21: 'A woman, when she is in labour, hath sorrow because her hour is come; but when she hath brought forth the child, she remembereth no more the anguish, for joy that a man is born into the world.

Chapter 40: Unicus et Pauper

It Was Winter. John 10:23: 'And Jesus walked in the temple, in Solomon's porch.'

Stones into Bread. Matthew 4:3: 'And the tempter coming said to him: If thou be the Son of God, command that these stones be made bread.'

Give Me Your Hand. John 20:27: 'Then he saith to Thomas: Put in thy finger hither and see my hands. And bring hither my hand and put it in my side. And be not faithless, but believing.'

Chapter 41: The Cellar Gallery

Christ the Good Samaritan. Luke 10:33: 'But a certain Samaritan, being on his journey, came near him: and seeing him was moved with compassion.'

Trying to Keep Awake. Luke 12:37: 'Blessed are those servants, whom the Lord, when he cometh shall find watching Amen I say to you that he will gird himself and make them sit down to meat and passing will minister unto them.'

The Mixed Sheaf. Matthew 13:30: 'Suffer both to grow until the harvest, and in the time of the harvest I will say to the reapers: Gather up first the cockle and bind it into bundles to burn, but the wheat gather ye into my barn.'

Chapter 42: Not Looking Back

Not Looking Back. Luke 9:62: 'Jesus said to him: No man putting his hand to the plough and looking back is fit for the kingdom of God.'

Following with Faint Hearts. Mark 10:32: 'And they were in the way going up to Jerusalem: and Jesus went before them. And they were astonished and following were afraid. And taking again the twelve, he began to tell them the things that should befall him.'

Chapter 43: A Big Thing

Under My Roof. 'Matthew 8:8: 'And the centurion making answer, said: Lord I am not worthy that thou shoudst enter under my roof: but only say the word and my servant shall be healed.'

The Rich Young Man. Mark 10:22: 'Who being struck sad at that saying, went away sorrowful: for he had great possessions.'

Don't Bury It. Matthew 25:18: 'But he that had received the one, going his way, digged into the earth and hid his lord's money.'

Chapter 44: Don't Bury It

The Angel of the Lord. Luke 2:9: 'And behold an angel if the Lord stood by them and the brightness of God shone round about them: and they feared with a great fear.'

The Eleventh Hour. Matthew 20:6-7: 'But about the eleventh hour he went out and found others standing. And he saith to them: Why stand you here all the day idle? They say to him: Because no man hath hired us. He saith to them: go you also into my vineyard.'

Chapter 45: Back To Nature

Thinking he was the Gardener. John 20:15: 'Jesus saith to her: Women why weepest thou? She saith to them: Because they have taken away my Lord; and I know not where they have laid him.'

I Am the Door. John 10:9: 'I am the door. By me, if any man enter in, he shall be saved: and he shall go in and go out, and shall find pastures.'

The Bent Woman Straightened. Luke 13:13: 'And he laid his hands upon her: and immediately she was straight and glorified God.'

Chapter 46: Beyond the Church

The Judgment. Matthew 13:48: 'Which, when it was filled they drew out: and sitting by the shore, they chose out the good into vessels, but the bad they cast forth.'

Chapter 47: Fire on the Earth

Fire on the Earth. Luke 12:49: 'I am come to cast fire on the earth. And what will I, but that it be kindled.'

Eularia Clarke   *Painter of Religion*

The Religious Collection

The following list constitutes the collection as it now stands. There are many secular sketches of landscapes and people and one or two oils that are not listed here as Eularia did not consider them to be part of her collection. All of her work, with one or two exceptions, is, at the time of writing, in the hands of her family who are in the process of establishing a Trust to take over ownership and care, and to provide access to them once again.

A Boy Here (1966)
A Manchild is Born (1969)
Across the Desert (1963)
All This Waste (1968 - not included in the original collection)
Angel of the Lord, The (1970)
Ash Wednesday in the Wilderness (1962)
Ash Wednesday in the Wilderness (copy)
Baptising in the Jordan (1968)
Bent Woman Straightened, The (1970)
Blessing the Babies (1963)
Buying the Wood (1962)
Candlemas (sketch 1959)
Candlemas (1960 - copy, original lost)
Cave, Shroud and Angels (1965)
Chairs to Mend (1965 - copy, original lost)
Christ the Good Samaritan (1969)
Christ the Vine Dresser (1968)
Christmas Gospel (1962)
Come Down Zaccheus (1967)
Coming up from the Water (1965)
Corpus Christi (1968)

Crucifixion (sketch, circa 1930)
Don't Bury It. (1969)
Easter Candles (1967)
Eleventh Hour (The) (1970)
Finding the Ex-Blind Boy (1968)
Fire on the Earth (1970)
Five Thousand, The (1962 - The Methodist Modern Art Collection)
Five Thousand, The (copy)
Flames on their Heads (1965)
Flames on their Heads (copy)
Following with Faint Hearts (1969)
Gethsemane, Vision of Failure (1963)
Give Me Your Hand (1969)
Glastonbury, Taking up the Crosses (1963)
He Shall Not Perish (1970)
His Head Touching the Stars (1970 - unfinished)
Hole in the Roof (1966)
Holy Tree, The (1970)
I Am the Door (1970)
I Say Unto You (1965)

Into Deep Waters (1968)
It Was Winter (1969)
Judgment, The (1970)
Kissing the Cross, Good Friday (1961)
Lepers, The (1965)
Lourdes, Communion for the Sick (1960)
Lourdes, Communion for the Sick (1960 - two sketches)
Lourdes, Going to Confession (1960)
Lourdes, Going to Confession (copy)
Lourdes, Going to Confession (1960 - sketch)
Lourdes, the Grotto (1960 - The Stokes Family)
Lourdes, the Grotto (copy)
Lourdes, the Grotto (1960 - sketch)
Lourdes, Inside the Grotto (1960)
Lourdes, Inside the Grotto (1960 - sketch)
Lourdes, Touching the Walls (1960)
Lourdes, Touching the Walls (1960 - sketch)
Lourdes, Water from the Spring (1960)
Lourdes, Water from the Spring (1960 - sketch)
Lourdes, Way of the Cross (1960 - The Stokes Family)
Lourdes, Way of the Cross (copy)
Martha and Mary (1967)
Mary Practises the Magnificat (1968)
Mass of the Circumcision (1962)
Master, Where do you Live? (1968)
Maundy Thursday (1965)
Mending their Nets (1967)
Miracle at Gadara (1966)
Mixed Sheaf, The (1969)
No More Wine (1968)
Not Looking Back (1969)
Oblates at Compline, the Taena Community (1961)
Palm Sunday (1961 - St Peter's Presbytery, Winchester)
Penitent Thief, The (1964 - copy, original lost)
Picnic on the Shore (1965)
Preaching from the Boat (1967)
Priest Brings Communion (1962 - The Stokes Family)
Priest Brings Communion (copy)
Rescuing Sheep (1964)
Rich Young Man, The (1969)
Sacred Heart Devotion (1967)
Saint Joseph (1964 - St Joseph's Presbytery, Aldershot)
Search the Highways (1967)
She-Ass and her Colt, The (1969)
Son Came Home, The (1968)
Sowers, The (1968)
Stations of the Cross, Holy Week (1961)
Stations of the Cross 18-inch (1965)
   Jesus is Condemned to Death
   Veronica Wipes the Face of Jesus
   Jesus Falls for the Second Time
   Jesus Clothes are Taken Away
Jesus is Nailed to the Cross
Stations of the Cross 8-inch (1965–66, all are included except no.12, Jesus Dies on the Cross)
Stations of the Cross 6-inch (1965–66, all are included except no.12, Jesus Dies on the Cross)
Stones Into Bread (1969)
Storm over the Lake (1963 - Methodist Modern Art Collection)
Storm on the Lake (copy)
Sunday Mass, Woodchester (1961)
Supper at Emmaus (1963)
Transfiguration in the Valley (1962)
Thinking He Was the Gardener (1970)
Trying to Keep Awake (1969)
Under My Roof (1969)
Valley of the Shadow, The (1968)
Village at Sunset (1966)
Vinegar Bottle, The (1964)
Walking on the Water (sketch - circa 1930)
Walking on the Water (1966)
Water from the Rock (1966)
Weighing the Catch (1964)
White and Dazzling (1968)
Widow's Dead Son (1968)
Winter Baptisms (1962)

Index

Index of Paintings

Eularia Clarke   *Painter of Religion*

Eularia Clarke   *Painter of Religion*

Eularia Clarke   *Painter of Religion*

23376638R00212

Printed in Great Britain
by Amazon